Cases in Managerial Finance

FIFTH EDITION

Cases in Managerial Finance

FIFTH EDITION

Eugene F. Brigham
University of Florida

Roy L. Crum
University of Florida

Chicago   New York   Philadelphia   San Francisco
Montreal   Toronto   London   Sydney   Tokyo
Mexico City   Rio de Janeiro   Madrid

The Dryden Press

Acquisitions Editor   Elizabeth Widdicombe
Editorial Assistant   Judy Sarwark
Project Editor   Kathleen Gleason
Design Director   Alan Wendt
Managing Editor   Jane Perkins
Production Manager   Mary Jarvis

Text and cover design by Muriel Underwood
Copy editing by Bernice Eisen

Address orders to:
383 Madison Avenue
New York, New York 10017

Address editorial correspondence to:
One Salt Creek Lane, Hinsdale, Illinois 60521

Library of Congress Catalog Card Number: 82-72310
ISBN 0-03-060101-0
Printed in the United States of America
345-090-9876543

CBS College Publishing
The Dryden Press
Holt, Rinehart and Winston
Saunders College Publishing

Preface

Although corporation finance can be fascinating, student interest in the subject must first be stimulated. Feedback from students, especially those not majoring in finance, suggests that many of them regard finance as either too mechanical or too theoretical. In an effort to overcome this attitude, we experimented with several different ideas. First, we learned from questionnaires and discussions that student attitudes toward finance closely reflect our ability to relate the subject matter to the "real world." If, in a lecture on a particular topic, we illustrate a point by referring to an actual situation, students' curiosity seems to intensify, their powers of concentration are sharpened, and we are able to impart more knowledge than we would if we dealt strictly with abstractions or hypothetical situations.

Recognition of the fact that we can improve the value of a course by increasing students' awareness of its relevance led us to experiment with the case method. We tried various types of cases, ranging from the Harvard-type case to simpler, more structured ones, without notable success. The Harvard cases were too complicated for our introductory students, who spent an inordinate amount of time trying to figure out what steps they should follow to solve the case and what data were actually necessary and useful in reaching the solution. A number of students became frustrated and simply gave up. Others, especially finance majors, were sufficiently interested in the cases to spend the perhaps excessive time required to learn something from them. On balance, we concluded that Harvard-type cases are suitable only for relatively advanced students. We also experimented with a number of the simpler cases that are available in published form. Some of these are quite good, and we had success with them. However, we found it difficult to use many of them because they were not designed to complement specific text assignments. This lack of direct relationship held even for the combined text-and-cases textbooks that some of us tried.

In informal discussions with our colleagues, we raised the question of whether we could devise a set of cases that would retain the virtues of the Harvard-type cases—that is, motivate students by putting the text material into a real world context—while overcoming the drawbacks mentioned above. Over the years, each of us had collected a number of examples that we used in our lectures to illustrate the text material. Most of these examples had come from consulting experiences, although some had been presented by corporate officers in executive development programs or were drawn from publications such as *Fortune*. We decided to restructure a limited number of these "case illustrations" into short but formal cases to see how useful they would be as teaching vehicles. As we proceeded, the following two rules were uppermost in our minds:

1. Each case should be keyed to a specific topic—ratio analysis, capital budgeting, dividend policy, and so on—to limit the scope of the case and thus make it correspond to a specific chapter in a textbook.
2. It should be possible for a student to work the case within a reasonable period of time. We used two hours as a target, and tried to design the cases so that a student could, after having studied the relevant chapter, work the case in roughly the desired time.

Our first experimental cases were used in both undergraduate and graduate introductory finance courses, as well as in the second undergraduate corporation finance course. The cases were utilized somewhat differently in the various courses. More emphasis was put on student presentation in the graduate and, especially, the intermediate undergraduate courses. In the introductory undergraduate course, students were generally instructed to read the case and familiarize themselves with the situation, after which the instructor presented the solution to the case in class in lieu of a lecture on the text material. In spite of the fact that these early cases had weaknesses, the instructors who used them received favorable evaluation reports from their students, and comments on the questionnaires distributed indicated that this favorable reaction came about in large part *because of the cases*. On the basis of the success of the experiment, we decided to go ahead with the project and write cases to complement each chapter in the major texts.

Although the initial cases had been highly successful, two problems were readily apparent. First, we concluded that it was virtually impossible to write a case that would not initially have a number of ambiguities, omissions of essential data, or outright errors. This led us to have each case worked thoroughly and independently by several teaching and research assistants before it was used in class. Even so, we made major modifications in every case after presenting it in class. Second, we found that the largest single problem with the early cases was that many students simply did not know how to begin solving them. We already had, of course, a written solution for each case, showing what decision the company had actually taken, as well as the steps used in reaching the decision. Because we wanted the students to understand how the text material was used in reaching the decision, we simply added a series of questions at the end of each case. These questions point out the direction of the decision process that was actually followed, but do not lead the student "by the hand" to the correct solution. The inclusion of these carefully structured sets of questions greatly improved the usability of the cases. This was especially true at the introductory level.

We, and others, found that using cases makes it much easier to motivate our students, majors and nonmajors alike. Students can now see the importance of finance in actual business decisions, and, for many students, the cases have transformed finance from a sterile, mechanical, "theoretical" subject into an interesting, pragmatic one. By showing the students why it is important to master theory, the cases actually *cause* them to learn more of the abstract, theoretical material than they would otherwise.

Changes in the Fifth Edition

Although earlier editions of the book met with more success than we had anticipated, they did have a number of errors and confusing sections. These problems have been corrected. Also, in earlier editions it was clear that some cases "worked out" better than others; some were more interesting and informative, and got their message across better. Upon examination, it turned out that the better cases were generally those that involved an extensive discussion of subjective, judgmental considerations as well as numerical calculations. In preparing the fourth edition, we reviewed each case and made sure that these subjective elements were present. In addition, we added questions where necessary to ensure that students think through these subjective considerations. This policy has been carried over to the new edition.

Almost half of the cases in the fourth edition were either completely new or extensively revised to reflect changes in the finance literature. This trend is continued here in the fifth edition where over forty percent of the cases have been revised substantially or are totally new. As is invariably true when extensive revisions are involved, errors and ambiguities tend to appear in some of the cases. We have taken particular care in this edition to eliminate such errors through extensive classroom testing. The cases that have not been modified drastically are those that are still consistent with the theoretical literature and "work out" well in class. These have simply been updated, and in some instances, streamlined. Among the new cases, several topics have been included for the first time. American Business Machines, Inc., not only gives students practice in determining relevant costs for use in an economic analysis, it also shows how acquisitions that change the timing of the cash flow stream can be valuable to a firm. In American Telephone and Electronics Company, the emphasis is on operating and financial leverage, but the case departs from the usual situation of an existing firm changing its operating or financial leverage and determining the effect on the value of its stock. Rather, we focus on a new fully-separated subsidiary, see how its initial value changes with leverage, and let the founders (the parent company) capture the gains from leverage.

Two other key features of the fifth edition are: (1) a major effort to reduce "busy work;" and (2) the inclusion of an appendix that provides partial answers to numerical questions. Some cases require extensive but somewhat repetitive calculations; for example, one simply cannot undertake a realistic leveraged lease analysis without making so many numerical calculations that the case cannot be worked in a reasonable length of time. In such situations, we have simply supplied most of the calculations, leaving enough blanks for students to fill in to ensure that they understand the calculating procedure. This allows for presentation of some important but numerically complex topics, and it also frees students to devote some time to the subjective issues embodied in the "essay questions" at the end of each case.

We are grateful to a number of individuals for giving suggestions that materially improved the book. Edward Altman, Abdul Aziz, Peter Bacon, Steven Bolten, William Brueggeman, Santosh Choudbury, David Ewert, Louis Gapenski, Anna Hackman, Irwin Harvey, Steven Hawk, Pearson Hunt, Keith Johnson, Donald Knight, Charles Kroncke, Harry Magee, Kathy McShane, Robert Moore, Kose John, James Pettijohn, Hugo Phillips, John Pinkerton, Robert Radcliffe, William Regan, Pietra Rivoli, Ellen Rose, Judith Rosenblum, Dayal Singh, Donald Sorenson, Milford Tysseland, Paul Vanderheiden, Steven Vincent, J. Fred Weston, and Elizabeth Wood all made helpful contributions. In particular, we wish to thank Linda Bricker and Chris Prestopino for their careful review and critique of the manuscript. The College of Business at the University of Florida provided us with intellectual support in writing and testing the manuscript, and Joyce Crum did her usual great job typing, proofing, and coordinating the many revisions and last minute changes that had to be made. Finally, we want to express our appreciation to The Dryden Press staff, especially Liz Widdicombe, Judy Sarwark, and Kathy Gleason for their support in bringing the book to completion.

The field of finance continues to undergo significant changes and advances. It is stimulating to participate in these developments, and we sincerely hope that these cases will help to communicate the important issues in finance to future generations of students.

Eugene F. Brigham
Gainesville, Florida

Roy L. Crum
Gainesville, Florida

Contents

Cases in Managerial Finance

FIFTH EDITION

Part 1: Financial Analysis, Planning, and Control

Case 1: *Financial Analysis*

Forest Resources Corporation

Laurie Phillips, vice-president and senior loan officer of the First Florida National Bank of Jacksonville, was recently alerted to the deteriorating financial position of one of the bank's long-standing clients, Forest Resources Corporation (FRC), via the bank's computer analysis program. The bank requires quarterly financial statements from each of its major loan customers. Information from such statements is fed into the computer, which then calculates key ratios for each customer, charts trends in these ratios, and compares the statistics for each company with the average ratios of other firms in the same industry and against any protective requirements in the loan agreements. If any ratio is significantly worse than the industry average, reflects a marked adverse trend, or fails to meet contractual requirements, the computer highlights the deficiency.

An analysis of FRC's financial statements revealed a number of significant trends (see Tables 1-5 for the financial statements and partial analyses thereof). Particularly disturbing were the 1979 current and debt ratios, which failed to meet the contractual limits of 2.0 and 55 percent, respectively. Because the current and debt ratios do not meet contractual requirements, the bank legally could call for immediate repayment of both the long- and short-term loans and, if they were not repaid within ten days, could force the company into bankruptcy. However, Phillips was reluctant to take such drastic action, preferring to approach FRC's management and persuade them to initiate immediate, decisive action to improve the company's financial position. Accordingly, she sent a copy of the computer output, together with her comments on the company's financial position, to George Whiting, founder and president of FRC, with a request that he review this material and submit to the bank proposals for immediate corrective action.

Forest Resources Corporation's common stock is traded over-the-counter. The company manufactures and distributes a wide range of forest products including building lumber, pulp and paper, plywood, and wood specialties.

3

Table 1   Forest Resources Corporation Balance Sheets
                December 31 ($ in thousands)

	1977	1978	1979
Cash	$ 807	$ 628	$ 612
Accounts receivable	2,682	2,896	4,605
Inventory	2,970	5,181	7,319
Current assets	$6,459	$ 8,705	$12,536
Land, buildings, plant and equipment (gross)	2,786	3,153	3,588
Accumulated depreciation	470	730	1,050
Net fixed assets	$2,316	$ 2,423	$ 2,538
Total assets	$8,775	$11,128	$15,074
Short-term bank loans	$ 500	$ 800	$ 2,860
Accounts payable	1,061	1,648	3,137
Accruals	540	800	1,150
Current liabilities	$2,101	$ 3,248	$ 7,147
Long-term bank loan	1,000	1,500	1,500
Mortgage	450	408	367
Long-term debt	$1,450	$ 1,908	$ 1,867
Total liabilities	$3,551	$ 5,156	$ 9,014
Common stock (3.65 million shares)	3,650	3,650	3,650
Retained earnings	1,574	2,322	2,410
Owners' equity	$5,224	$ 5,972	$ 6,060
Total liabilities and owners' equity	$8,775	$11,128	$15,074

a. Market price of shares: 1977—$2.79; 1978—$1.52; 1979—$0.16.
b. Price-earnings (P/E) ratios: 1977—6.7; 1978—5.6; 1979—5.0.
c. Assume that all changes in interest-bearing loans and gross fixed assets occur at the start of the relevant years.
d. The mortgage loan is secured by a first mortgage bond on land and buildings.

Major markets for the company's products are in the residential housing, commercial/industrial construction, and packaging products areas. The company purchases part of its raw timber requirements and obtains the balance from its own forests. With some exceptions, the company's products are not subject to deterioration or technological obsolescence over a period of from three to five years.

During the eight years prior to 1977, FRC had sustained fairly stable rates of growth in assets, sales, and earnings. During the last quarter of 1977, the

Table 2   Forest Resources Corporation Income Statements
Years Ended December 31 ($ in thousands)

	1977	1978	1979
Net sales	$26,820	$28,966	$30,703
Cost of goods sold	21,216	23,550	26,140
Gross profit	$ 5,604	$ 5,416	$ 4,563
Administrative and selling expenses	2,006	2,407	2,648
Depreciation	250	260	320
Miscellaneous expenses	318	558	898
Total operating expenses	$ 2,574	$ 3,225	$ 3,866
Earnings before interest and taxes	3,030	2,191	697
Interest: Short-term loans	50	88	286
Interest: Long-term loans	—	150	150
Interest: Mortgage	41	37	33
Net income before taxes	$ 2,939	$ 1,916	$ 228
Taxes (48 percent)	1,411	919	110
Net income after taxes	1,528	997	118
Dividends on common stock	382	249	30
Retained earnings	$ 1,146	$ 748	$ 88

a. Earnings per share (EPS): 1977—$0.419; 1978—$0.273; 1979—$0.033.
b. Interest rates on borrowed funds:
   Short-term loan: 1977—10 percent; 1978—11 percent; 1979—10 percent.
   Long-term loan: 10 percent for each year.
   Mortgage: 9 percent for each year.
c. For case purposes, assume that expenses other than depreciation and interest are all variable.

company experienced some difficulty in marketing its full production. Although FRC did achieve an 8 percent growth in sales for that year, management noticed a slight softening of the market and encountered some resistance when it tried to cover rising costs through increasing selling prices. However, management had expected a revitalization of demand in 1978 and had therefore increased production towards the end of 1977. When sales continued to fall dramatically during the first half of 1978, the company started offering price discounts and more liberal credit terms in an effort to stimulate demand. Even though the decline in the market was steeper than anticipated, it was still considered to be a temporary phenomenon. Despite these sales promotion moves, the company was unable to dispose of the increased production. 1979

Table 3 Forest Resources Corporation Ratio
Analyses December 31

	1977	1978	1979	Industry Average
Liquidity ratios:				
Current ratio	3.1	2.7	1.8	2.5
Quick ratio	1.7	1.1	.93	1.0
Leverage ratios:				
Debt ratio (%)	40.5	46.3		50.0
Times-interest-earned	33.5	8.0	1.5	7.7
Asset management ratios:				
Inventory turnover (cost)[a]	7.1	4.5	3.6	5.7
Inventory turnover (selling)[b]	9.0	5.6	4.2	7.0
Fixed assets turnover	11.6	12.0	12.1	12.0
Total assets turnover	3.1	2.6	2.0	3.0
Average collection period (days)	36.0	36.0	54	32.0
Profitability ratios:				
Profit margin (%)	5.7	3.4	4	2.9
Gross profit margin (%)	20.9	18.7	14.9	18.0
Return on total assets (%)	17.4	9.0	.8	8.8
Return on owners' equity (%)	29.3	16.7	2	17.5
Dividend payout ratio (%)	25.0	25.0		20.0
Potential failure indicators:				
Altman Z factors[c]	6.8	4.8	2.9	1.81/2.99

a. Uses cost of goods sold as the numerator.
b. Uses net sales as the numerator.
c. The 'Altman Z factor' range of 1.81/2.99 represents the so-called 'zone of ignorance'. Refer to Appendix 6A of Eugene F. Brigham, *Financial Management: Theory and Practice*, 3rd ed., (Hinsdale, Ill.: Dryden Press, 1982), for details concerning the Z factor.
d. Year end balance sheet values were used throughout in the computation of ratios embodying balance sheet items.
e. Assume constant industry-average ratios throughout the period 1977–1980.

witnessed a continuation of the relatively depressed 1978 market conditions, yet management still increased production in anticipation of a surge in demand. By the fourth quarter of 1979, demand had increased somewhat, mainly due to favorable housing markets in the sunbelt states. At this point, FRC had more than adequate inventory to meet any surge in demand.

Table 4   Forest Resources Corporation Statements of Changes
In Financial Position Years Ended December 31
($ in thousands)

	1978	1979
Sources of funds:		
Net income	$ 997	$ 118
Depreciation	260	320
Funds from operations	1,257	438
Long-term loan raised	500	—
Net decrease in working capital	—	68
Total sources	$1,757	506
Applications of funds:		
Mortgage repayments	$ 42	$ 41
Fixed asset additions	367	435
Dividend payments	249	30
Net increase in working capital (refer below)	1,099	—
Total applications	$1,757	$ 506
Analysis of Changes in Working Capital		
Increase (decrease) in current assets:		
Cash	$ (179)	$ (16)
Accounts receivable	214	1709
Inventories	2,211	2138
Net increase (decrease) in C.A.	$2,246	$ 3831
Increase (decrease) in current liabilities:		
Accounts payable	$ 587	$ 1489
Short-term loans	300	2060
Accruals	260	350
Net increase (decrease) in C.L.	$1,147	$ 3899
Net increase (decrease) in working capital	$1,099	$ (68)

After he received the computer output and Laurie Phillips's letter, George Whiting realized the potential danger of losing the company's line of credit, and he actively began to seek a solution to the company's problems. As he delved into the situation, Whiting realized that the problem was even more serious than Phillips had indicated; he had recently signed a contract for a plant expansion that would require another $1,000,000 of capital, which he had planned to obtain as a short-term bank loan to be repaid from profits generated by the expansion. Even though FRC had been a good customer of

Table 5   Forest Resources Corporation Common-size
              Financial Statements 1977–1979

Income Statements	Percentages of Net Sales		
	1977	1978	1979
Net sales	100.0	100.0	100.0
Cost of goods sold	79.1	81.3	85.1
Gross profit	20.9	18.7	14.9
Interest	0.3	0.9	1.6
Administrative and selling expenses	7.5	8.3	8.6
Depreciation	0.9	0.9	1.0
Miscellaneous expenses	1.2	2.0	2.9
Total expenses	9.9	12.1	14.1
Net income before taxes	11.0	6.6	0.8
Taxes	5.3	3.2	0.4
Net income after taxes	5.7	3.4	0.4

Balance Sheets	Percentages of Total Assets		
	1977	1978	1979
Cash	9.2	5.6	4.0
Accounts receivable	30.6	26.0	30.6
Inventory	33.8	46.6	48.6
Current assets	73.6	78.2	83.2
Fixed assets (gross)	31.7	28.3	23.8
Accumulated depreciation	5.3	6.5	7.0
Net fixed assets	26.4	21.8	16.8
Total assets	100.0	100.0	100.0
Short-term loans	5.7	7.2	19.0
Accounts payable	12.1	14.8	20.8
Accruals	6.2	7.2	7.6
Current liabilities	24.0	29.2	47.4
Long-term loan	11.4	13.4	10.0
Mortgage	5.1	3.7	2.4
Long-term debt	16.5	17.1	12.4
Total liabilities	40.5	46.3	59.8
Common stock	41.6	32.8	24.2
Retained earnings	17.9	20.9	16.0
Owners' equity	59.5	53.7	40.2
Total funds	100.0	100.0	100.0

the Jacksonville bank for over 20 years, Whiting began to question whether the bank would continue to supply the existing lines of credit, let alone grant an additional one million dollar short-term loan. He was especially troubled by the fact that during the last quarter of 1979, the Federal Reserve System had tightened bank credit, forcing the bank to ration credit even to its best customers.

Whiting is confident that the company's financial position can be improved, particularly in light of recent trends in the housing market. He has asked you to assist in the preparation of a proposal for corrective action that can be submitted to Laurie Phillips, supporting both the continuation of the existing credit lines and a $1,000,000 increase in short-term loans. Whiting is of the opinion that net sales and the cost of goods sold will each grow by 8 percent in 1980, and he plans to reduce both accounts receivable and inventories during 1980 to levels that would yield ratios in line with industry averages by the year end. (Inventories are to be related to the cost of goods sold, rather than to sales, for this purpose.) He also plans to embark on an immediate economy drive, without influencing the quality of the firm's products or the level of its marketing and promotional activities, designed to reduce administrative and selling expenses to 7.5 percent of sales and miscellaneous expenses to 1.2 percent of sales for 1980. (These are the relationships that existed in 1977, prior to the decline in the firm's performance.) To appease suppliers, future bills are to be paid more promptly. Tax rates and interest rates on borrowed funds are not expected to change during the coming year. The additional $1 million short-term loan, which is required at the start of 1980, would, if granted, probably bear interest at a rate of 16 percent. To conserve funds, Whiting plans to oppose the payment of cash dividends during 1980. Finally, Whiting is of the opinion that all of the planned improvements should cause the investment community to reassess the company's investment worth. This, he thinks, should increase the company's P/E ratio to about 6.5 by the end of 1980.

Questions

1. For 1979:
   a. calculate FRC's key financial ratios, and
   b. prepare a Statement of Changes in Financial Position (sources and uses of funds statement).
2. Based on the case data and the results of your analysis in Question 1, what are FRC's strengths and weaknesses? What are the causes thereof? (Use of the duPont system would facilitate analysis and strengthen your answer.)
3. If the bank were to maintain the present credit lines and grant an additional $1 million short-term loan with interest effective from January 1, 1980, would the company be able to retire all short-term loans existing on December 31, 1980? (To answer this question, consider profits, deprecia-

tion, and the amount of inventory and accounts receivable that would be carried if inventory utilization and the average collection period were at industry level; that is, if the company generated funds by reducing inventories and receivables to industry averages. Also, assume that all of Whiting's plans and predictions concerning sales and expenses materialize. Cash is a residual balancing figure, and FRC's tax rate is 48 percent.) Table 6 is included as a worksheet to facilitate analysis.

4. On the basis of your analyses, do you think that the bank should:
    a. extend the existing short- and long-term loans and grant the additional $1 million loan, or
    b. extend the existing short- and long-term loans without granting the additional $1 million loan, or
    c. demand immediate repayment of both existing loans?

    If you favor (a) or (b) above, what conditions (collateral, guarantees, or other safeguards) should the bank impose to protect itself on the loans?

Table 6   Forest Resources Corporation 1980 Worksheet

Income Statement ($ in thousands)		Balance Sheet ($ in thousands)	
Net sales	$	Cash	$
Cost of sales	$	Accounts receivable	$
Gross profit	$	Inventory	$
Interest—notes	446	Current assets	$
Interest—long-term	150	Fixed assets (gross)	4,588
Interest—mortgages	30	Accumulated depreciation	1,430
Interest	$ 626	Net fixed assets	$3,158
Administrative and selling		Total assets	$
expenses	$	Short-term loans	$3,860
Depreciation	$ 380	Accounts payable	2,509
		Accruals	1,459
Miscellaneous expenses	$	Current liabilities	7,828
Total expenses	$	Long-term loan	1,500
		Mortgage	330
Net income before taxes	$	Total liabilities	$9,658
Taxes	$		
Net income after taxes	$	Common stock	$3,650
Dividends	$	Retained earnings	$
Retained earnings	$	Owners' equity	$
		Total claims	$

5. If the bank decides to withdraw the entire line of credit and demands immediate repayment of the two existing loans, what alternatives would be open to FRC?
6. Under what circumstances might the validity of comparative ratio analysis be questionable? Can you think of an actual company or industry for which it might be rather difficult to establish a meaningful set of comparative industry averages?

Case 2: *Break-Even Analysis and Leverage*

Sparkle Toy Company

After receiving his M.A. in chemistry, with a specialty in plastics, Ken Sparks joined the plastics division of a major chemical firm. His wife, Barbara, had managed the toy department of Shield's, a large department store in Chicago, before their marriage in 1960. As a hobby, Mrs. Sparks designed and Mr. Sparks produced certain toy items which they gave to their friends on Christmas, birthdays, and other occasions. These toys were very well received, and a number of the Sparks's friends asked to buy additional ones that they could use as gifts. Mrs. Sparks's successor in Shield's toy department also urged them to produce additional quantities to be marketed through the store.

In the summer of 1970 the Sparkses decided to devote their full time to the commercial production of toys, and, on January 1, 1971, the Sparkle Toy Company, named after their pet cat, commenced operations. The initial plans were well laid. Sales during the first year totaled one million dollars, and by 1981 they had grown to $10.5 million. The annual sales for the firm's first 11 years, together with certain other operating statistics, are presented in Table 1.

Total toy industry sales are quite stable, but because of fads and fashions, individual firms experience considerably more instability than the industry does as a whole. Sparkle Toys, for example, "missed the market" in 1976 and 1979, when its new designs were not especially well received, and sales dropped significantly during both these years.

Sales instability presents a financial planning problem in the toy industry, and this problem is heightened by the seasonal nature of the business. About 80 percent of all sales are made during the months of September and October, when stores are stocking up for the Christmas season, but collections are not generally made until January and February, when stores have received their Christmas receipts and are able to meet their obligations to the toy manufacturers.

Toy manufacturers have a choice of production techniques. They can either produce heavily during the April to September period in anticipation of the

Table 1 Operating Data, 1971–1981 ($ in thousands)

	1971	1972	1973	1974	1975	1976	1977	1978	1979	1980	1981
Sales	$1,000	$1,250	$1,500	$1,950	$2,350	$2,000	$3,600	$4,800	$4,200	$7,500	$10,500
Less variable costs:											
Cost of sales	770	962	1,155	1,502	1,810	1,540	2,772	3,696	3,233	5,775	8,084
Selling and administrative expenses[a]	50	63	75	98	118	100	180	240	210	375	525
Total variable costs	$ 820	$1,025	$1,230	$1,600	$1,928	$1,640	$2,952	$3,936	$3,443	$6,150	$ 8,609
Contribution to overhead and profits	$ 180	$ 225	$ 270	$ 350	$ 422	$ 360	$ 648	$ 864	$ 757	$1,350	$ 1,891
Less fixed operating costs:											
Rent	$ 59	$ 80	$ 81	$ 116	$ 131	$ 152	$ 55	$ 96	$ 148	$ 241	$ 437
Depreciation	8	13	10	19	16	18	179	216	301	388	443
Taxes, property							32	61	90	116	180
Total fixed operating costs	$ 67	$ 93	$ 91	$ 135	$ 147	$ 170	$ 266	$ 373	$ 539	$ 745	$ 1,060

Earnings before interest and taxes	$ 113	$ 132	$ 179	$ 215	$ 275	$ 190	$ 382	$ 491	$ 218	$ 605	$ 831
Less interest	5	5	13	11	16	16	24	21	22	31	40
Earnings before taxes[b]	$ 108	$ 127	$ 166	$ 204	$ 259	$ 174	$ 358	$ 470	$ 196	$ 574	$ 791
Less income taxes[b]	$ 38	$ 48	$ 67	$ 84	$ 111	$ 70	$ 158	$ 212	$ 80	$ 262	$ 366
Profit after taxes	$ 70	$ 79	$ 99	$ 120	$ 148	$ 104	$ 200	$ 258	$ 116	$ 312	$ 425
Less dividends	$ 40	$ 40	$ 40	$ 40	$ 40	$ 40	$ 40	$ 40	$ 40	$ 40	$ 40
Additions to retained earnings	$ 30	$ 39	$ 59	$ 80	$ 108	$ 64	$ 160	$ 218	$ 76	$ 272	$ 385
Net profits after taxes as a percentage of sales	7.0%	6.3%	6.6%	6.2%	6.3%	5.2%	5.6%	5.4%	2.8%	4.2%	4.0%

a. Figured at 5 percent of sales.
b. Taken as 20 percent on the first $25,000, 22 percent on the next $25,000, and 48 percent on the balance.

Christmas sales, or they can follow a practice of level production during the year, storing output produced during the off-season period. The advantages of uniform production are that plant capacity, and thus fixed-assets requirements, is reduced and better personnel can be obtained because of the full-time employment. Seasonal production, on the other hand, reduces the danger of obsolescence due to style changes, decreases the storage problem, and reduces the need for financing to carry off-season inventories. Sparkle Toys has been following a seasonal production pattern, producing about 70 percent of its output during the April through September period and 30 percent during the remainder of the year.

Although the company has been continuously profitable, costs have been getting out of hand in recent years. The main plant was built in 1974, and additional capacity has been provided for in various rented buildings in the west Chicago area. Inefficiencies associated with the lack of centrally located production facilities and the need to train new labor during the peak production period are considered to be the primary reasons for the disproportionate increase in costs and the declining profit margin on sales. Barbara Sparks is convinced that the firm should buy some land adjacent to the present plant, construct an automated and integrated production complex, and produce at a more uniform rate throughout the year. She also thinks the firm should build a plant large enough to meet projected sales demand for some years into the future.

Ken Sparks, on the other hand, is worried about increasing fixed costs in a firm characterized by sales fluctuations. He believes that it would be sounder practice to slow down the firm's rate of expansion and consolidate its present position. Ken believes that his wife's approach, which would enable the firm to maintain its rapid growth and perhaps even make the family quite wealthy, could also jeopardize the continued existence of the firm.

It is estimated that variable costs would amount to approximately 85 percent of sales during 1982 if the present production setup is maintained. Fixed costs for 1982 under the existing setup would be about $1.2 million, and $485,000 of this would be depreciation. If Barbara Sparks's expansion proposal—which calls for expenditures of approximately $3,000,000 for plant, equipment, and increased working capital, all to be financed by a ten-year loan from an insurance company—is carried out, variable costs would fall to approximately 75 percent of sales. At the same time, fixed costs would rise to $2.2 million per year. Depreciation in this case would be an estimated $1.4 million per year.

Economics of expansion dictate that the Sparkses must take the steps all at once if they are going to take them at all, because expansion in stages is too costly. If the expansion is not undertaken, Barbara Sparks believes that a larger profit margin can be restored by concentrating on cost control.

Since 1975, sales have been increasing at a rate of about 29 percent compounded annually. The Sparkses do not expect sales to continue to grow at this rate, but they do anticipate that a 20 percent annual sales increase can be attained over the next several years if the $3 million expansion is undertaken. Without this expansion the Sparkses agree that sales growth after 1981 would only be about 15 percent.

Questions

1. **a.** Calculate the break-even point in dollars for 1982 assuming that present production methods are maintained. (Hint: the break-even point based on sales occurs where selling price times quantity sold, or total sales volume, equals fixed costs divided by 1.0 minus the ratio of variable costs to sales. $P \cdot Q = \text{Sales} = FC/(1 - VC/\text{Sales})$.) Also, calculate estimated 1982 sales, and express the break-even point as a percentage of 1982 sales. Under the expansion program, estimated 1982 sales are $12.6 million, and Sparkle breaks even at a sales level of $8.8 million, or 70 percent of estimated sales. (Note: since Sparkle Toys sells many different items at different prices, the break-even point must be expressed in terms of dollar sales, not quantity in units.)
   b. Assuming that the expansion program is undertaken, what is the estimated EBIT for 1982? If the expansion program is not instituted, estimated 1982 earnings before interest and taxes would be $611,250. (Hint: EBIT = estimated total revenue − VC − FC).
2. Complete the linear break-even chart given in Figure 1 by: (1) labeling the lines and key points for the present production methods as shown; and (b) adding the appropriate lines for the expansion situation.
3. At what level of sales would operating profits be equal under the two production methods?
4. Assuming that the expansion program is instituted, what would happen to EBIT if 1982 sales fell from the 1981 level by about the same rate (roughly a 13 percent decline when rounded to the nearest whole number percentage) that sales fell in 1979? If the expansion program were not instituted, EBIT would be $170,250 if sales fell by the same percentage.
5. Assuming that depreciation is the only noncash charge, what is the operating cash break-even sales level for the no-expansion alternative? The cash break-even sales level for expansion is $3.2 million.
6. Assuming that both variable cost percentages and total fixed costs remain constant from 1982 to 1984, estimate 1984 before-tax earnings with and without expansion. The projected sales levels in 1984 are $18,144,000 and $15,969,188 for expansion and no expansion, respectively.
7. Assume that sales in 1982 increase by 20 percent over the 1981 level if the expansion is carried out. What is the degree of operating leverage for this new sales level? If the expansion is not undertaken, sales will increase by 15 percent over the 1981 level, and the degree of operating leverage will be

Figure 1   Break-even Chart

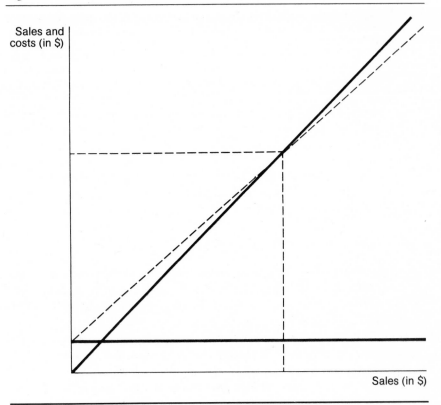

2.96. Use expected, or "formula," cost figures rather than actual income statement figures.[1] What is the significance of these figures?

Note: Question 8 assumes a knowledge of elementary probability theory, and Question 9 assumes a knowledge of financial leverage and the combined leverage effect. If students have not been exposed to these topics, instructors may want to omit either or both of these questions.

8. The sales level is a random variable. Under the expansion alternative, 1982 sales are expected to be $12.6 million; this is the mean of a normal

---

1. Degree of operating leverage $= \dfrac{\text{Percentage change in profit}}{\text{Percentage change in output}}$

$$= \frac{Q(P - VC)}{Q(P - VC) - FC} = \frac{QP - QVC}{QP - QVC - FC}$$

$$= \frac{\text{Sales} - \text{Total variable costs}}{\text{Sales} - \text{Total variable costs} - \text{Fixed costs}}.$$

probability distribution with a standard deviation of $2.53 million; that is, μ = $12.6 million and σ = $2.53 million.

a. Points A, B, C, and D in Figure 2 represent expected EBIT, break-even sales, $\mu - \sigma$, and μ, respectively. Put the dollar values associated with these points on the graph.

b. Find the shaded area under the probability distribution curve; that is, calculate the probability of at least breaking even. What does this tell you about the probable success of the expansion program? If the expansion program is not undertaken, 1982 sales are expected to be $12,075,000 with a standard deviation of $2,390,000. Assume that the probability of breaking even if they do not expand is 95.59 percent.

9. Assume that interest expenses will remain at $40,000 in 1982 if the expansion is not undertaken, but will increase to $340,000 if Sparkle chooses to expand. Calculate the degree of financial leverage and the combined leverage effect for the estimated 1982 level of sales assuming

Figure 2 Probability Distribution for Sales Level and EBIT Comparison, Assuming Expansion

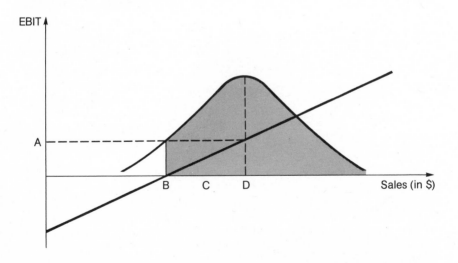

Note: (1) This figure has "profits" on the vertical axis. The graph is derived from a linear break-even chart, which would show total operating costs (VC + FC) equal to sales revenues at point B, losses to the left of B, and operating profits to the right of B. Thus B is the break-even point on a conventional break-even chart. (2) The probability distribution for sales is simply superimposed on the EBIT sales graph. Point D is the expected level of sales; hence A represents the expected value for EBIT.

they choose to expand.[2] If Sparkle does not expand, the values are 1.07 and 3.17 for financial leverage and the combined leverage effect, respectively. What is the significance of these leverage figures?

10. Do you think Sparkle Toys should expand? Summarize the reasons for your decision.

---

2. Degree of financial leverage $= \dfrac{\text{EBIT}}{\text{EBIT} - \text{I}}$

and

Combined leverage effect $=$ (Degree of operating leverage) $\times$ (Degree of financial leverage)

$$= \frac{Q(P - V)}{Q(P - V) - F} \times \frac{Q(P - V) - F}{Q(P - V) - F - \text{I}}$$

$$= \frac{Q(P - V)}{Q(P - V) - F - \text{I}}.$$

Case 3: *Financial Planning and Forecasting*

Structural Analytics Corporation

Structural Analytics Corporation was organized in 1964 to produce a line of nondestructive testing equipment for use in the aerospace, nuclear, and ship-building industries. Robert Davis, who received an M.S. in metallurgical engineering and, in 1962, a Ph.D. in physics from Georgia Tech, had developed and patented a revolutionary magnetic flux "fingerprint" process to reveal hidden structural stress flaws in critical machine components. A unique feature of this process was the incorporation of digital circuitry that gave the testing equipment the ability to project on a video screen a computer map of internal stress areas for the component under analysis. As external forces were applied to the part, the changes in the stress map could be observed instantly.

Marvin Richards, an aeronautical engineer and a close friend of Davis's, had worked with him in designing and building several special purpose testing machines for applications such as stress and fatigue analysis of aircraft turbine blades, and quality analysis of nuclear reactor primary coolant system valves and piping. These machines had several advantages over other existing technologies for nondestructive testing, particularly in terms of cost per test and of processing time for test results, but the cost of the equipment was higher than that of other machines. Thus, there appeared to be a receptive market for the equipment, but strong competition would limit pricing flexibility and result in a lower sales price than might otherwise be charged.

On the basis of the patent on the process, the prototype machines, their production plans, and firm contracts from several major aerospace defense contractors, Davis and Richards constructed a business plan for their proposed firm, Structural Analytics Corporation. The company was incorporated in the state of Georgia in February 1964. To make the firm more attractive to wealthy investors, the 100,000 shares of stock were issued in accordance with Section 1244 of the Internal Revenue Code. This permitted losses on the stock to be written off as ordinary losses rather than as capital losses in the event that the company failed and had to be liquidated. Based on the business plan, Davis and Richards were able to secure the financial backing of John Corgel, who had been in a highly lucrative real estate business in the Atlanta area and had a sizable net worth. Corgel's function in the new enterprise was simply to supply venture capital in return for a percentage of the operation. The resulting distribution of equity had Corgel owning 35 percent of the stock, Davis and Richards each owning 30 percent, and Kathryn Price, an accountant brought in to handle the controllership functions, owning 5 percent.

The new business was an immediate success. Production began in the summer of 1964, and the first deliveries were made in August. Revenues for the five months of 1964 totaled only $125,000, with an operating loss of $70,200, but sales jumped to $4,875,000 in 1973, with a profit of $339,900, and reached a total of $12,000,000 and a net income of $619,800 by 1980. A large-scale physical expansion took place in 1970, when capacity at the Atlanta home plant was increased. This expansion was financed by a public stock issue, Davis and Richards not wanting to utilize debt capital as long as they could raise additional equity capital while still retaining 51 percent of the voting stock. After the company went public, Davis and Richards each owned 26 percent of the stock. Corgel held 30 percent, Price owned 4 percent, and 14 percent was held by the general public.

Because of the space shuttle program and the desire of the major airlines for new fuel-efficient aircraft, in 1980 a production facility was built near Los Angeles to service the aerospace industry more directly. At the time financing was being arranged, Structural Analytics stock was selling (over-the-counter) below book value per share, interest rates were very high, and credit was extremely tight. Davis and Richards adamantly opposed another equity issue not only because of the depressed stock price but also because it would cause them to lose their absolute majority ownership. Thus, they considered a debt issue to be necessary.

A 15-year term loan was negotiated with a major insurance company at an interest rate of prime plus 4 percent. Although high, this rate was reasonable and in line with prevailing market rates. However, onerous indenture provisions were imposed on Structural Analytics because the insurance company was bargaining from the stronger position. For example, the loan required the firm to maintain a current ratio of 2.55 to 1 and forbade any additional long-term financing. Moreover, the loan contract contained a provision that called for the payment of an extremely severe penalty in the case of prepayment. Thus, if the company wanted to repay the loan before its due date (for example, the firm might want to refinance its debt at lower interest rates), it would have to pay a certain sum in addition to the principal. Although normal prepayment penalties usually amount to one year's interest, Structural Analytics was forced to agree to a provision calling for a sum equal to four years' interest.

The business prospered, but certain frictions began to develop among the major stockholders. Davis and Richards, the president and chairman of the board respectively, dominated the affairs of the company, while Corgel and Price were cast in the role of dissenting minority shareholders. Specifically, Davis and Richards were both satisfied with receiving large salaries from the firm and did not want to distribute profits as dividends. Corgel and Price, on the other hand, preferred to distribute some of the profits as dividends, believing that this would enhance the value of the stock. Further, Davis and Richards did not want to issue additional shares of stock because that would result in their loss of absolute control of a majority of the voting stock. Corgel and Price both desired wider public ownership that would lead to listing on one of the major stock exchanges and greater marketability of their shares. This, they argued, would also enhance the value of the stock and hence its price in the market. Finally, both Corgel and Price had objected to the insurance company term loan in 1980 because they felt that the prohibition on additional long-term debt financing, together with the current ratio requirement, would hamstring the firm in its future expansion plans.

Events during 1981 seemed to bear out Corgel's and Price's position. The number of new orders exceeded projections, and the new, recently installed plant facilities already appeared to be inadequate. It was obvious that additional expansion would be required if the firm were to attain its full growth potential.

At the directors' meeting in September 1981, Corgel and Price made a joint presentation of their views on the company and its position. From a production and marketing standpoint, they conceded that the firm's policies had been excellent. However, from a financial standpoint, management had been much less satisfactory. The major problems on the financial side, they maintained, involved a failure to plan for growth and to arrange financing in the most advantageous manner. The two minority directors felt that the company would need additional external capital—amounts in excess of what could be supplied by retained earnings—and that it was imperative that plans should be made to raise the needed capital by coordinated equity and debt offerings. They pointed out that the provisions in the term loan agreement would make additional long-term debt financing difficult, even though additional equity raised through the sale of stock would enable the company to take on additional debt without creating an imbalance in its financial structure. However, the problem of raising additional equity could not be avoided even if there were no restrictions on long-term debt; preservation of absolute control by Davis and Richards was inconsistent with realizing the growth potential of the firm. The other option available to the company was to use short-term debt to finance the expected growth, but this would create problems in terms of the current ratio requirement and increase the risk of financial stress if the short-term notes could not be renewed. The two minority directors charged that these points should have been considered before the term loan was finalized the previous year. This past mistake, they argued, made it even more important to construct a well-thought-out financial plan for the next few years at the present time.

For the purposes of such a plan, both Corgel and Price believed that the 1981 sales projection should be adjusted in light of the sales figure for the first eight months. Assuming that approximately as much business would be done in the last four months of 1981 (in terms of percentage) as had been done in the same period of 1979 and 1980, total sales for Structural Analytics for 1981 were projected at $13,880,000, with a 5 percent profit margin. Davis and Richards agreed that this was a realistic estimate. All four stockholders felt that a sales goal of $16,880,000 was reasonable for 1982, and that $19,750,000 was an appropriate figure for 1983. The profit margin for both years was assumed to be 5 percent.

Although the two majority stockholders admitted that some formal financial plan was necessary, they believed that any needed expansion funds could come from retained earnings, perhaps supplemented by minor amounts of short-term debt if required. Davis indicated that this was possible because of the large increase in expected profits. Corgel and Richards held that the projected growth of the firm was in excess of the amount that could be supported by internally generated funds, and that, to realize its potential, the firm would have to acquire external capital, at least some of which was equity. All four stockholders agreed that high sales and profit growth were their first objectives. Therefore, it was decided that the company should: (1) make a projection of financing needs; and (2) make plans for obtaining outside funds, if necessary to support growth, well in advance of the time they were needed.

Questions

1. Use the percent-of-sales formula (using 1980 percentages)[1] to forecast financial needs for 1981, 1982, and 1983 (see Tables 1 and 2). Assume that no dividends are paid during the period.

---

1. $\quad \begin{bmatrix} \text{Additional} \\ \text{funds} \\ \text{needed} \end{bmatrix} = \begin{bmatrix} \text{Required} \\ \text{increase} \\ \text{in assets} \end{bmatrix} - \begin{bmatrix} \text{Spontaneous} \\ \text{increase in} \\ \text{liabilities} \end{bmatrix} - \begin{bmatrix} \text{Increase in} \\ \text{retained} \\ \text{earnings} \end{bmatrix}$

$$\text{AFN} = \left(\frac{A}{S}\right)\Delta S \quad - \quad \left(\frac{L}{S}\right)\Delta S \quad - \quad MS_1(1 - d).$$

Here,

AFN = additional funds needed.

A/S = assets that increase spontaneously with sales as a percent of sales, or required dollar increase in assets per $1 increase in sales.

Table 1   Structural Analytics Corporation
Balance Sheet ($ in thousands)

$S = 1050$ $S = 4875$ $S = 12,000$

	1968	1973	1980
Assets			
Cash	$ 41	$ 174	$ 395
Accounts receivable	334	1,376	3,300
Inventory	375	1,600	2,856
Total current assets	$ 750	$ 3,150	$ 6,551
Net plant and equipment	395	2,725	6,345
Total assets	$1,145	$ 5,875	$12,896
Liabilities and Net Worth			
Accounts payable	$ 205	$ 1,400	$ 2,465
Notes payable	0	0	0
Total current liabilities	$ 205	$ 1,400	$ 2,465
Long-term debt	0	0	3,935
Common stock	845	1,770	1,770
Retained earnings	95	2,705	4,726
Total liabilities and net worth	$1,145	$ 5,875	$12,896

2. For 1968, 1973, and 1980, calculate the percentages of: (a) total assets to sales; (b) current liabilities to sales; and (c) current assets to sales. The company calculated similar percentages for all the intervening years and then ran a simple linear regression. The following projections were obtained for 1981, 1982, and 1983: 108.3, 107.9, and 107.7 percent for total assets to sales; 21.1, 20.9, and 20.8 percent for current liabilities to sales; and 54.9, 54.4, and 54.1 percent for current assets to sales, respectively. Use the projected total asset and current liability percentages to determine the financial needs for 1981, 1982, and 1983 by the percent-of-sales method. Then check the current ratio in each year to ensure that Structural Analytics does not violate the terms of the loan agreement.

L/S = liabilities that increase spontaneously with sales as a percent of sales, or spontaneously generated financing per $1 increase in sales.

S_1 = total sales projected for next year. Note that S_0 = last year's sales.

ΔS = change in sales = $S_1 - S_0$

M = profit margin, or rate of profits per $1 of sales.

d = percentage of earnings paid out in dividends, or the dividend payout ratio.

Table 2   Structural Analytics Corporation
             Income Statement ($ in thousands)

	1968	1973	1980
Net Sales	$1,050	$4,875	$12,000
Variable operating costs:			
Sales and administration	75	348	1,200
Cost of goods manufactured	630	2,925	6,960
Gross Margin	$ 345	$1,602	$ 3,840
Fixed operating costs:			
Fixed production costs	77	217	766
Research and development	66	208	541
Depreciation	79	345	769
Other	10	45	100
Net operating income (EBIT)	$ 113	$ 787	$ 1,664
Interest	6	133	472
Taxable income	$ 107	$ 654	$ 1,192
Tax	51	314	572
Net income	$ 56	$ 340	$ 620
Earnings per share	$ 0.56	$ 2.91	$ 5.31
Price per share	$14.00	$34.97	$ 53.10

3. Given your answers in Question 2 concerning the 2.55-to-1 mandatory current ratio, how much, if any, short-term financing could be used by Structural Analytics in each year to obtain an exact 2.55-to-1 ratio?

4. Prior to the September 1981 director's meeting, Corgel and Price (using data not given in the case) ran a simple linear regression in an attempt to predict with more accuracy the inventory levels necessary to support various levels of sales. Here is their resulting equation: Inventories = $500,000 + 0.1947 (sales). Construct a graph comparing this method of inventory prediction with the percent-of-sales method. For the percent-of-sales method, use the 1980 inventory/sales ratio, and note that the line must be linear and pass through the origin. Explain which method appears to be a more accurate and reliable model upon which to base this type of business decision.

5. Are the assumptions involved in applying the percent-of-sales method valid when forecasting financial needs for Structural Analytics in 1981, 1982, and 1983? Explain.

6. Outline a two-year financial plan for the company showing which option is preferred—debt or equity financing—and why it is superior. Be sure to cover the following points: (a) the plan must not violate the existing loan

agreement; and (b) sufficient funds must be on hand to support the target growth rates. Assume that the industry average debt ratio is 30 percent and that the insurance company would renegotiate the loan agreement and provide more debt capital if more equity were raised.

7. If the bond agreement stated that a 2-to-1 rather than a 2.55-to-1 current ratio must be maintained, in what position would Structural Analytics be with relation to additional use of short-term debt financing?

8. Structural Analytics has engaged in research and development activities that have led to the introduction of other equipment and have diversified somewhat the product line. However, much of the sales revenue still comes from the primary line of test equipment. Profit margins in this line have been kept fairly low to increase cost competitiveness of the equipment and thus gain market share. It is rumored in the industry that several firms are working on a new process, based on the emerging technology of moving holographs, that uses light interference patterns to produce images similar to those produced by Structural Analytics's magnetic flux process. Neither Davis nor Richards believes that this new technique can be made operational sooner than 1985, at which time Structural Analytics is expected to have a new generation of equipment ready to meet the competition. However, if certain technological breakthroughs were made sooner than anticipated, the holographic equipment could enter the market as early as late 1982. If this were to occur, 1982 and 1983 sales projections would have to be revised downward by at least 20 and 35 percent respectively. In light of this consideration, should any changes be made in your suggested long-range financing plan? Explain.

Case 4: *Financial Planning and Control*

Sharman Industries, Inc.

Sharman Industries, Inc., a Fortune 500 company which began in 1964 with the reorganization of a troubled $10 million brick and tile manufacturing firm, is a multi-market corporation with products ranging from yogurt to pollution control equipment. Vertical integration has been achieved in some areas such as the tire division, which has rubber plantations, tire manufacturing plants, and retail outlets. The conglomerate's divisions are run on a decentralized basis, with each division or profit center being evaluated in terms of its profitability, efficiency, and return on investment. Under this system, Sharman achieved a high growth rate in total assets, earnings, and stock prices throughout the 1960s and 1970s.

However, two years ago, in 1980, these favorable trends were reversed: The corporation experienced some major problems and was suddenly faced with declining earnings, unstable stock prices, and a generally uncertain future. This situation persisted to early 1982, at which time a new president, John Tinbergen, was appointed by the board of directors. Tinbergen, a C.P.A. who had served for a time on the financial staff of I.E. du Pont, used the du Pont system to evaluate the various divisions. All showed definite weaknesses.

Tinbergen reported to the board that the principal reason for the poor overall performance was a lack of control by central management over each individual division's activities. He was particularly disturbed by the consistently poor results of the corporation's budgeting procedures. Under Sharman's current system, each division manager draws up a projected budget for the next quarter, along with estimates of sales, revenues, and profits. Funds are then allocated to the divisions, basically in proportion to their budget requests. However, actual budgets seldom match the projections—they are usually off by a wide margin, either over or under the projected budget. These discrepancies, of course, result in a highly inefficient use of capital.

In an attempt to correct the situation, Tinbergen asked the firm's chief marketing officer, who was also serving temporarily as executive vice-president, to draw up a plan to improve the planning, budgeting, and control processes. When the plan was submitted, its basic provisions included the following:

1. Growth rate targets for each division's sales and earnings would be set by the central headquarter's staff in accordance with the corporate strategic plan. The division would then be required to develop programs to meet these targets.
2. To improve the quality of the divisional budgets, the division managers would be informed that the continuance of wide variances between their projected and actual budget figures would result in dismissal.
3. A system would be instituted under which funds would be allocated to divisions on the basis of their average return on investment (ROI) during the last four quarters. Since funds are short, divisions with high ROI's would get most of the available cash.
4. Only about half of each division manager's present compensation would be received as salary. The rest would be in the form of a bonus related to the division's average ROI for the quarter.
5. Each division would have to submit all capital expenditure requests, production schedules, and price changes to the central office for approval. Thus the company would be recentralized.

Tinbergen believed that drastic actions had to be taken soon to reestablish proper control. As he reviewed the suggested procedures, however, he had an uneasy feeling that something was not quite right.

Questions

1. a. Is it reasonable to expect the new procedures to improve the accuracy of budget forecasts?
   b. Should all divisions be expected to maintain the same degree of accuracy?
   c. In what other ways might the budgets be made? Should central management have a role in the preparation of the budget? If so, what role?
2. a. What problems would be associated with the use of the ROI criterion in allocating funds among the divisions?
   b. What effect would the period (four quarters, one quarter, two years, and so on) used in computing ROI have on the effectiveness of this method?
   c. What problems might occur in evaluating ROI performance by managers of the rubber plantation and the tire manufacturing division? Between the yogurt products and pollution control equipment divisions?

3. What problems would be associated with rewarding each manager on the basis of his division's ROI?
4. How well would the proposed policy of recentralization work in a highly diversified corporation such as Sharman Industries, Inc., particularly in light of the four other proposals?
5. Should uniform assumptions be made about the national economy (i.e., interest rates, inflation, unemployment, GNP growth, etc.) or should each profit center be required to make its own economic assumptions?

Case 5: *Cash Budgeting*

Lenox Furniture Company

When he returned from his coffee break at 10:30 a.m. on Monday, Robert Saxon, assistant treasurer of Lenox Furniture Company, found a note from Lydia Mitchell, financial vice-president and treasurer, asking him to come to her office as soon as possible. When Saxon arrived, he found Mitchell and Steve Lewis, controller of the company, pouring over a set of worksheet figures. Saxon quickly learned that because of the tight money situation that hit in the fall of 1981, Lenox's bank was requesting that all of its major loan customers estimate loan requirements for the remainder of 1981 and the first half of 1982.

Mitchell had a luncheon appointment with John Collier, the bank loan officer who handled Lenox's account, on the following Thursday—three days away. Mitchell wanted Lewis and Saxon to provide her with an estimate of financial requirements for the period in question. She would be leaving on a business trip that same afternoon and would not return until Thursday morning, just before the luncheon appointment. Lewis was tied up with an IRS audit of the firm's federal income tax returns, so he would not be able to contribute much to the forecast. Accordingly, the primary responsibility for the estimate would fall on Robert Saxon.

At the Monday morning meeting, Mitchell, Lewis, and Saxon agreed that what was needed was a cash budget. The firm had, of course, used cash budgets in the past, but one had not been prepared recently, making it necessary to start from scratch. Just as the three were beginning to discuss the mechanics of the actual cash budget preparation, Mitchell's secretary came into the office with two messages: first, Mitchell had 45 minutes to catch her plane; and second, two IRS agents were waiting for Lewis in his office, and becoming more irritated every minute. A few minutes later, Saxon was back at his desk, scratching his head and wondering how to begin the preparation of the cash budget.

On the basis of information already at hand, Saxon decided that no bank borrowing would be required before January. So he decided to restrict the cash budget analysis to the period January 1, 1982 through June 30, 1982. The following sales forecast was obtained from the marketing department.

Note: All dollars here and elsewhere in the case are in thousands; thus, November sales are forecasted to be $25 million. Ignore the three missing zeroes to simplify the arithmetic. Also, the sales shown below are <u>before</u> *discounts.*

1981	November	$25,000
	December	40,000
1982	January	50,000
	February	60,000
	March	70,000
	April	95,000
	May	65,000
	June	50,000
	July	25,000
	August	20,000

Lenox Furniture Company's credit policy (1/10, net 30) allows a 1 percent discount on cash purchases made within ten days of the sale. Otherwise, payment in full is due 30 days after the invoice date. Past experience indicates that 20 percent of the customers will take the discount, 70 percent will pay the next month, and 10 percent will be late, paying the following month (60 days after purchase).

The manufacturing process begins two months before the anticipated delivery date. The costs of production consist of material purchases and labor expenses. These total 60 percent of the forecasted sales, 20 percent for materials, and 40 percent for labor. All materials are purchased two months before sale and delivery of the finished products. Lenox pays 50 percent of the invoice in the month it receives the materials (i.e., the second month prior to the sale), and the balance the following month. Labor expenses are incurred according to a similar schedule; 50 percent incurred and paid for 2 months before the sale, 50 percent the next month.

General and administrative salaries amount to $8,000 a month. The current lease agreements call for $3,000 per month and will not expire until December 31, 1992. Fixed assets are depreciated at $4,000 monthly, and miscellaneous expenses are estimated at $2,500 a month. The $100,000 of outstanding bonds have a 10 percent annual coupon, paid semiannually, in January and July. Also, in June the company expects to replace an old machine with a $50,000 purchase of equipment. The old machine will have no salvage or book value. Taxes are estimated at $7,500 quarterly, paid in December, April, June, and September. The minimum desired cash balance is $30,000, which the company will have on hand, as shown in Table 1.

Table 1   Pro Forma Balance Sheet, December 31, 1981

Assets		Claims on Assets	
Cash	$ 30,000	Accounts payable	$ 9,500
Liquid assets	46,000	Bank loans	20,000
Accounts receivable	22,000	Current liabilities	$ 29,500
Inventory	77,000	Bonds (10%, 20 years)	$100,000
Current assets	$175,000	Common stock ($1 par)	100,000
Fixed assets (net)	250,000	Retained earnings	195,500
Total assets	$425,000	Total claims on assets	$425,000

Questions

1. Prepare Lenox Furniture Company's cash budget for the first half of 1982. In constructing your cash budget, disregard both the interest on any bank loan you need or income on surplus funds. Also, assume that sales all occur on the 15th of the month. Note that cash from some sales made in November and December will not be collected until January.

2. Estimate the required financing (or surplus funds) for each month during the budget period. Lenox has a $50,000 line of credit established with its bank. Will this amount be sufficient to cover the forecasted deficits? Suppose Lenox discovers that it must obtain funds elsewhere. Where might you suggest the company seek alternative financing?

3. Saxon also decides to prepare a daily cash budget for the first two weeks of January and weekly budgets for the remainder of the month. January's cash budget is shown in Table 2. Assume sales are made at a constant rate throughout the month (i.e., 1/30 of sales made daily. For ease of computation, assume January to have only 30 days, and also assume that Lenox is open seven days a week.) Daily sales are collected according to the 20 percent, 70 percent, 10 percent breakdown. Purchasers taking the 1 percent discount will always take full advantage of the ten-day discount period. Likewise, the "on-time" purchasers will wait for the "net 30" period to pay. The lease payment is made on the first. Materials are delivered on the first, and payment is made on the fifth. Labor costs and general administrative salaries are paid on the 15th and the 30th. Interest on the bonds is paid on the 15th. The desired cash balance remains at $30,000. Show how the indicated items were calculated and fill in the missing items in Table 2. Discuss the daily, weekly, and monthly cash budgets, indicating their

Table 2 Daily Cash Budget, January 1982

	1	2	3	4	5	6	7	8	9	10	11
Sales	1,667	1,667	1,667	1,667	1,667	1,667	1,667	1,667	1,667	1,667	1,667
Discount	264	264	264	264	264	264	264	264	264	264	330
"Net"	933	933	933	933	933	933	933	933	933	933	933
Late	83	83	83	83	83	83	83	83	83	83	83
Daily receipts	1,280	1,280	1,280	1,280	1,280	1,280	1,280	1,280	1,280	1,280	1,346
Payments:											
Materials											
Labor											
General and administrative											
Lease											
Miscellaneous											
Taxes											
Interest											
Total											
Net Cash		1,197	1,197	1,197	1,197	1,197	1,197	1,197	1,197	1,197	1,263
Cash on hand	30,000										
Cumulative cash		29,394	30,591			21,182	22,379	23,576	23,576	24,773	25,970
Less: Desired level of cash	(30,000)	(30,000)	(30,000)	(30,000)	(30,000)	(30,000)	(30,000)	(30,000)	(30,000)	(30,000)	
Bank loans											
Surplus cash											

Table 2 Continued

| | | | | | Week Ending | | |
| | | | | | Jan. 21 | Jan. 28 | |
	12	13	14	15	16–21	22–28	29–30
Sales	1,667	1,667	1,667	1,667	10,002	11,669	3,334
Discount	330	330	330	330	1,980	2,310	660
"Net"	933	933	933	933	5,598	6,531	1,866
Late	83	83	83	83	498	581	166
Daily receipts	1,346	1,346	1,346	1,346	8,076	9,422	2,692
Payments:							
Materials							
Labor							
General and administrative							
Lease							
Miscellaneous							
Taxes							
Interest							
Total							
Net Cash	1,263	1,263	1,263		7,578	8,841	(14,474)
Cash on hand	27,233	28,496	29,759			17,863	26,704
Cumulative cash	(30,000)	(30,000)	(30,000)	(30,000)			
Less: Desired level of cash							
Bank loans							
Surplus cash							

purposes and usefulness to management in anticipating financing needs. (Notice that due to rounding errors, loans outstanding on January's daily cash budget differ slightly from the figure calculated in Question 1.)

4. Management is also interested in utilizing its cash efficiently. It is considering a proposal which will incorporate seasonal cash balances. During heavy production months when cash needs are greatest, Lenox would have more cash on hand. Conversely, in slower months the balance would be lowered. How would this policy affect the cash budget? How might compensating balances affect the policy? Comment also on the applicability of such a policy on daily cash budgets.

5. Since cash is a nonearning asset the company invests in marketable securities whenever it has a sufficient cash surplus. Lenox wants to generate income from its investment portfolio, but realizes the necessity of quick conversion without loss. Suggest an investment policy that will provide the necessary liquidity and earnings. Be sure to mention the type of investment instrument, desired maturity, expected yield, and risk. Would your suggested investment policy be affected if Lenox's sales and earnings were valued in thousands instead of millions of dollars? Explain.

Part 2: Asset Management

Case 6: *Credit Policy and Accounts Receivable Management*

Kendall Dairies

Kendall Dairies is a small, independent company which produces a line of specialty ice cream products distributed regionally in the midwestern United States. Under the leadership of its founder and president, C. P. Kendall, the company experienced a moderate but steady rate of growth in sales through the fifties and sixties. In 1970, the product line was expanded to include dietetic ice milk. Traditionally, this market segment has had a severely limited choice of flavors: namely chocolate, vanilla, and strawberry. When Kendall entered this market, it included a number of innovative ice milk flavors such as "Peanut Blossom" and "Swiss-Mist."

Kendall's ice cream is regarded by consumers as being a premium grade product. The selling price is substantially higher than that of competing national brands, but Kendall does offer a large flavor selection along with high quality. Kendall's use of only natural ingredients, and the absence of preservatives, also enhance the "homemade" quality capitalized upon in the company's advertising campaigns. However, with high inflation in food prices, many retail stores are shifting their promotional emphasis away from Kendall's high margin ice cream to lower cost brands. The rationale behind this change is that it is becoming increasingly difficult to persuade price conscious customers to buy the more expensive premium brands. Thus, sales growth in the past two years has fallen off dramatically, and sales for 1982 are actually projected to be at about the same level as they were in 1981.

Dan Cody, the new vice-president of marketing who recently joined the company, has been reviewing the marketing strategy, and he has concluded that one major problem area is Kendall's credit policy. Cody views trade credit as being an important selling device, but one that Kendall has not been exploiting adequately. The current credit terms are 2/10, net 35. This policy was established in the late fifties, and the previous marketing managers had never examined its implications in view of the changing consumer patterns of the seventies and eighties. Presently, bad debt losses are 1 percent of gross sales; 60 percent of the customers who pay (59.4 percent of all customers) take the discount; and the average collection period is 20 days.

At present, gross sales (before bad debts) for Kendall are $1,000,000 per year, with variable costs amounting to 70 percent of sales. The company uses a 10 percent cost-of-capital for investments in receivables, and there is sufficient productive capacity to supply up to 40 percent more sales.

At the April 15, 1982 board meeting, Cody presented his views about stimulating sales by a proper tailoring of credit terms. He then proposed a new, easier credit policy which he believed would result in an increase in sales and profits. The new policy would be 3/10, net 60, with a more liberal attitude toward granting credit. Based on his knowledge of the dairy industry in general and Kendall Dairies in particular, Cody concluded that the new credit terms would result in an increase in gross sales of $200,000 per year. The average collection period was expected to be increased to 35 days, with 50 percent of the paying customers taking the discount, and 5 percent of the total gross sales becoming bad debt losses.

At this point, Grete Laine, vice-president of finance, stated that she was opposed to the change in credit policy advocated by Cody. While the others had been talking, Laine had quickly calculated that Kendall Dairies could not support a 75 percent increase in the collection period and absorb the increased bad debt losses without decreasing the profitability of the firm. These calculations are shown in Table 1. She agreed with Cody that trade credit can be a powerful tool to stimulate sales, but increased sales can be harmful if they do not generate sufficient revenue to cover the expenses they involve. With high interest rates in the economy and Kendall's deteriorating cash flow position, Laine believed that great caution had to be exercised.

At this point, Kendall asked Cody and Laine to investigate the matter more thoroughly and to try to agree on credit policy for the firm. They were asked to present a formal analysis of the proposed change at the board's next meeting.

From their work sessions, a revised credit policy emerged that both Cody and Laine believed to be a reasonable compromise. It called for changing the credit terms to 3/10 net 45 and relaxing credit standards slightly, though not as much as Cody had originally envisioned. They estimated that under the compromise policy, sales would increase by $110,000 and bad debts would rise to 3 percent of gross sales. Customers taking the discount would fall to 55 percent of collectable sales with the remaining 45 percent paying the net amount on day 45.

Questions

1. What is the average collection period (ACP) under the revised new policy agreed upon by Cody and Laine?

2. Construct a new table like Table 1 to show the effect of the new (compromise) credit policy on the firm.

3. Under the new policy, what is the maximum that Kendall Dairies could afford to pay to an outside collection agency to collect sufficient bad debts to bring the percentage down to 1 percent?

4. Of the variables used in this analysis, which are most likely to be subject to forecasting error? Would an implementation plan calling for new credit terms to be applied in only one or two markets be a feasible means of reducing this uncertainty?

5. What would be the likely reaction of competitors to each of the proposed changes in credit policy?

6. Should Kendall Dairies switch to the new policy?

Table 1 Analysis of Cody's New Credit Policy

	Present Policy (Original sales, original policy) $	New Policy (New sales, new policy) $	Change (New minus original) $(Decline)
Sales:			
Gross sales	1,000,000	1,200,000	200,000
Less uncollectable	10,000	60,000	50,000
Collectable gross sales	990,000	1,140,000	150,000
Discount customers	594,000	570,000	(24,000)
Less: discount	11,880	17,100	5,220
Net discount sales	582,120	552,900	(29,220)
Net customers' sales	396,000	570,000	174,000
Total net collectable	978,120	1,122,900	144,780
Add back: uncollectable	10,000	60,000	50,000
Total net sales	988,120	1,182,900	194,780
Cost of Sales:			
Discount customers	415,800	399,000	16,800
Net customers	277,200	399,000	121,800
Uncollectable	7,000	42,000	35,000
Total cost of sales	700,000	840,000	140,000

Earnings Before Bad Debts:	288,120	342,900
Less: bad debts..................	10,000	60,000
Net Earnings Before Fixed Costs	278,120	282,900

	54,780
	50,000
	4,780

Less Financing Costs Of:

$$\text{Increased investment in receivables} = \left(\begin{array}{c}\text{Cost of} \\ \text{original sales}\end{array}\right)\left(\frac{ACP_N - ACP_O}{360}\right)\left(\begin{array}{c}\text{cost of} \\ \text{capital}\end{array}\right)$$

$$= (\$700,000)\left(\frac{35-20}{360}\right)(0.10) = (\$2,917)$$

$$\text{Deferred receipt of contribution}^{[a]} = \left(\begin{array}{c}\text{contribution} \\ \text{margin}\end{array}\right)\left(\frac{ACP_N - ACP_O}{360}\right)\left(\begin{array}{c}\text{cost of} \\ \text{capital}\end{array}\right)$$

$$= (\$300,000)\left(\frac{35-20}{360}\right)(0.10) = (\$1,250)$$

$$\text{Cost of additional sales} = \left(\begin{array}{c}\text{Cost of} \\ \text{new sales}\end{array}\right)\left(\frac{ACP_N}{360}\right)\left(\begin{array}{c}\text{cost of} \\ \text{capital}\end{array}\right)$$

$$= (\$140,000)\left(\frac{35}{360}\right)(0.10) = (\$1,361)$$

Net change in profits[b]   ($ 748)

a. The −$1,250 represents the cost of deferring receipt of the contribution margin (gross sales minus total cost of sales) from the existing receivables under the new credit terms. Since the ACP is extended, Kendall Dairies will have funds tied up in receivables for a longer period of time.

b. The net change in profits can also be calculated by using equations to determine the incremental investment in receivables (ΔI), and then the change in profits (ΔP):

$$\Delta I = (S_O/360)(ACP_N - ACP_O) + V(ACP_N)(\Delta S/360)$$

$$= \left(\frac{\$1,000,000}{360} \right) (35 - 20) + (0.7)(35) \left(\frac{\$200,000}{360} \right) = \$55,277.78$$

$$\Delta P = \Delta S(1 - V) - (D_N S_N P_N(1 - B_N) - D_O S_O P_O(1 - B_O)) - (B_N S_N - B_O S_O) - k(\Delta I),$$

$$= (\$200,000)(1 - 0.7) - [(0.03)(\$1,200,000)(0.5)(1 - 0.05) - (0.02)(\$1,000,000)(0.6)(1 - 0.01)] -$$

$$[(0.05)(\$1,200,000) - (0.01)(\$1,000,000)] - (0.10)(\$55,277.78) = (\$747.78)$$

where the subscripts N and O denote "new" and "old," and where

S = gross sales; ΔS = change in gross sales

ACP = average collection period

D = discount percentage

B = bad debts percentage

P = percentage of customers who take discounts

V = variable cost percentage

k = cost of capital

Case 7: *Inventory Management*

Barracuda Marine Corporation

Barracuda Marine is a large manufacturer of powered fiberglass sport and fishing boats ranging from a 16-foot open cruiser to a 34-foot sports-fisherman. The production process at the firm's North Carolina plant can be described as a labor intensive, assembly line operation that must be balanced carefully to prevent bottlenecks. One of the most important considerations for smooth functioning of the lines, which is critical if costs are to be kept under control, is the inventory management system. In fact, the "bottom line" profitability of Barracuda depends directly on how well the inventory control system functions to keep the production process from bogging down.

Production is subdivided into four sequential steps. In the molding room, after a part is removed from its mold, a careful inspection is made to ensure that no damage has been inflicted on the mold surface. If none is found, the mold is carefully cleaned and waxed with a release agent that permits easy removal of the next part. Gelcoat, the cosmetic outer layer, is then sprayed into the mold and permitted to dry. If the dry gelcoat is found to be defective when inspected, it is removed from the mold by a blast of air, resulting in a loss of from $75 to $350, depending on the size of the boat. The process then starts over. If the gelcoat is satisfactory, a precut fiberglass "kit" is obtained from the stockroom and laid on by hand to build the various pieces for the boat. Flotation foam pieces are bonded into the hull and deck at this time. After the parts have dried, they are removed from the mold, inspected, and sent to the assembly room. The process is then repeated to get the molds ready for the next boat.

The individual pieces from the molding room are trimmed and brought together for assembly in production lines. In the assembly room, decks are joined to their hulls, engines and electrical wiring are installed, wood joiner work is incorporated, and all other operations necessary to complete the boat are performed in a rigid sequence. Quality control is accomplished by inspection and testing after each production step.

After the final line inspection, the boat is sent to the water-testing facility. In a building with what appears to be a very large indoor swimming pool, all boats are placed in the water to check for leaks and proper operation of engines, controls, and other similar equipment. Only after water certification are the boats readied for shipment. They are cleaned, installed in shipping cradles, and placed on trucks for shipment to dealers throughout the United States and Canada.

It should be easy to see why efficient inventory control is so important for the profitability of Barracuda Marine. If the stocks of gelcoat, fiberglass, resin, or flotation foam were to run out, the molding room could not operate and all lines would soon have to shut down. Without engines, wiring harnesses, steering systems, etc., at least some of the lines would have to stop operation because a critical sequential step could not be performed. This would disrupt the production of boats, would slow the shipment to dealers, and could cause lost sales. Because selling prices are fixed, the extra expense of rush orders would have to be absorbed by the company, and it is not inconceivable that these costs could exceed the profit margin on the boats.

Barracuda Marine carries over 50,000 different items in inventory, ranging from diesel engines to upholstery tacks. These items vary widely in price, in required ordering lead time, and in terms of the consequence of a stock out. To manage such a diverse assortment of raw materials, the firm employs the ABC method of inventory control in conjunction with "red line" or "two bin" storage for some items and informal methods for others. The process is fully computerized. To begin, for each item in inventory a "multiplier value" is assigned as a function of the ordering lead time and consequences of a stock out; multiplier values are given in Table 1. The raw materials are then identified by a numerical "value," as shown in Table 2, as follows:

Table 1   Multiplier Values

Lead Time Classes	Lead Time Multiplier
0–30 days	0
1– 3 months	4
3– 6 months	8
6– 9 months	12
9–12 months	16
Over 1 year	20

Stock Out Effects Class	Stock Out Multiplier
1. Unimportant	1
2. Average	15
3. Critical	30

Note: The values in this table are judgmental, although they are based on an analysis of past data.

Table 2   Raw Materials Classification Table

Inventory Item	Average Annual Usage	Average Cost Per Unit ($)	Maximum Lead Time Multiplier	Penalty Class for Stock Out Multiplier	Value Assigned to Item
Engines	10,000	900.00	12	15	243,000,000
Stern Drives	7,500	350.00	8	15	60,375,000
Fiberglass	500,000 lbs.	0.60	0	30	9,000,000
Resin	40,000 drums	250.00	0	30	300,000,000
Cleats	40,000	2.50	4	1	500,000

$$\begin{bmatrix} \text{average} \\ \text{annual} \\ \text{usage} \end{bmatrix} \begin{bmatrix} \text{average} \\ \text{cost per} \\ \text{unit} \end{bmatrix} \begin{bmatrix} \text{lead time} \\ \text{multiplier} \end{bmatrix} + \begin{bmatrix} \text{stock out} \\ \text{multiplier} \end{bmatrix} = \text{value assigned.}$$

Each inventory item is arrayed from highest to lowest production values, and graphed as in Figure 1. Then the inventory items are separated into three classes, labeled A, B, and C. Notice that the 10 percent of the inventory items in the A category involve 50 percent of the cumulative inventory value, and that the 40 percent of the items in A and B constitute 82 percent of the total dollar value. By concentrating attention on the items identified as most critical in terms of cost, lead time requirements, or the effect of a stock out, the firm can better utilize its managerial resources. These items tend to be concentrated in class A and class B. Based on the information on the value of each class A and B component, a rational, tailor-made safety stock and ordering policy can be established.

For most class C items, either the two-bin system or the red line method is used. With the two-bin system, parts such as cleats, chocks, running lights, step pads, etc., are stored in two locations or bins. The first bin contains the normal inventory, the safety stock is in the second. As soon as the stock in the first bin is depleted, an order is placed. Upon receipt of the order, the safety stock is replenished, the first bin is filled, and the process repeated. The red line method is a variation of the two-bin system that can be used for bulk items such as tacks, bolts, screws, etc. A red line is painted toward the bottom of the storage bin, and an order is placed as soon as usage depletes the supply to the point where the line is visible.

For class A inventory, Barracuda Marine has the policy of ordering a two-month supply every two months. Similarly, a three-month supply of class B inventory is ordered every three months. Class C items are ordered as necessary in accordance with the two-bin system; usually, a quantity equal to six month's usage is ordered. The control process thus concentrates attention on all class A and B inventory, where dollar values are high, ordering lead times are long, or stock out penalties are high.

Figure 1   ABC Classification Graph

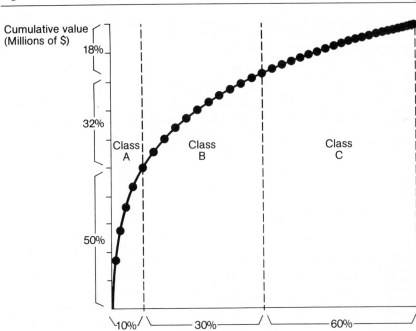

Although the process has worked reasonably well for over ten years, Craig Heath, the new vice-president of finance, believes that too much capital is wastefully employed in excess inventory. He points to the fact that the firm has never even been close to a stock out, even when strikes had shut off deliveries of critical items. He believes that ordering points and order quantities for class A items should be determined by more sophisticated techniques than are now employed, and that safety stock levels should be reviewed in light of experience. His preliminary calculations show that inventory turnover can be increased by about 25 percent if this is done. As Heath's assistant, you are asked to help him prepare a presentation to demonstrate the new techniques to the board of directors and to show the savings that can be realized with the switch. He asks you to concentrate your analysis on the class A item described in Table 3. Manufacturer A is currently the primary supplier of steering systems.

Questions

1. Calculate the economic order quantity for hydraulic steering systems under the assumptions of ordering from: (a) manufacturer A (the current supplier), and (b) manufacturer B.

Table 3   Information for EOQ Analysis

Item: Hydraulic steering systems
Expected Annual Usage: 12,500 units per year
Expected Average Cost Per Unit: $250

Inventory Carrying Costs (In percentages):

Depreciation and obsolescence	10.00
Storage and handling	5.25
Interest (Current bank rate)	9.50
Property taxes	0.75
Insurance	0.50
Total	26.00

Inventory Delivery Times and Fixed Ordering Costs:

From Manufacturer A, 15 days delivery	$120.00
From Manufacturer B, 20 days delivery	$ 90.00

---

2. How many orders should be placed each year under the assumption that they are made: (a) through manufacturer A, or (b) through manufacturer B? Assume that the company has a large enough stock on hand to permit deliveries to arrive, and note that in a "steady state" situation there will always be "goods in transit."

3. Assuming that 1,050 steering systems are now on hand, what is the initial reorder point; that is, how low should inventories be permitted to fall before a new order is placed, assuming it is placed with: (a) manufacturer A, or (b) manufacturer B? Use 360 days in a year and define the reorder point as "inventory on hand plus on order." (Hint: Find the daily usage and multiply by the delivery time to determine steering system usage between the time an order is placed and the time it arrives.) Also, *what is the actual inventory physically on hand*, in the steady state situation, when an order is placed?

4. Assume that a safety stock of two months' usage must be kept on hand at all times to provide insurance against running out of stock because of strikes or shipping delays, or because of abnormally high sales during a period when the firm is awaiting receipt of shipments. How should this affect: (a) average inventory held; (b) the cost of ordering and carrying inventory; and (c) the reorder point? Answer (b) and (c) in words; do not work out the numbers.

5. Assume a safety stock of two months' usage. What is the average inventory, including the safety stock, in both dollar amounts (at cost) and units under each of the two alternatives?

6. What is the total cost of ordering and carrying inventories under each of the two new alternatives and under the present method? Use the following equation:

Total cost = dollar carrying cost per unit × average units of inventory + ordering costs per order × number of orders placed

Assume that the current safety stock is set as two months' production, and that the firm orders two months' supply every two months, so that the current average inventory is 3,150 units. What is the magnitude of the savings that could be enjoyed by shifting from the present to the EOQ methodology in terms of both dollars and increased turnover of the item, where turnover is based on cost of goods sold?

7. Which method of ordering inventories should be used?
8. Would a seasonal sales pattern be likely to affect the analysis? If so, how could it be handled?
9. In calculating the cost of carrying inventories, the current rate of interest on bank loans was used. Is this an appropriate procedure? Explain your answer.

Case 8: *Working Capital Policy*

Brownsville Crate Company

Brownsville Crate Company was founded to manufacture a new type of wooden and reinforced fiber board box used to pack fresh fruits and vegetables. The company has expanded rapidly since 1965, when its first plant was established in the Rio Grande Valley of south Texas. In 1970 the company placed two other plants on line, one in Arizona and another in north central Florida. Capacity has been increased annually at all three plants. Because Brownsville Crate produces different types of boxes for various products, its sales are not affected extensively by seasonal variations in the yield of particular crops. Brownsville Crate's primary problem has been increasing production fast enough to meet the demand for its products. Although the company has been expanding rapidly, it has frequently lost sales because of insufficient production. Recognizing this problem, Miguel Robledo, president and chief executive officer, called a meeting of the top officers and interested directors to consider ways to increase production. Those present at the meeting included Raul Escobar, vice-president for operations; George Grayson, vice-president for finance and accounting; and Fred Simmons, director and banker. Robledo began the discussion by describing the problem and asking for suggestions from the participants.

Raul Escobar, the operations head, reported that although the sales department had indicated it could sell over 6 million number 16 boxes during the current grapefruit season in Texas, he must limit production to 3.6 million. This cutback is necessary in order to get the plant ready to produce number 8 and number 9 boxes, used to pack lettuce, celery, and other vegetables, prior to the start of the seasons for these crops. The production of number 8's and number 9's, in turn, will have to be curtailed before demand for them is fully satisfied in order to ready the production line for number 12's, to be used for the tomato crop. This situation, which has existed in the past, will continue in the future unless additional manufacturing equipment is installed.

Fred Simmons, the banker, agreed that it is important to obtain more equipment, but he indicated that the company will have difficulty obtaining additional long-term debt financing at the present time. Brownsville Crate's debt ratio is, in Simmons's opinion, as high as long-term lenders will permit without charging a healthy risk premium on the new debt. He suggested that the proposed expansion be financed by a new issue of common stock.

Robledo interrupted at this point, stating that a stock offering was probably out of the question. The current shareholders are not in a position to buy additional stock, and a sale to outsiders would raise serious control problems.

George Grayson, who has responsibility for finance and accounting, entered the discussion at this point. First, he was not convinced that Brownsville Crate could not borrow additional long-term capital, but if neither long-term debt nor common stock could be increased enough to finance purchasing of the needed equipment, the only avenues open were leasing, short-term borrowing, increasing retained earnings, or reducing working capital. Restrictions in the company's long-term loan agreements made leasing difficult, and to increase retained earnings by cutting the dividend would worsen stockholder relations and increase the danger of control problems. Thus, Grayson stated, the best way to obtain funds for expanding plant capacity would be in the working capital area. Current liabilities might be increased and/or current assets might be decreased to generate the needed funds.

Simmons interrupted, stating that there were definite limits on the company's ability to increase current liabilities and reduce current assets. If these limits were exceeded, the risk level would become excessive. There would be too high a probability of a default problem if the firm's liquidity position fell below a "safe" level.

Grayson interjected that working capital management is a function of several relationships, including those between: (1) current and fixed assets; (2) long- and short-term debt; and (3) total debt and total equity. Further, working capital policy is profoundly influenced by the willingness of stockholders and management to take risks. Grayson stated that Brownsville Crate's working capital policy was, in his opinion, quite conservative. To support this contention, he presented Table 1, which he had constructed for the meeting. According to this table, Brownsville Crate has more current assets and, consequently, a higher current ratio than the average firm in the industry. If the industry average is defined as "normal," Brownsville Crate is definitely conservative. Grayson concluded by stating that a shift to the industry average would make available a considerable amount of money that could be used to increase plant capacity.

Reflecting his background, Simmons indicated apprehension about any change in working capital policy, but then left the group to attend a meeting of his bank's board of directors. Robledo asked if the ratios of sales to fixed assets, and of expenses to sales, as shown in section C of Table 1, would change if a new working capital policy were adopted. Escobar stated that these ratios

Table 1   Working Capital Policy

	Current Balances		Industry Averages
A. *Balance Sheet*:			
Current assets	$14,400,000	40%	36%
Net fixed assets	21,600,000	60%	64%
Total assets	$36,000,000	100%	100%
Current liabilities (16%)	$ 4,680,000	13%	13%
Long-term debt (18%)	14,400,000	40%	40%
Common equity	16,920,000	47%	47%
Total claims	$36,000,000	100%	100%
B. *Income Statement Data*:			
Sales	$48,000,000		
Operating expenses	40,800,000		
Earnings before interest and taxes			$ 7,200,000
Interest	$ 3,340,800		
Taxable income			$ 3,859,200
Taxes (50%)	$ 1,929,600		
Net income			$ 1,929,600

C. *Significant Ratios*:

	Brownsville Crate	Industry
Sales/fixed assets	2.22X	2.15X
Current ratio	3.08:1	2.77:1
Rate of return on equity	11.4%	10.51%
Expenses other than interest and taxes to sales	85.0%	86.0%
Debt/total assets	53.0%	53.0%
Times-interest-earned	2.16X	2.05X

could be maintained if fixed assets were not increased more than 30 percent above their present levels. He did not want to commit himself if the increase in fixed assets exceeded 30 percent.

It became clear to the group that more analysis would be required before a decision could be made. Three alternatives were identified: policy C, under which the firm's current conservative stance would be maintained; policy I, calling for a movement toward the industry average by reducing current assets to the industry average percentage and using the funds so generated to purchase fixed assets, with no change in liabilities or capital; and policy A, an aggressive policy calling for decreasing current assets by 20 percent, increasing current liabilities by 20 percent, and using the funds obtained to purchase new fixed assets. Long-term debt and equity would be maintained at present levels under all three policies. Brownsville Crate can borrow short-term funds at 16 percent, and long-term funds at 18 percent.

Grayson was asked to prepare an analysis of these possibilities for the next meeting of the group, and it was agreed that the group would meet to discuss the alternatives in two weeks. It was further agreed that if a decision were reached to change the basic working capital policy, subsequent decisions would have to be made regarding the specific current asset components—cash, accounts receivable, marketable securities, and inventories—that would have to be changed. However, Grayson was asked to omit these considerations at the present time.

Questions

1. Prepare an exhibit that will illustrate the effects of the alternative policies on Brownsville Crate's financial position. Show each of the following items for each policy: (a) balance sheet; (b) income statement; (c) the ratios: current, total debt/assets, times-interest-earned, and rate of return on equity. In preparing the exhibit, hold common equity and long-term debt constant. Do not add in retained earnings. Also, assume that the firm's ratios of sales to fixed assets and of expenses to sales will remain constant under all three alternatives. This means that for the balance sheet, fixed assets are the residual balancing factors.
2. Compare the times-interest-earned and current ratios under the three alternative policies. What do you consider to be the primary factors influencing the relative riskiness of the alternative policies? Discuss their influence in the present case, quantifying the factors where possible, and indicating the type of data needed to quantify the risks (and the feasibility of obtaining such data) where it is not given in the case.
3. Which policy should Grayson recommend at the next meeting? Explain your answer.
4. The data given in the case indicate that the yield curve is upward sloping. (A "yield curve" is a graph showing the interest rate for a given debt instrument on the vertical axis and the years to maturity of the particular instrument on the horizontal axis.)
   a. Do yield curves always slope upward?
   b. How do expectations about future interest rates affect the shape of the yield curve?
   c. If expectations are for no change in the general level of interest rates, which factors would probably impart an upward slope to the yield curve?
   d. How would Grayson's personal feelings about future yield curves influence his feelings about maturity-structure-of-debt aspects of Brownsville Crate's working capital policy?

Case 9: *Disposal of Excess Working Capital*

Eastex Resources Corporation

John Jeffries, a partner in the management consulting firm of Arthur McKinney and Company, is reviewing the recent financial statement of the Eastex Resources Corporation, one of his clients. Because of adverse developments in one of Eastex Resources' major divisions, sales and profits have recently experienced a serious decline. Jeffries's company has been retained to help Eastex Resources decide what action, if any, should be taken as a result of these developments.

The East Texas Company was formed in the 1870s by a group of farmers and cattlemen who owned substantial acreage in the Gulf Coast region of Texas. The original purpose of the company was to obtain greater economies of scale in clearing and developing land, purchasing livestock, and marketing the group's products. However, the nature of the company changed markedly in the 1930s when oil was discovered on the property. At that time the company was split into two divisions, a land use division that concentrated on farming and cattle operations, and an oil division that simply leased mineral rights to the company's oil to major oil companies. Within a very few years after the discovery of oil on the property, the oil division, which was very small in terms of the number of people employed, was contributing about 80 percent of the firm's revenues and profits.

As the firm's original founders died, and as their estates were split up among their descendants, the stock gradually changed from being closely held to being publicly owned. In the late 1930's the stock was listed on the New York Stock Exchange. Although the company had a broad ownership and its oil revenues made it one of the larger companies in the country, the East Texas Company was managed in a most unimaginative manner until the early 1960's. In 1962 the major stockholders concluded that the company was not using its assets in a sufficiently profitable manner, and Charles Hamner, an individual with broad experience in the oil industry, was brought in as president and chief executive officer.

Hamner decided to use the cash flows generated by East Texas to acquire firms in other industries, principally manufacturers of farm equipment. As a signal to the capital markets that corporate thinking had been redirected to a new strategic path, the firm's name was changed to the Eastex Resources Corporation. The expansion program did increase sales and profits, but the manufacturing division, although profitable, was not a notable success. In fact, because the problems experienced with the new companies in the manufacturing division proved to be so vexing, Eastex Resources suspended its acquisition program. Jeffries, and most other sophisticated observers of the business scene, regarded Eastex Resources as a big, blundering company fortunate enough to hold title to some very valuable properties.

Sales in the farm equipment industry tend to be cyclical, moving up or down depending on factors such as weather conditions, government price supports, conditions in export markets, and the like. In 1979 farmers and manufacturers of farm equipment had a fairly good year. However, in 1980, there was a sharp downturn in sales and profits for farm equipment manufacturers, and 1981 was one of the worst years for them since the end of World War II. As a result of these industry-wide trends, Eastex Resources' manufacturing division experienced a sharp decline in sales and earnings between 1979 and 1981. In fact, the manufacturing division actually suffered losses in 1980 and 1981, but steady profits in the oil division were sufficient to enable the company to show an overall profit of $48 million.

As sales declined, accounts receivable also declined, and inventories were liquidated somewhat to reflect the lower level of sales. Although part of the funds generated by the reduction of accounts receivable and sales was invested

Table 1   Balance Sheet Year Ended December 31 (in millions)

	1979	1980	1981
Cash	$ 55.2	$ 83.2	$112.4
Marketable securities	——	55.6	112.8
Accounts receivable	220.0	166.4	140.8
Inventories	274.8	249.6	197.2
Total current assets	$550.0	$554.8	$563.2
Fixed assets	412.8	418.0	424.8
Total assets	$962.8	$972.8	$988.0
Total current liabilities	$175.6	$134.8	$137.6
Long-term debt (8%)	60.0	60.0	60.0
Common equity (stock plus surplus)	727.2	778.0	790.4
Total liabilities and net worth	$962.8	$972.8	$988.0

Table 2   Selected Information

	1979	1980	1981
Sales (in millions)	$1,924.0	$1,812.0	$1,712.0
Profits (in millions)	112.0	74.8	48.0
Dividends (in millions)	24.0	24.0	35.6
Earnings per share	18.0	12.0	7.72
Dividends per share	3.84	3.84	5.72
Price of stock per share	180.0	120.0	85.0

in short-term marketable securities, Eastex Resources' cash balances in banks still increased substantially between 1979 and 1981. These trends are shown in Table 1. The declining volume of business caused a significant reduction in profits and earnings per share, which, in turn, caused a drop in the price of Eastex Resources' stock. These trends are shown in Table 2.

In his report to the directors, Jeffries intends to make some recommendations for significant and fundamental changes in Eastex Resources' operations which he believes will cause profits to rise substantially above the 1981 level within a few years. If the recommendations are followed, the funds currently in excess will be profitably employed in fixed assets. However, the final report is not scheduled for completion for another six months, at which time the directors will have to decide what to do and then take some action. All this will take a year, but Jeffries believes that action should be taken immediately to reduce the excessive and unprofitable liquidity of the company. Therefore, he plans to submit a partial report containing suggestions for disposing of excess working capital. He lists the following alternatives for the consideration of Eastex Resources' directors:

1. The long-term debt could be retired. The insurance company that holds the bonds, which are due in 1996, is willing to permit the company to retire the bonds at the present time without penalty.
2. Some of the cash could be used to buy additional short-term marketable securities, such as treasury bills, commercial paper, certificates of deposit and the like. Treasury bills are currently yielding 14 percent, while commercial paper is yielding 15 percent.
3. The company could buy long-term bonds. Long-term governments are yielding 16½ percent, and the corporate bonds of companies with about the same degree of risk as Eastex Resources are yielding 18½ percent.
4. The company could buy high quality preferred stock with yields of about 20 percent.
5. The company could buy common stock of other companies.

6. The company could buy its own stock in the open market.

7. The company could increase dividends.

Questions

1. Discuss the pros and cons of the alternatives, and make a specific recommendation, including the dollar amounts involved, for the disposal of excess liquidity. Be sure to indicate how much excess liquidity you think the firm now has. The current ratio for the average firm in the industry is 2.50. Notice that Eastex Resources is in a 50 percent tax bracket.

Case 10: *Replacement Decisions*

Precision Control and Engineering, Inc.

Robert Hartley, president and chief executive officer of Precision Control and Engineering, Inc., leaned back in his chair and stared off into space. 1981 had not been a good year for PC&E. A few months earlier it had been Hartley's unpleasant task to report to the shareholders that for the first time since the Second World War, both sales volume and earnings per share had decreased during the year. Now, halfway through 1982, the picture was even more gloomy. The economic upturn that had been anticipated had not yet materialized, and unless the third and fourth quarters showed a strong upsurge in sales for PC&E, 1982 could end with the firm showing a net loss.

Precision Control and Engineering is a major producer of fluid control systems, pressure and flow regulators, and other specialized hydraulic components. These products have a wide range of applications in such fields as sanitation control systems, chemical and petroleum production, pipeline transportation, industrial process cooling systems, and hydroelectric power generation. Although some of the control systems are specifically designed for individual customers, most are standard items that sell in the range of $50,000-$200,000. Historically, the majority of PC&E's sales have been to companies who were expanding their operations and therefore needed additional fluid control capabilities. However, as a result of high interest rates in the past three years and a softening of demand for their products, companies have been increasingly reluctant to enlarge their facilities, so the major sales target shifted to retrofitting and upgrading existing plant and equipment.

Because PC&E's product line consists of highly specialized precision instruments that are used in conjunction with many different types of industrial equipment, a high degree of technical expertise is needed to match the appropriate control equipment with a particular application. Consequently, the PC&E sales force tends to be dominated by engineers or persons with at least some engineering background. The sales force works closely with potential customers to demonstrate the advantages of using PC&E equipment. Since most sales involve a number of separate components or complete systems, the total dollar volume that can be generated from a single order makes it well worthwhile for the salespersons to devote considerable time and effort to closing each sale.

The immediate cause of Hartley's preoccupation was a report he had received that afternoon from Andrea Lovenstein, the recently appointed vice-president for marketing. In an attempt to discover ways to bolster the firm's sagging sales, Hartley had requested and Lovenstein had prepared an in-depth analysis of business conditions in the industry and changes in the competitive positions of the leading firms—including PC&E. She soon discovered that all of PC&E's competitors were experiencing a decline in sales volume, but more importantly, it appeared that PC&E was also steadily losing market share. Two other companies were found to be increasing their share of the market, and their decline in sales had not been as pronounced as for other firms in the industry. On the basis of her analysis, Lovenstein concluded that the primary cause of the market share erosion the firm is now experiencing is the change in target market profile characteristics along with PC&E's failure to adapt its marketing strategy to reflect the changed environmental conditions.

Up to now, PC&E's marketing strategy had focused only on the engineering aspects of the products, and the firm's promotional literature reflects this orientation. Such an emphasis is considered to be appropriate because engineering excellence has always been the hallmark of PC&E. The strategy worked well until the late 1970s, partly because expenditures on control equipment for new facilities tend to be a very small fraction of the total capital outlay for the larger project and therefore are not usually subjected to a separate rigorous analysis, and partly because capital was readily available at reasonable rates to finance the purchases. As interest rates started to rise dramatically toward the end of 1979, however, the sales force found it much more difficult to convince customers to buy PC&E equipment solely on the basis of engineering performance characteristics.

Increasingly, economic aspects of the proposed purchase have begun to dominate the sales effort. As customers' expansion plans were cut back, the control equipment was no longer looked upon as only a small piece of a much larger project. Rather, prospective purchasers started to view expenditures on control equipment as involving, in their own right, a significant commitment of scarce and expensive capital resources. Since, in almost all cases, the new equipment would replace an existing control system that was still serviceable, PC&E salespersons were compelled to demonstrate that the economic benefits from replacing the equipment immediately would more than offset the capital cost. By not recognizing the implications of this fundamental shift in the requirements for effective selling in a different target market and then adapting the marketing strategy and promotional material accordingly to better support the sales force, PC&E placed itself at a competitive disadvantage.

Other companies were quick to seize and exploit the opportunity, and they succeeded in taking customers away from PC&E.

Lovenstein uncovered two additional pieces of information that Hartley believed to be of particular significance. First, the two companies in the industry that appeared to be gaining market share were also the ones that stressed to the greatest extent the economics of replacement decisions in their promotional literature and sales presentations. Both used a discounted cash flow (DCF) approach to convince potential customers of the advantages of replacing old control systems with the new, more efficient types the companies were now selling. Second, the most successful of PC&E's salespersons in the past three years were engineers who had received formal college training in engineering economics. These individuals, who were trained in the use of DCF methodology, had employed their knowledge to refine their own sales approach and develop supplemental material. By doing so, they were able to generate substantially more sales than their untrained peers.

Because of these facts, Lovenstein concluded that as soon as possible, PC&E should develop appropriate promotional literature and train all its sales force in the use of discounted cash flow capital budgeting techniques. Hartley admitted that this appeared to be a sound recommendation, and he saw no reason why it should not be implemented immediately. As he pondered the information in Lovenstein's report, though, he had the uneasy feeling that the implications of the decision were far more pervasive than they appeared to be on the surface.

DCF techniques had never been used at PC&E for any purpose, the payback method being the preferred tool for capital expenditure analysis. The more he reflected on Lovenstein's report, however, the more Hartley started to question whether this was a wise policy. PC&E's clients included some of the largest and best run companies in the world. If they required an economic analysis based on discounted cash flow methodology for their own capital budgeting decision, then perhaps PC&E was making a strategic error and should reconsider its position. Hartley had learned the mechanics of DCF calculations at an Executive Development Seminar in the mid 1970s, but he really did not understand why DCF is considered to be superior to other economic evaluation methodologies or how using payback could lead to less effective resource allocations.

At the Executive Committee meeting the next afternoon, Hartley explained his reservations about total reliance on payback and his thoughts concerning the introduction of discounted cash flow techniques in PC&E's internal budgeting and marketing operations. He quickly discovered that no one in the room knew much more than he did about the strengths and weaknesses of the various economic analysis techniques. James Quinton, vice-president for finance, was generally supportive of the suggested changes, but he proposed that a feasibility study be conducted as a first step. A second-year MBA student with several years of work experience in the finance area, Elizabeth Wood, had just started a summer internship in his division, and Quinton believed this to be an excellent project for her to undertake. Lovenstein interrupted to remind Hartley of the pressing need for prompt action in her division to develop promotional literature and train the sales force in the use of DCF techniques. Only after this had been done, she asserted, should the broader implications for PC&E's internal operations be considered.

Hartley decided that the best course of action was first, to find out how well Wood is versed in capital budgeting techniques, and second, if the training proves to be adequate, to ask her to work on the marketing division project during her internship. When Hartley questioned Wood, he was delighted to learn that not only had she worked in the economic evaluation department in her former job, she also had taken an entire course dealing with capital budgeting. (Wood, for her part, was surprised to learn that PC&E was still using the payback method.) She readily agreed to the assignment in the marketing department, and she and Lovenstein decided to start by analyzing one of the standard control devices—a unit that sells for $140,000 delivered. The following facts, which Lovenstein indicated were fairly typical, were to be used in the illustrative material:

1. The equipment has a delivered cost of $140,000. An additional $10,000 is required to install and test the new control system. The installation charge is added to the cost of equipment for purposes of computing depreciation.
2. The new control device is classified by the IRS as 5-year property, although it has a 25-year estimated service life. At the end of 25 years, the salvage value will be less than 10 percent of the original investment, so it can be ignored in the depreciation calculation. The best estimate of salvage value is zero—the scrap value will be exactly offset by removal costs.
3. The existing control device has been in use for approximately 30 years, and it has been fully depreciated (that is, its book value is zero). However, its net value for scrap purposes is estimated to be $5,000. This gain represents a recapture of depreciation, hence is taxable at ordinary rates.
4. Although accelerated depreciation based on the Accelerated Cost Recovery System (ACRS) can be utilized, for the promotional literature, straight-line depreciation and a 25-year life will be used for the new equipment.
5. The new control device requires lower maintenance costs and frees personnel who would otherwise have to monitor the system. In addition, it reduces product wastage. In total, it is estimated that the yearly savings will amount to $31,500 if the new control device is used.
6. The illustrative firm's cost of capital is 12 percent.
7. A 10 percent investment tax credit is permitted.
8. The applicable tax rate for the illustrative firm is 40 percent.

Questions

1. Develop a capital budgeting schedule that evaluates the relative merits of replacing the old control device with the new one. Use the net present value method.

2. Suppose one of the salespersons was making a presentation to a potential customer who used the internal rate of return method in evaluating capital projects. What is the internal rate of return on this project?

3. Suppose you were making a presentation to a potential client who used the payback method in evaluating capital projects. What is the payback period (using after-tax cash flows) for the investment in a new control device?

4. Explain why the payback method puts long-term investments such as hydraulic control devices at a relative disadvantage vis-a-vis short-term investment projects.

5. What would be the effect on net present value and on internal rate of return if accelerated depreciation, rather than straight-line depreciation, was used? Give direction of change, not precise figures.

6. Suppose one of PC&E's potential customers had a 50 percent marginal tax rate. Do not repeat the calculations to get a new solution, but determine (a) what items would be changed and (b) whether the IRR and NPV would be raised or lowered by the shift in tax rates.

7. For assets classified by the IRS as 5-year property, the Accelerated Cost Recovery System (ACRS) permits the company to depreciate the asset over 5 years at the following rates: year 1 = 15 percent, year 2 = 22 percent, years 3-5 = 21 percent. If the service life of the asset is 25 years and the company chooses to use the ACRS depreciation rates, what is the proper life to use in the economic study? Now assume that ACRS depreciation is used and the service life of the asset is 25 years, but that the company plans to retire and sell the asset in 10 years. What is the proper life to use in the economic study in this situation? Based on your answer to the first two parts of this question, can you suggest a general rule that can ascertain the correct study life when evaluating independent (that is, not mutually exclusive) projects?

Case 11: *Capital Budgeting: Relevant Costs*

Lastinger Implement Company

"It doesn't make a bit of sense!" fumed Dan Boyd, director of marketing. "Bob (Robert Lastinger, president of Lastinger Implement Company) says that he wants to increase profits in all product lines, and he shifted more of the salary of the outside sales force to a commission basis, but your people can't even produce enough to keep up with the orders we're bringing in now!" As they walked back to their office after the executive committee meeting, Boyd and Ralph Speir, vice-president for operations, discussed the controversy that had consumed most of the two-hour session.

"Don't blame me for not being able to expand production," Speir said. "I told Bob last year that the city government was not about to let us expand the Russell plant" (the factory on Russell Street where the firm's line of garden cultivators is produced). "But no, he wanted to try to enlarge the plant rather than move the operation out of town! Now we're in a bind, and he's putting the pressure on us to bail him out. It's a good thing my staff has been working on a contingency plan in case the Russell plant expansion fell through."

By the time he had gotten back to his office, Speir had decided to ask the treasurer, Beverly Hoover, to help him prepare a formal proposal for presentation to the Executive Committee at next week's meeting. He hoped that his staff had been able to get all the necessary information, because Boyd correctly noted that action had to be taken as soon as possible to prevent the competition from eroding Lastinger's share of the garden cultivator market.

Lastinger Implement Company was started in 1884 by Robert Lastinger's grandfather, Adolphe Lastinger, to produce a line of specialized agricultural equipment for fruit orchardists. By the time Bob's father, Earle Lastinger, assumed the presidency in 1918, the firm had grown significantly and had expanded the product line to include more generalized equipment used on small family farms. Under Earle Lastinger, the firm continued to grow, and a second production facility was added (the Russell Street plant) to manufacture a more complex line of mechanical cultivators. When Bob Lastinger became president in

1954, the company's operations were divided between the "main plant" and the smaller "Russell plant." Today, there are three profit centers in the firm: the garden cultivator division (Russell plant), the orchard equipment division (main plant), and the repair and overhaul facility (main plant). Central management offices are spread over both plants, an arrangement that has worked well over the years.

The controversy that had occupied most of the meeting of the Executive Committee that day was precipitated by the rapidly growing sales of garden cultivators. These versatile yet relatively inexpensive cultivators are particularly well suited for the average suburban gardener who cannot justify spending more money for a power rotary tiller. The "organic gardening" phenomenon had proved to be a real boon for the company, and sales of the cultivator doubled in less than five years. With three shifts, seven days a week, maximum production is 100,000 units per month. Average sales for 1981 were 99,500 units per month, and orders received in August 1981 through January 1982 averaged 108,000 per month. Clearly, a backlog of orders was being generated, with the amount increasing all the time. Dan Boyd, the marketing manager, believed that demand could easily be increased to 150,000 units per month within a few years if the firm were to engage in a coordinated national advertising campaign.

Ralph Speir, the production manager, realized over a year ago that capacity at the Russell plant would be insufficient even in the short run if demand were to grow as forecast. He also recognized that having production in two locations would not be feasible, so he proposed that a larger facility be leased or purchased as soon as possible. Speir did not believe that the city would grant a permit to expand the present facility because the town council was already on record as opposing further industrialization in the Russell Street section of the city. Also, there was no vacant land adjacent to the plant, and none of the surrounding buildings were really suitable for a large-scale manufacturing facility. Nevertheless, Bob Lastinger was opposed to moving the operation away from Russell Street except as a last resort, and he directed the production department to prepare expansion plans for submission to the city commission.

The expansion permits were denied and the denial had been upheld in court. Rather than file a further appeal, Lastinger directed Speir to examine other locations where it would be feasible to move the Russell facility. As Lastinger saw it, there were two options available to the company:

1. Continue operations at the Russell plant and forego the added sales. If this alternative were chosen, perhaps the selling price of the cultivators could be raised to increase the contribution from each unit sold. This would decrease demand to the level at which the company was able to produce.
2. Shut down the Russell plant and move the operation to a new suburban location. If this were done, both the manufacturing operations and the central management staff housed in the Russell facility would have to be transferred.

With an eye to future expansion of the orchard equipment division; Lastinger directed that if the Russell facility were closed, a building sufficiently large to accommodate the cultivator division, central staff personnel, and the repair and overhaul facility (now in the main plant) be acquired. If the repair and overhaul facility were to be relocated, space would then be available in the main plant to expand orchard equipment production.

To increase garden cultivator production to 150,000 units per month, additional equipment with a tentative cost of $41 million would be required. However, the orchard equipment division has an automated milling machine that is carried on the books at $50,000 and which should last at least 10 more years, but which is no longer required for their operations. It is unused and is occupying space in the main plant that could be put to better use. A buyer has been found who is willing to pay $110,500 for the machine if it is removed from the plant, crated, and sent to the railroad loading dock. It is estimated that removal from its present location would cost $1,000, crating $400, and transportation to the depot $100. However, close inspection of the operating specifications of the machine shows that it can be used by the cultivator division, thus reducing the capital outlay required to expand production by $1 million, to a total of $40 million. It would cost $5,000 to remove the machine from the main plant, transport it to the new plant, and reinstall it in the proper place. Current depreciation on this machine is $5,000 per year for the next ten years.

It has been estimated that the cultivator division requires about 60,000 square feet of space to achieve a production of 150,000 units per month. The repair and overhaul facility requires about 30,000 square feet, and the office space requirements are for at least 9,000 square feet. Speir's staff has located several buildings that will meet the firm's requirements. They are recommending a new building in the Suburban Industrial Park that has 100,000 square feet of usable space and has the further advantage of being located next to the railroad siding—a definite plus for deliveries of raw materials and shipping out finished products. The lease payment for the new building is $2 million per year, an increase over the $750,000 now paid annually for the Russell plant.

The engineering and cost accounting departments have been able to supply various direct and allocated costs for both the Russell plant and the proposed new facility. Their estimates appear in Table 1. Since sales are not constant, Table 2 gives estimates of marketing costs and working capital requirements for various levels of sales. With the new facility, Dan Boyd estimates that in 1982, sales will average 112,500 units per month for the entire year; 125,000 for 1983, 137,500 for 1984, and 150,000 per year thereafter. Included in the figure for 1982 is a provision for the approximately 45 days of lost production resulting from the move to the new facility.

Ralph Speir gathered together all of this information, then took it to Beverly Hoover, the treasurer. It would be the task of Beverly's department to perform the economic analysis and to present the results at the next Executive Commit-

Table 1   Estimates of Direct and Allocated Costs

	Russell Plant	**New Facility**
Production capacity	100,000 units/mo.	150,000 units/mo.[a]
Fixed production costs	$12,500,000/year	$18,200,000/year
Variable cost per unit	$ 80	$ 75
Selling price per unit	$ 115	$ 115
Lease payment per year	$ 750,000	$ 2,000,000
General overhead allocated to the cultivator division per year	$ 100,000	$ 300,000
Depreciation per year for existing cultivator division assets	$ 5,000,000	$ 5,000,000

a. Expandable to 175,000 units by storing raw materials in a warehouse on available land adjacent to the factory.

tee meeting. As Speir's discussion with Hoover progressed, a number of differences of opinion arose concerning the treatment of such items as: (1) the investment value to be assigned to the milling machine to be transferred from the orchard equipment division if the project is accepted; (2) whether or not the total lease payment for the new facility should be charged to the garden cultivator division, since two other operations are to be housed there; and (3) whether allocated general overhead costs should be included in the economic evaluation. Before these differences could be resolved, Speir was called away to a meeting with Lastinger and the firm's auditors.

Hoover knew that Speir wanted to move to the new facility, so if her analysis indicated otherwise, there would be sharp questioning when she presented the results before the Executive Committee. As Hoover's assistant, you must perform the economic analysis, paying particular attention to questions listed below on which she is sure to be questioned closely.

Other data relevant to the decision are as follows: the project's life is ten years; straight line depreciation to a zero salvage value is appropriate; the firm

Table 2   Estimated Annual Marketing Costs and Working Capital Requirements

Sales Level (units/mo.)	Annual Marketing Costs	Average Working Capital Investment
100,000	$2,450,000	$11,800,000
112,500	$2,650,000	$12,850,000
125,000	$2,840,000	$13,875,000
137,500	$3,055,000	$15,000,000
150,000	$3,240,000	$16,420,000

can take an investment tax credit of 10 percent on all new assets purchased; the firm uses 15 percent as a discount rate for this type of project; and the corporate marginal tax rate (federal plus state) is 55 percent. Also, the first year's lease payment is not due until period 1; the cost of moving equipment—except for the automated milling machine, whose moving cost must be analyzed separately—is included in the $40 million investment; and the initial increment of additional working capital is not required until period 1.

Questions

1. If the expansion (and move) is undertaken, Lastinger must spend $40 million (gross), less an adjustment for applicable tax credits which you must calculate, plus an additional amount for revenue foregone in moving the milling machinery rather than selling it. You must determine a "net cash outlay," or initial investment, for use in a discounted cash flow (DCF) analysis. (a) What investment value for the old automated milling machine should be included in the total net cash outlay? (b) What total net cash outlay should be used in the DCF analysis?
2. Calculate the incremental after-tax cash flows to the firm for the life of the project. In answering this question, be sure to consider whether the full $2 million lease cost should be considered in the analysis, or whether some other amount is more appropriate given that the repair facility will utilize 30 percent of the space. Also, assuming that the increase in general overhead is a direct result of the move to the new facility (that is, the increase will not be incurred if the decision is made to remain at the Russell plant), should it enter the analysis?

   (Hints: Calculate the net cash flows that would exist during each year under the "expand" and "don't expand" alternatives. The increment cash flow, or ICF, for each year is the difference in these two cash flows. Be sure to take account of working capital requirements. Also, in this analysis, assume that the cultivator operation is terminated at the end of ten years.
3. On the basis of your answers to the first two questions, conduct a DCF analysis to determine if the firm should move to the new facility. Explain fully.
4. If the company decides to remain at the Russell plant, it has been suggested that the selling price be increased to $120 per unit with demand reduced accordingly to a level of about 100,000 units per month. Assuming that this is a feasible alternative, do you come to the same conclusion that you did in Question 3? Explain.
5. It was stated that the automated milling machine is no longer required by the orchard equipment division and is occupying needed space. Suppose it was not obsolete but simply represented excess capacity that the orchard equipment division will not need for four years. Thus, if the cultivator

division takes the machine (that is, moves to the new facility), a new one will have to be purchased in four years by the orchard equipment division. However, if the cultivator division does not take the equipment and remains at the Russell plant, it will be eight years before the orchard equipment division has to purchase another machine. Describe how you would have handled this situaiton in your present analysis (no calculations are required).

Case 12: Capital Budgeting with Unequal Project Lives; Competitive Bidding

Fibertech Labs, Inc.

Most government projects are put up for competitive bidding, the winner of the contract being the firm with demonstrated competence and the lowest bid. However, in some instances, special rules are made to give minority-owned businesses a better chance for securing government jobs. Fibertech Labs, Inc., a minority firm located in Melbourne, Florida, is currently reviewing a request for proposal (RFP) from NASA that falls into this category.

With the launch of the space shuttle Columbia from Cape Canaveral, a new era of manned U.S. space flight began. The labor force at the Kennedy Space Center again started to grow, and it is predicted that in a few years activity will at least equal and perhaps even exceed that when the Apollo program was in its heyday. Opportunities for business are also mushrooming as NASA moves ahead on the ambitious shuttle program. One project of particular concern is space station construction—building hugh space stations in orbit for a variety of purposes. The shuttle would be used as the transport vehicle as well as the construction platform on which to build such structures.

To equip each shuttle for carrying the materials and machinery necessary to assemble these vast orbiting laboratories and power plants, special modular storage bins that fit into the cargo bay of the shuttle must be designed and built. Requirements for maximum strength and minimum weight direct attention to fiber reinforced plastic materials and, in particular, to high density carbon fibers in a rigid multilayered structure. These containerized cargo bins would have the strength and weight desired, and they shoud also be relatively inexpensive to construct, making it feasible to jettison the bins after their contents have been removed and they are no longer useful.

Fibertech Labs, Inc. has almost ten years experience in the reinforced plastics business and the president, Aaron Jackson, believes that they can get the cargo bin contract—if their bid is made with care. With this in mind, he asked the chief engineer, James Cook, to work up a bid.

NASA requests delivery of ten units per year for the next five years. The units are, to some extent, "custom made" for each launch, so premanufacture and stockpiling is not feasible. James Cook notes that the contract is to run for five years, with only a remote chance of renewal. Although Fibertech Labs is a minority firm, Cook knows that several other black- and Cuban-American-owned companies are bidding on the contract, so he will have to submit the lowest cost estimate that will permit a sufficient return to the firm.

He identifies two processes that can be used to meet the design specifications for the cargo containers. From an engineering standpoint, Cook believes that the processes are equal, so Jackson directs him to choose the method that would allow Fibertech Labs to submit the lowest per-unit bid. Both processes require about 100,000 square feet of floor space which can be leased for $2 million per year. Also, the firm uses straight line depreciation and the required rate of return is 12 percent after a 40 percent tax.

The first process which Cook investigated is a continuous filament (CF), high-pressure molding technique that automatically forms a "beehive" sandwich of small hexagonal pockets. This increases the strength of a panel dramatically without sacrificing the weight advantage. Production equipment to implement this process costs $2,550,000, has a design life of five years, and an expected salvage value of zero at the end of the fifth year. With the CF method, raw materials are expected to cost $65,000 per unit ($650,000 per year) and direct labor expense is $5,000 per unit, or $50,000 per year. General overhead, including a maintenance agreement on this rather complex piece of equipment, is $1,550,000 per year.

The other production method, called the woven mat (WM) process, involves the hand lay-up of carbon fiber mats with preformed corrugated inner sections for strength yet lightness. The WM process requires equipment that costs $1,500,000 and has a design life of three years. At that time, the salvage value is zero and the machine would have to be replaced to continue production. Neither Jackson nor Cook expect any new developments in machinery technology in the next three years, and they also believe that the price of the machinery will be somewhat stable. If Fibertech Labs were to sell the WM machine at the end of two years, a market value of $500,000 should be realized. With the WM method, preformed corrugated inner sections must be purchased, so the raw material cost would be $74,000 per unit or $740,000 per year. Similarly, more hand labor would be involved, so direct labor costs would be $10,000 per unit, or $100,000 per year. The machinery is not as complex as for the CF process, so a maintenance agreement would not be necessary, and general overhead would be only $1,500,000 per year.

If the CF process is chosen, the firm can take an investment tax credit of 3 percent of the original cost. Since the life of the WM equipment is only three years, no investment tax credit may be taken on it.

Questions

1. Which production process would you advise Jackson and Cook to select? At what price per unit should Fibertech Labs submit a bid to NASA?
2. How would each of the following factors affect your recommendation?
   a. Inflation in the price of labor, raw materials, and machinery is expected to accelerate.
   b. Fibertech Labs is subject to severe capital rationing.
   c. Technology in the molding equipment industry is advancing rapidly.
   d. Fibertech Labs' cost of capital rises dramatically.
   e. NASA expects to receive funding and therefore to extend the life of the contract indefinitely.

Case 13: *Capital Budgeting*

Tarheel Forwarding, Inc.

Tarheel Forwarding, Inc. is a family operation owned by the three Jenkins brothers. Adrian Brooks, son-in-law of the oldest Jenkins brother, recently assumed the position of assistant to the financial vice-president. Although Brooks's primary responsibility is to evaluate capital investment projects, he was also asked to review the firm's capital structure and the effect of that capital structure on the cost-of-capital.

Brooks is presently undertaking a detailed analysis of the four major capital investment proposals available to Tarheel for the coming year. A description of each project, together with its cost and expected cash flow data (after-tax profit plus depreciation), is presented in Table 1. The four projects are all equally risky, and their risk is about the same as that of the firm's other assets.

Project A: Expanded Facilities at the Charlotte Terminal

Tarheel Forwarding operates primarily as a bonded freight forwarder, and the firm must provide rapid delivery on short notice for cargo temporarily stored in its bonded warehouse. The four existing loading docks are often insufficient for the rapid loading necessary to make prompt deliveries.

Tarheel has not been able to meet schedules on several occasions. Although the business lost so far has not been substantial, a continuation of the problem would have a serious effect on sales.

Project A calls for the construction of an annex to the existing warehouse; the addition would provide four new loading docks and additional storage space, which would speed up freight handling operations.

Project B: Alternative Plan for Expansion of the Charlotte Terminal

After tentatively deciding to go with Project A, an alternative, Project B, was proposed. Brooks noted that Project A will provide some additional storage space, but that this space is not urgently needed. Therefore, he determined

Table 1   Characteristics of Investment Proposals

Cost	Project A $750,000	Project B $750,000	Project C $1,500,000	Project D $750,000
Inflows (Year)				
1	$216,400	$575,000	$ 458,900	$261,900
2	216,400	425,000	458,900	261,900
3	216,400	142,900	458,900	261,900
4	216,400	80,000	458,900	261,900
5	216,400		458,900	261,900
6	216,400		458,900	
7	216,400		458,900	
8	216,400		458,900	
9	216,400		458,900	
10	216,400		458,900	

that it would be possible (Project B) to solve the problem at hand by simply adding four more loading docks to the existing building. These new docks could be operational in the very near future, but they would cost approximately as much as Project A because the construction would necessitate extensive modifications.

Project C: Purchase of Four New Tractor-Trailer Rigs

An increase in business has been forcing Tarheel Forwarding to hire lease drivers (individuals who own and operate their own rigs) on a short-term basis. Although it is desirable to have lease drivers available on short notice to help meet peak requirements, the high cost of employing these individuals renders frequent utilization of their services unfeasible. Project C would alleviate this situation by having the firm purchase new rigs and provide more systematic and exacting maintenance of all equipment in service.

Project D: Special Equipment for Handling Coal

A profitable capital investment made in 1970 would be upgraded under project D. The installation of a movable conveyor system to increase railroad car loading efficiency would bring additional profitability by reducing labor costs. Frontloaders are presently being used for car loading and represent a somewhat inefficient utilization of man and machine hours.

On the basis of the pro forma income statement for the coming year, Brooks estimates that approximately $2,250,000 will be available for capital investment from internally generated sources (depreciation plus retained earnings). A 20 percent cost-of-capital has been used in the past for internal funds, and

Brooks sees no reason for departing from this figure. Under the existing capital structure, any additional funds used for capital budgeting purposes will have to come from the three Jenkins brothers, and to make these funds available, they will be required to liquidate personal security holdings.

The firm has a policy that Brooks has been trying to change, so far unsuccessfully, of not using any debt. Brooks proposes to complete the current analysis utilizing the existing capital structure, but then to lower the cost-of-capital for illustrative purposes by including long-term debt in the capital structure. He hopes to demonstrate to the Jenkins brothers the advantages of debt financing and to show them the effect a change in the capital structure would have on the capital budget. (See Table 2).

From discussions with the Jenkins brothers, Brooks concludes that their opportunity cost on outside investments is 26 percent. In other words, funds over and above the $2,250,000 that will be generated internally are available, but the marginal cost of any additional funds is 26 percent rather than the 20 percent cost of internal funds. The Jenkins brothers have thus far refused to introduce debt into the capital structure, but they have agreed to at least listen to Brooks's thoughts on the subject.

Brooks is also working on a five-year financial plan for the company, developing estimates of capital investment opportunities and financial sources for this period. The plan at present is only in its formative stages, so he cannot formally incorporate it into his capital budgeting recommendations for the present year. However, he is reasonably confident of two things. First, he thinks he will be able to persuade the Jenkins brothers to use debt financing

Table 2   Capital Structure and Cost-of-Capital

Present, December 31, 1982

	Amount	Weight	Component Cost	Percent
Debt	0	0	0	0
Preferred stock	0	0	0	0
Common equity	$2,975,000	1.00	20%	20.0
Weighted average cost-of-capital			=	20.0%

Proposed, December 31, 1983

	Amount	Weight	Component Cost	Percent
Debt	$1,250,000	0.250	16.0%	4.0
Preferred stock	0	0	0	0
Common equity	3,504,375	0.750	20.0	15.0
	$4,754,375	1.00		
Weighted average cost-of-capital			=	19.0%

and that this will lower the firm's cost-of-capital. Second, he feels that a recently initiated employee incentive program designed to generate new investment ideas will bear fruit, with the result that Tarheel Forwarding will be able to invest more money at higher rates of return in the future than it has been able to invest in the past.

Questions

1. Calculate: (a) the internal rate of return (IRR) for each project; and (b) the net present value (NPV), using both 20 and 26 percent. (Hint: for Project B's IRR, try 34 percent.)
2. Based on your calculations in Question 1, what projects should Tarheel Forwarding accept for the coming year? (Note: Projects A and B are mutually exclusive.)
3. Draw a graph of NPV versus discount rate for Projects A and B (a net present value profile) using, in part, your answers for (a) and (b) in Question 1. Which project is superior?
4. To develop his firm's investment opportunity schedule (IOS), Brooks will plot each project's IRR on the vertical axis and its required dollar outlay on the horizontal axis, starting with the highest IRR project. By plotting the IOS on a graph with the firm's MCC schedule, Brooks can determine the optimum capital budget. The intersection of the investment opportunity schedule (IOS) and the MCC curve indicates the proper amount of capital investment for the next year. Figure 1 illustrates this process.

   Following the procedure outlined above, develop Tarheel Forwarding's optimum capital budget for 1983. Assume that in addition to the four available projects, funds can be invested in government securities yielding 18 percent.
5. a. Now reconsider the mutually exclusive Projects A and B. At Tarheel Forwarding's marginal cost of capital (MCC), which project should be accepted? (Refer to your answers to Questions 1 and 3.)
   b. Suppose that Brooks discovered a mistake in the projected cash flows for Project D—they should have been $290,400 per year, and D's IRR should have been 27 percent. Determine the effect this change would have on both Tarheel Forwarding's capital budget and its marginal cost-of-capital. Would this situation bear on the decision regarding the mutually exclusive projects? Explain.
6. Assuming that the return on Project A is representative of investment opportunities generally found in the trucking industry, would it be reasonable for Brooks to claim that Project B will generate a return of approximately 34 percent over its four-year life? Explain in terms of available reinvestment rates.

Figure 1

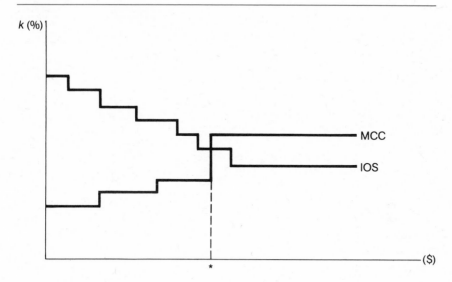

7. If Brooks is confident that he will be able to generate more and better projects in the years to come, but relatively doubtful that he will be able to persuade the Jenkins brothers to employ debt financing, how might this influence his recommendations? Could there ever be a situation in which Project D would be advisable? Explain.
8. Assume that if Project A is adopted, a new warehouse will be constructed in five years to augment the present facility. Adoption of Project B would lead to construction of a new warehouse in one year with the existing structure becoming a maintenance shop. Are these facts of relevance for the current decision? If you believe that they are, explain why they are relevant and indicate how they should be incorporated into the analysis.

Case 14: *Capital Budgeting*

American Business Machines, Inc.

In late 1982, the senior executives of ABM, a major office equipment manufacturer and one of the leading firms in the computer mainframe industry, scheduled a meeting to consider a significant change in corporate strategy. At present, ABM's strategic plan calls for it to concentrate on large computers, which are connected to terminals distributed throughout its customers' operations, rather than on smaller stand-alone computers. However, technological and marketing developments in the early 1980s, including the rapid growth of the home computer market, have led ABM's management to reconsider this decision. They are now thinking of making a major thrust into the small computer business.

ABM's officers are examining a proposal for a two-step, strategic move into small computers. Stage 1 calls for the construction or purchase of a relatively unsophisticated, no-frills manufacturing plant which could go on line almost immediately. Stage 2 calls for the development of a major facility which would house the entire small computer division—research and development, manufacturing, software development, marketing, and general management. Of course, should things not work out well during Stage 1, the Stage 2 expansion could be delayed or cancelled—this is one reason for the staged entry plan.

The decision now at hand concerns Stage 1, and, specifically, the best way to obtain manufacturing facilities during Stage 1 if the decision is made to proceed with the proposed entry into the small computer market. To date, ABM has spent $7 million on R&D, including design and market studies, on the new small computer. Of the $7 million total, $2 million has been expensed, while the remaining $5 million has been capitalized and will be amortized over the operating life of the Stage 1 operation. Under an IRS ruling, $2 million of the expenditures was the maximum that could be expensed; the remainder had to be capitalized and then amortized after the project becomes operational and begins to generate cash revenues. If the small computer project is abandoned, these capitalized R&D expenditures will have produced no information or designs that can be used elsewhere either in other divisions of the company or by anyone else. In this case, they can and will be written off immediately.

Two alternative plant setups are being considered for manufacturing during Stage 1. Under Plan 1, ABM would construct a completely new plant. With Plan 2, ABM would acquire an existing plant, complete with most of the required machinery as well as the necessary working capital, from Computel Corporation.

If ABM decides to build its own plant, it will require a 20-acre site on January 1, 1983 (t = 0). The company currently owns a tract of land in an industrial park which would be suitable for the new plant. However, this particular land is owned by the semiconductor division, which plans an expansion in 1988 (t = 5). This tract cost $1 million, which is also its current market value; other similar sites are available at the same price in the park. If the small computer division takes over the semiconductor division's tract, provisions will have to be made for a replacement. For a payment of $100,000 on January 1, 1983, ABM can obtain an option on a similar 20-acre tract in the same park; exercise of the option would call for the payment of $1.3 million for the property on January 1, 1988. It is estimated that the tract will have a market value of $1.5 million in 1988, so similar tracts should be available for that price in 1988.

If ABM were to build its own plant, most of 1983 would be spent obtaining approvals and so forth; land acquisition at t = 0 would be the only material expenditure during 1983. Actual construction would occur during 1984, and the cost would be $8 million. (Assume that the $8 million expenditure would occur on January 1, 1984, which is t = 1.) The plant would be depreciated, starting on January 1, 1986, by the 175 percent declining balance method[1], over a 15-year period. The building would have a $1.5 million salvage value. Although the depreciable life is 15 years, the plant would actually be used to produce small computers for only five years, from January 1, 1986 through December 31, 1990 (t = 4 through t = 8). It is estimated that the land and buildings would have a market value of $5.3 million at the end of 1990, when the operation would be closed and manufacturing would be shifted to the Stage 2 plant. The $5.3 million is equal to the book value that would exist on December 31, 1990.

The necessary manufacturing equipment, under the build alternative, would be installed during 1985 at a cost of $12 million (assume payment would be made on January 1, 1985, which is t = 2). An investment tax credit of 10 percent is available. The equipment would be depreciated by the 150 percent

1. The 175 percent declining balance method is the maximum rate of depreciation for buildings permitted under the 1981 Tax Code. It is like the double declining balance method, except that 1.75 is used rather than 2.0.

declining balance method over a five-year life toward a zero salvage value. (Assume that removal cost would equal scrap value.)

If ABM builds the Stage 1 plant, an initial investment in net working capital equal to 30 percent of estimated first-year sales would be required in 1986 (assume the investment would be made on December 31, 1985, at t = 3). Additions to net working capital in each subsequent year would be 30 percent of any increase in sales from the previous year. Assume that this investment would be made on December 31 of the preceding year; for example, any additional net working capital needed to support any projected 1988 sales increase would be paid for on December 31, 1987.

ABM's marketing department has projected sales of the new computer at 27,500 units annually, with a range, depending on market conditions, of 15,000 to 40,000 units. The sales price per unit would be set within a range of $1,500 to $2,500, again depending on market conditions, with an expected price of $2,000. The production department has estimated manufacturing costs as follows:

> Variable Costs: 65 percent of sales
> Fixed Costs: $7.5 million annually,
>   excluding depreciation

The sales price, variable costs, and fixed costs other than depreciation are projected to increase with the rate of inflation, which is expected to be 8 percent per year. All operating cash flows are assumed to occur at the end of the year.

If the already existing plant is purchased from Computel Corporation, it will be on a turn-key basis, with payment being made on January 1, 1983, which is t = 0 in this analysis, and with ABM immediately taking over the plant and starting to operate it. (The contract would call for ABM to hire most of the Computel employees and to have access to the plant for training, as needed, prior to the January 1, 1983 closing.) This plant would have a net cost of $50.0 million, and it would be expected to produce after-tax cash flows of $9.625 million per year for eight years. It would have a salvage value of approximately $4 million, which includes a return of the working capital included in the $50.0 million. The salvage value would be expected to equal book value, so no taxes should be involved. Also, the cash flows as given include all tax effects from the $5 million of capitalized R&D costs.

ABM's effective tax rate is 46 percent; its target debt ratio is 40 percent; its cost of new debt is 11 percent; its next expected dividend, D_1, is $1.80; its current stock price, P_0, is $45; and the firm's expected growth rate, g, is 10.37 percent. ABM uses its overall weighted average cost-of-capital in evaluating average risk projects, and it adjusts this figure up or down by 2 percent for more or less risky individual projects. Plan 1 (build the plant) is considered to be above average risk, while Plan 2 (purchase the plant) is considered to have average risk.

Assume that you are a newly graduated MBA who has just joined the capital budgeting staff of ABM. Analyze the facts as given above and reach a conclusion as to (1) whether or not ABM should proceed with the small computer project and, (2) if so, whether it should go with Plan 1 or Plan 2. In developing your decision, use the depreciation schedules and worksheets that follow and answer these questions:

Questions

1. What cost of capital, or discount rate, should ABM use? (Hint: the weighted average cost of capital is equal to $k_a = w_d (k_d)(1 - t) + w_e k_e$, where w_d and w_e are the fractions of debt and equity in the capital structure, k_d and k_e are the respective costs of debt and equity, and t is the corporate tax rate.

2. How should the R&D expenditure be handled under Plan 1? (Assume that this expenditure has already been handled properly in the cash flows given under Plan 2.)

3. What procedure should the semiconductor division use to transfer its land to the small computer project, should that decision be made? If the small computer project is abandoned, what action, if any, should the semiconductor division take?

4. Explain how the depreciation schedules were developed, and then complete the attached schedules.

5. Complete the attached schedule of cash flows.

6. When two mutually exclusive alternatives are being considered, it sometimes happens that one project is preferable if the corporation's cost of capital is relatively low, while the other ranks higher if the cost of capital is relatively high. What conditions can cause such a ranking change? Are those conditions present in this case? If so, at what corporate cost of capital would the two projects have the same ranking?

7. As a new member of ABM's capital budgeting staff, what are your recommendations for this proposed project? Base your decisions on an NPV analysis, but also include your estimation of each project's IRR.

Table 1   Schedule of Depreciation

Building

Cost:	$8,000,000
Salvage value:	1,500,000
Useful life:	15 years
Method:	175% declining balance

Year	Depreciation ($ in thousands)	Balance
1985	—	$8,000
1986	?	
1987	$824	
1988	728	
1989	643	
1990	?	
1991	501	
1992	443	
1993	392	
1994	346	
1995	306	
1996	270	
1997	238	
1998	211	
1999	95	
2000	—	1,500

Table 2   Schedule of Depreciation

Equipment

Cost:	$12,000,000
Salvage value:	0
Useful life:	5 years
Method:	150% declining balance

Year	Depreciation ($ in thousands)	Balance
1985	—	$12,000
1986	?	
1987	$2,520	
1988	1,960	
1989	?	
1990	?	-0-

Note: Switched to straight line in 1988.

Table 3 American Business Machines, Inc.
Analysis of Proposed Investments
($ in thousands)

	1983	1984	1985	1986		1987	1988	1989	1990
PLAN 1	t = 0	t = 1	t = 2	t = 3	t = 4	t = 5	t = 6	t = 7	t = 8
Sales						$59,400		$69,284	
Variable costs						38,610		45,035	
Fixed costs						8,100		9,448	
Depreciation						12,690		14,801	
R & D related	($2,300)					3,344		2,603	
						1,000		1,000	
Earnings before tax						8,346		11,198	
Tax (46%)						3,839		5,151	
Net Income						4,507		6,047	
Depreciation						3,344		2,603	
Amortization						1,000		1,000	
Cash flow						8,851		9,650	
Investment in fixed assets		($ 8,000)	($10,800)a						
Investment in working capital				($16,500)		(1,426)		(1,663)	
Salvage									
Recovery of working capital									
Net cash flow	($ 3,300)	($ 8,000)	($10,800)	($16,500)		$ 7,425		$ 7,987	
IRR									
PLAN 2									
Net cash flow	($50,000)	$ 9,625	$ 9,625	$ 9,625	$ 9,625	$ 9,625	$ 9,625	$ 9,625	$13,625
NPV									
IRR									

a. Cost of equipment less 10% I.T.C.

Case 15: *Capital Budgeting under Uncertainty*

Datronix Corporation

Michael Sullivan is about to make his first major decision as president and chief executive officer of Datronix Corporation, a computer leasing and software firm organized in 1977 by three former Monolithic Business Machine employees. The fledgling company's records of growth and profitability were extraordinary during the period 1977–1980, with earnings amounting to over $30 million in the third year of operation. Because investors assumed that this earnings trend would continue, the company's stock sold at approximately 20 times earnings during 1980, giving the firm a total market value of $600 million. At this point, each of the company's three founders held about 10 percent of the stock and had a paper net worth of approximately $60 million on an initial investment of about $60,000. The remaining 70 percent of the stock was owned by public stockholders, principally mutual funds and bank pension trust managers.

The extraordinary expansion during the first three years of the new company's life was financed partly by the sale of stock now owned by the public and partly by bank credit. Most of the bank credit consisted of short-term loans used to finance equipment that the company purchased and then leased to clients. Each client leased a package which included computer hardware plus programs especially designed and written by Datronix's programmers to meet the client's specialized needs.

The three founders made two mistakes. First, they put up their own stock in the company as collateral for personal bank loans which they used to buy the stock of other computer companies. Second, Datronix purchased a large quantity of computer hardware just before the announcement that the dominant computer manufacturing company was releasing a new and significantly different computer that would make Datronix's recently acquired equipment obsolete. After this announcement, Datronix was forced to lease its old equipment at much lower rates than had been anticipated. At the same time, it had to revamp a number of its older computer programs at considerable cost. The net result was that profits skidded from $30 million in 1980 to $520,000 in 1981, then to a loss of $24 million in 1982.

The sharp earnings decline, coming at a time when the general market was also weak, drove the price of the stock down from its 1980 high of $200 to a low of $10 per share. The fall in the price of the stock reduced the value of the stock that the three founders had put up as collateral for their personal bank loans. When the market value of the securities dropped below the amount of the loan, the bank, acting under a clause in the loan contract, sold the pledged securities on the open market to generate funds to repay the bank loan. This very large sale further depressed the price of Datronix's stock, so the proceeds from the stock sale were not sufficient to retire the bank loan. The bank then sued the three founders for the deficit and won a judgment which required the founders to turn their other stocks over to the bank. This additional stock was not sufficient to pay off the loan in full, and the final result was bankruptcy for the three men. Thus, in just six years, each of the founders saw his net worth go from $60,000 to $60 million to zero.

The corporation itself was badly damaged by this series of events, but it remained intact. When the three major stockholders lost their shares in the company, the large institutional investors, who now had control of the firm, decided to put in a completely new board of directors and to install Mike Sullivan as president and chief executive officer. The institutions would naturally have preferred to sell their holdings of the stock, but they realized that if they attempted to do so they would further depress the market; they were "locked in," in other words.

Sullivan was given significant stock options in the company and was told that he was expected to restore the firm's lost luster. At the last annual meeting, there was some debate among the institutional stockholders concerning the firm's underlying philosophy. The more aggressive institutions wanted the company to take more chances, while the conservative holders preferred a more cautious approach. The issue was never resolved, and Sullivan concluded that he could decide the risk posture of the firm for himself.

Sullivan was certain that his own position would be on solid ground if he followed a high-risk, high-return policy—and was successful. His stock options under these conditions would be extremely valuable, and his salary would be assured. He also knew that he would be out of a job if he followed such a policy and the company was not successful. On the other hand, he was not altogether sure what his position would be if he followed a conservative policy. The company could survive and make a modest profit, but he might still end up losing his job.

The first major decision Sullivan must make involves a system for transmitting data from clients, storing the data, and retrieving it for later processing. Three alternative systems are available. Some information on these methods is presented in Table 1. With Project A, the U.S. Telephone and Telegraph

Table 1   Alternative Methods for Data Handling Systems

Outflows

| | Project A | | Project B | | Project C |
Probability	Cash Outflows	Probability	Cash Outflows	Probability	Cash Outflows
1.0	$30,000,000	0.10	$30,000,000	0.06	$40,000,500
		0.20	27,500,000	0.15	32,500,000
		0.40	25,000,000	0.35	25,000,000
		0.20	22,500,000	0.30	21,500,000
		0.10	20,000,000	0.14	18,035,500

Inflows

Probability	Project A Cash Inflows	Project B Cash Inflows	Project C Cash Inflows
0.050	$ 9,998,000	$12,790,000	$16,100,000
0.360	7,998,000	9,790,000	12,100,000
0.360	5,998,000	6,790,000	8,100,000
0.167	2,798,000	1,180,000	− 600,000
0.050	− 204,000	− 4,410,000	− 7,100,000
0.013	− 3,002,000	− 8,010,000	− 11,900,000

Company would provide Datronix with all necessary receiving, storage, and switching equipment, and transmission facilities for $30 million. The actual cash inflows from this system would depend partly on sales of the new service and also on the level of mainly variable operating costs incurred by Datronix. Project B calls for Datronix to purchase all switching, receiving, and network access hardware, but to lease transmission facilities from U.S. Telephone and Telegraph. Initial costs with this system are not known with certainty, and it will obligate the firm to cover a substantially higher level of fixed operating costs than would be required for Project A. Project C calls for the purchase of satellite ground stations and switching systems for several hub cities and leasing satellite half circuits from American Satellite Communications Corporation. Local telephone loops would be used to connect Datronix's customers to the ground stations. Installation costs are quite uncertain as are cash flows from the service. Operating costs for the satellite system are mainly fixed.

Sullivan noted that if the worst possible cash inflows resulted from Project C, Datronix would be insolvent and would be forced to declare bankruptcy. All of the projects' cash outflows will be incurred in the first year. He estimates that the actual first-year cash flow from each project, whatever the flow turns out to be, will continue for the entire ten-year life of each project. Of course, if the large first-year loss on Project C is incurred, the service will be dropped because the company will be bankrupt.

Questions

1. Sullivan realizes how important this first major decision is, not only to Datronix Corporation, but also to his own future. Therefore, he has requested that all quantifiable data upon which he will base his final decision be compiled and presented to him. The data needed are shown in the following table. Complete the blank cells:

	Expected Cash Flow ($\bar{x}$)	Standard Deviation of Cash Flow (σ)	Coefficient of Variation of Cash Flow (v)	Expected Cost ($\bar{x}$)	Standard Deviation of Cost (σ)	Coefficient of Variation of Cost (v)[a]
Project A	$5,956,500	$2,631,463	0.4418	$30,000,000	0.0	0.000
Project B	$6,480,730	$4,395,420	0.6782	$25,000,000	$2,738,613	0.1095
Project C						

a. The coefficient of variation is equal to $\sigma/\bar{x}$.

Based on these data, which project appears to be most risky? Least risky?

2. Calculate the internal rate of return on each project based on expected values of the inflows and outflows.

3. Determine the expected net present value of each project based on expected values of inflows and outflows assuming that a 20 percent cost-of-capital is appropriate for Datronix Corporation.

4. With the cash flow patterns given in the case, could the net present value (NPV) and internal rate of return (IRR) result in conflicting rankings? (Hint: Drawing the present value profile for each project all on the same graph would be helpful.)

5. Is it reasonable to use a 20 percent cost-of-capital for each project even though their costs and return probability distributions differ? What methods of dealing with risk are available to Sullivan? Assuming that 20 percent was a reasonable cost of capital for an average project in the computer services industry, what are reasonable costs of capital for these projects? Explain, and discuss other required information, if any.

6. Assume that Sullivan instructs you to use different risk-adjusted discount rates for each project, and that he suggests that 16 percent is reasonable for Project A, 20 percent for Project B, and 30 percent for Project C. Calculate the risk-adjusted net present values for each project. Do conflicting rankings in terms of the risk-adjusted NPV and IRR occur? If so, why? If 20 percent is used to evaluate B, what costs of capital for A and C would make them appear equally as good as B?

7. Assume that Sullivan's job as president of Datronix is to maximize the value of the firm and thereby maximize the stockholders' wealth. Disregard his personal situation and feelings. Which approach do you think should be taken, an aggressive one or a conservative one? Now go on to consider how Sullivan's personal situation might affect his decision; that is, could his personal situation cause him to make a decision that is not in the best interest of the stockholders?

8. Which of the projects do you think Sullivan should accept (a) if he operates strictly with stockholders' interest in mind, and (b) considering his personal situation? Assume that one of the projects must be chosen.

9. If the returns from Projects A, B, and C had strong negative correlation with the normal expected earnings of most firms in the economy, would this affect your estimates of expected NPV? Would you still consider C to be the riskiest project? How would it affect the overall riskiness of the firm? The overall cost-of-capital?

10. (Optional question: The solution requires a knowledge of the Hillier model for finding σ_{NPV} when cash flows are independent over time.) Assume that the cash flows for each project in year t are independent of cash flows in year $(t - 1)$. What is σ_{NPV} for Project A? Would this σ_{NPV} be larger or smaller if the cash flows were completely dependent, i.e., if the cash flows in year 1 were random, but then cash flows in years 2-10 were exactly equal to the level of cash flows achieved in year 1? Note: use $R_F = 14$ percent; $\sigma_{NPV(B)} = \$8,203,442$; and $\sigma_{NPV(C)} = \$12,242,066$.

Part **3:** Financial Instruments and Markets

Case 16: *Short-Term Credit*

Ashford Cycle Works, Inc.

In reviewing financial projections for 1982 together with actual balance sheets for 1980 and 1981 (see Table 1), James Mosley, financial vice-president of Ashford Cycle Works, Inc., saw some rather significant trends developing. While he was pleased with projections of the rate of return on net worth, he was disturbed by the declining profit margin on sales, the falling rate of return on assets, and, especially, the deteriorating liquidity position and markedly higher projected debt ratio. These ratios and appropriate industry averages are shown in Table 2.

Ashford Cycle Works, a nationally known producer of top quality bicycles, is located in Elk Grove, Illinois. Established in 1920, the company has grown steadily since that time. In 1980, however, the decision was made to embark on a rapid expansion program to take advantage of the growing market for mopeds. This product line expansion called for increases in assets of approximately 50 percent in both 1981 and 1982.

As Mosley studied the projections provided by his financial staff, his concern increased. The liquidity position at the end of 1981 was below the level prescribed by the company's board of directors. The level projected for the end of 1982 is completely unacceptable; something will have to be done to increase the current and quick ratios. The debt ratio is worrisome, to say the least, but Mosley had anticipated this development. In fact, the rising debt ratio was discussed at the last directors' meeting, and the decision was made to let the ratio climb to the level shown for 1982. The directors tentatively agreed, however, to consider a cut in the dividend until the debt ratio can be reduced to approximately the level of the industry average, but final action has not been taken on this point.

Mosley had not foreseen either the declining profit margin on sales or the falling rate of return on assets. In fact, he had counted on increases in both of these items because of the increased level of efficiency resulting from the plant modernization and expansion program. As he studied the figures, however,

Table 1 Ashford Cycle Works, Inc.

	1980	1981	Estimated 1982
Cash and securities	$ 1,400,000	$ 1,800,000	$ 4,932,000
Accounts receivable	6,820,000	9,030,000	14,250,000
Inventories			
Raw materials	698,000	1,220,000	1,538,000
Work in process	5,947,000	10,131,000	18,265,000
Finished goods	375,000	649,000	1,047,000
Total inventories	$ 7,020,000	$ 12,000,000	$ 20,850,000
Total current assets	$15,240,000	$ 22,830,000	$ 40,032,000
Net fixed assets	12,760,000	19,170,000	22,968,000
Total assets	$28,000,000	$ 42,000,000	$ 63,000,000
Accounts payable[a]	$ 2,750,000	$ 6,800,000	$ 17,700,000
Notes payable (Bank 12%)	3,110,000	4,071,000	4,700,000
Total current liabilities	$ 5,860,000	$ 10,871,000	$ 22,400,000
Long term debt	5,401,000	10,305,000	15,000,000
Common equity	16,739,000	20,824,000	25,600,000
Total claims	$28,000,000	$ 42,000,000	$ 63,000,000
Sales	$70,000,000	$90,268,000	$125,350,000

a. Accounts payable are reported net of discounts even if not taken.

Mosley realized why these declines had occurred. During 1981, the company abandoned its policy of taking cash discounts on all purchases. (The firm purchases materials on terms of 3/10, net 30.) This loss of discounts contributed to an increase in costs and a resulting decline in the profit margins and rate of return.

Table 2 Significant Industry Ratios

Key Ratios	1980	1981	Estimated 1982	Average Industry (1981)
Current ratio	2.6X	2.1X	1.80X	2.2X
Quick ratio	1.4X	1.0X	0.86X	1.2X
Debt ratio	40.0%	50.0%	59.00%	43.0%
Profit margin on sales	6.0%	5.3%	5.3%	6.0%
Rate of return on assets	15.0%	11.4%	10.6%	11.0%
Rate of return on net worth	25.0%	23.0%	26.0%	23.0%

Mosley's conviction that some important changes must be made, and quickly, is reinforced when his secretary brings him a letter from the insurance company that holds Ashford's long-term debt. The insurance company voices some concern over the declining liquidity position and points out that the agreement under which the loan was made requires the company to maintain a current ratio of at least 2 to 1. The letter closes by stating that Ashford Cycle Works is expected to correct the liquidity position in the very near future. As Mosley interprets it, if he can devise a plan whereby the liquidity ratios will be corrected within a reasonable period of time, the insurance company will give the firm time to correct the deficiency.

Mosley first questions whether the company should slow down its expansion program. However, the more he thinks about it, the more difficult this alternative appears. In the first place, the company has already contracted for the fixed-assets expansion, so it is impossible to reduce the $23 million figure anticipated for 1982. The company could slow down its rate of growth in sales by turning down orders, and this would enable it to reduce the estimated figures for 1982 for working capital: cash, accounts receivable, and inventories. However, if orders were turned down, the company would fail to make profitable sales. This would obviously hurt the profit figures and, in addition, would create some ill will that could harm future operations if crucial retail outlets were lost. He concludes that the alternative of slowing down sales is highly undesirable.

Turning to the liability side of the financial statement, Mosley recognizes that the anticipated level of accounts payable will present two problems. First, the $17.7 million accounts payable that the staff has projected for 1982 is based on the assumption that accounts payable will not be paid until 30 days past their due date. Although Mosley realizes that such delays are common in the industry, he feels that delayed payments could also hurt the company's reputation for being an excellent customer. Its suppliers make every effort to give the company not only quick delivery, but also first call on available supplies during shortage periods. Further, because of its reputation as a responsible company, Ashford Cycle Works has been able to negotiate favorable prices in its supply contracts. If it becomes a slow-paying account, as the current projections prepared by his staff would have it, these intangible benefits could be lost. The second problem with the accounts payable projections, of course, is that the firm would continue to lose trade discounts, as it did during 1981.

One way of reducing the accounts payable would be to increase notes payable to banks. In 1981 Ashford Cycle Works attempted to borrow additional funds from the Grove State Bank, with which the firm has been dealing since it was founded. However, the bank was not able to make additional loans to the company because it has capital and surplus of only $82 million, and the bank cannot lend more than 10 percent of this amount to any one customer. Because of this limitation, Mosley has been considering establishing relations with a larger bank in Chicago. Eugene Collier, president of Grove State Bank, suggests that it is feasible that additional bank loans at a 12 percent rate, discount interest, with a 10 percent compensating balance, could be gotten from Northern Trust of Illinois. Under the terms of the proposed bank loan, Ashford Cycle Works would be required to give a blanket pledge on all assets that are not already used as security for existing loans. Further, the bank loan could not be granted if either accounts receivable pledging or factoring is employed.

Mosley also has been informed that he can obtain a loan secured by accounts receivable from a major finance company. The interest rate on such a loan would be 15 percent if accounts receivable are pledged for the loan, or 14 percent plus a 5 percent discount from the face value of each accounts receivable invoice if the credit is obtained by factoring the receivables on a nonrecourse basis. Since his company has its own well-developed credit department, Mosley questions the wisdom of factoring accounts receivable.

As another alternative, Mosley is also considering the use of commercial paper. He has noted in recent issues of the *Wall Street Journal* that commercial paper rates at the present time are approximately 13 percent. For the past few years commercial paper dealers had contacted Mosley every two or three months to ask whether he was interested in obtaining funds through the commercial paper market, but he has not received any solicitation from these dealers for the last six months.

Finally, Mosley wonders about the possibility of obtaining credit secured by his inventories. They are projected to rise to almost $21 million by the end of 1982, and if a lower rate of interest could be obtained by virtue of the fact that the loan would be secured by his inventories, Mosley would be willing to use them as collateral.

There is no possibility of selling additional long-term debt. The loan agreement with the insurance company calls for Ashford Cycle Works to receive an additional $4.695 million during 1982, but it specifies that the company can obtain no other new long-term debt financing. Because of the directors' desire to maintain their control position, the board of directors has decreed that there will be no new common stock issues during 1982.

Questions

1. Does the commercial paper market now present a feasible alternative to the Ashford Cycle Works? Explain your reasoning.
2. Discuss the feasibility of Ashford's using its inventory as collateral for a loan. If this form of financing is undertaken, what type of security arrangements would probably be used?
3. What are the advantages and disadvantages of allowing accounts payable to build up, as the financial staff has suggested? Discuss specifically the firm's

declining liquidity position and its use of "spontaneous" financing through trade credit.

4. Discuss the pros and cons of Ashford's using accounts receivable financing at the present time. If the company elects to use receivables financing, would it be better off factoring its receivables or pledging its accounts receivable?

5. Assume that Ashford Cycle Works does not go along with suggestions of building up accounts payable to 60 days (reflected in the 1982 pro forma balance sheet in Table 1) but opts instead to start paying in 10 days and taking discounts.

   a. What is the revised amount of Ashford Cycle Work's projected year-end 1982 accounts payable?

   b. Calculate the amount of funds Ashford Cycle Works would have to borrow in order to take discounts. Assume at this point that bank borrowing, at 12 percent discount interest and with a 10 percent compensating balance requirement, is used. Also assume that all asset accounts, including the cash and securities now on hand, cannot be reduced. Base your answer on Ashford's "steady state" borrowing requirements, which means disregarding the one-time funds requirements to account for the fact that accounts payable are currently carried at net, yet most of them will have to be paid off at gross.

   c. What are the net savings that Ashford will realize from borrowing to take the discounts? Note that accounts payable are recorded net of discounts. (Hint: Find the annual gross purchases as the initial step.)

6. What effect would Mosley's decision to accept cash discounts have upon the current ratio, quick ratio, and profit margin? No further calculations are required for this question.

7. Should Ashford Cycle Works establish relations with and arrange a line of credit from Northern Trust of Illinois or another large Chicago bank?

8. What specific actions do you think James Mosley should recommend for Ashford Cycle Works during the coming year?

Case 17: *Refunding a Bond Issue*

Cumberland Gas and Electric

Paul Malone, financial vice-president of Cumberland Gas and Electric, is reviewing the minutes of the last meeting of the firm's board of directors. The major topic discussed was whether or not Cumberland should refund a $500 million issue of 26-year, 16 percent, first mortgage bonds issued 11 months earlier. Three of the board members had taken markedly different positions on the question. At the conclusion of the meeting, Martha Seligman, chairman of the board, requested that Malone prepare a report analyzing the alternative points of view.

The bonds in question had been issued the previous October, when interest rates were at their peak. At that time, Malone and the board of directors thought that interest rates were at a high and would likely decline in the future, but they had no idea that the slump would come so soon and be so sharp. Now, less than a year later, A rated utility bonds, such as those of Cumberland, can be sold to yield only 12½ percent.

Since Malone anticipated a decline in interest rates when the $500 million issue was sold, he had insisted that the bonds be made immediately callable. The investment bankers handling the issue wanted Cumberland to make the bonds noncallable for a five-year period, but Malone resisted this proposal. (If he had inserted the five-year call protection provision in the loan contract, the firm would have received an interest rate of approximately 15 percent, 1 percentage point less than the actual 16 percent.) The bankers insisted on a call premium of 10 percent if any bonds were called during the first year, with the premium declining by ½ percent a year until the twentieth year, after which the bonds could be called with no premium whatsoever.

Malone estimates that Cumberland could sell a new issue of 25-year bonds at an interest rate of 12½ percent. The call of old and sale of new bonds would take place in about five to seven weeks. The flotation cost on a refunding issue would be approximately ½ of 1 percentage point of the issue, and there would be a period of approximately three weeks during which both issues would be outstanding. During this overlap period, the excess funds could be invested in short-term Treasury securities yielding 10 percent.

Malone had proposed, at the last directors' meeting, that the company call the 16 percent bonds and refund them with a new 12½ percent issue. Although the refunding cost would be substantial, he believes that the savings of 3½ percent a year for 25 years on a $500 million issue would be well worth the refunding cost. Malone did not anticipate adverse reactions from the other board members, but three of them voiced strong opposition to the refunding proposal. The first, Henry Halstead, a long-term member of the board and chairman of Halstead, Babcock, and Company, an investment banking house catering mainly to institutional clients such as insurance companies, pension funds, and the like, argued that calling the bonds for refunding would not be well received by the major financial institutions that hold the firm's outstanding bonds. Halstead pointed out that no utility, at least within his memory span, had called a bond issue in less than three years. According to Halstead, the institutional investors that hold the bonds had purchased them on the expectation of receiving the 16 percent interest rate for at least three years, and these investors would be very much disturbed by a call after only one year. Since most of the lending institutions hold some of Cumberland's bonds, and since the firm typically sells new bonds or common stock to finance its growth every two or three years, it would be most unfortunate if institutional investors develop a feeling of ill will towards the company.

The second, George Parker, a relatively new member of the board and president of a local bank, also opposed the call but for an entirely different reason. Parker believed that the decline in interest rates was not yet over. He stated that a study by his bank suggested that the long-term interest rate might fall as low as 10 percent within the next six months. Under questioning from the other board members, however, Parker admitted that the interest rate decline could in fact be over and that interest rates might, very shortly, begin to move back up again.

The third, Frank Erickson, president of a management consulting firm specializing in utility operations, stated that he was not opposed in principle to refunding operations, but questioned whether the proposed refunding would be profitable in view of: (1) the very high call premium that would be incurred; (2) flotation costs on the refunding issue; and (3) the firm's 14.5 percent overall average cost-of-capital. Erickson suggested that a formal analysis using discounted cash flow (DCF) techniques be employed to determine the feasibility of the refunding. As he reflected on Erickson's proposal, Malone wondered whether it might not be better to modify the DCF analysis, if it were followed, by using Cumberland's cost-of-debt rather than its average cost-of-capital. Further, if the cost-of-debt were used, he wondered whether a before- or after-tax figure should be employed.

Questions

1. Calculate the net present value of the savings, assuming that Cumberland Gas and Electric goes ahead with the refunding. Assume that the firm has a 40 percent marginal tax rate and that $2,625,000 of unamortized flotation costs remain for the old issue. (Hint: the PVIFA of 7½ percent for 25 years is 11.1469.)
2. Give a critique of each of the positions taken by the various board members.
3. Should the refunding operation be undertaken at this time?
4. How would the subjective probability distribution of expected future interest rates affect the decision to refund now or to wait? Draw a distribution curve that suggests refunding be immediate and one that suggests that the refunding be deferred.
5. Discuss the discount rate used to evaluate future interest savings. What are the relative merits of using the after-tax current bond rate as opposed to the after-tax average cost-of-capital? Use hypothetical probability distributions of cash flows from the refunding operation versus cash flows from a "typical" project to illustrate your answer.
6. If the yield curve were downward sloping, and if Malone felt that "the market knows more than I do" about the future course of interest rates, how might this affect his decision to recommend immediate refunding or to defer the refunding?

Case **18:** *Investment Banking*

Ariel Electronics, Inc.

Last year, three executives of Hoffman Technology, Ltd., one of the largest privately owned corporations in the world, decided to break away from Hoffman and set up a company of their own. The principal reason for this decision was capital gains. Hoffman Technology stock is all privately owned, and the corporate structure makes it impossible for executives to obtain stock purchase options. Hoffman's executives receive substantial salaries and bonuses, but this income is all taxable at normal tax rates, and no capital gains opportunities are available.

The three men, Norman Scott, Frank Ryan, and Keith Bernhardt, located a medium-size electronics manufacturing company available for purchase. The stock of this firm, Ariel Electronics, Inc., is all owned by the founder, Ralph Lucas. Although the company is in excellent shape, Lucas wants to sell it because of his failing health. A price of $8,250,000 based on a price-earnings ratio of 12 and annual earnings of $687,500, has been established. Lucas has given the three prospective purchasers an option to buy the company for the agreed price, the option to run for six months, during which time the men are to arrange financing.

Bernhardt has contacted Lane Carlson, a partner of the New York investment banking firm of Carlson, Warren and Company and an acquaintance of some years' standing, for aid in obtaining the funds necessary to complete the purchase. Scott, Ryan, and Bernhardt each have some money available to put into the new enterprise, but they need a substantial amount of outside capital. There is some possibility of borrowing part of the money, but Carlson has discouraged this idea. For one thing, Ariel Electronics is already highly leveraged. If the purchasers were to borrow additional funds, there would be a very serious risk, in the event of a recession in the electronics industry, that they would be unable to service this debt. Although the firm is currently earning $687,500 a year, this figure could quickly turn into a loss in the event of a few canceled defense contracts or cost miscalculations. Carlson's second reason for discouraging a loan is that Scott, Ryan, and Bernhardt plan not only to operate and expand Ariel internally, but also to use the corporation as a vehicle for making further acquisitions of electronics companies. This being the case, Carlson believes it would be wise for the company to keep any borrowing potential in reserve for use in later acquisitions.

Carlson proposes that the three partners obtain funds to purchase Ariel Electronics, Inc. in accordance with the figures shown in Table 1. Ariel would be reorganized with an authorized six million shares, 1,350,000 to be issued at the time the transfer takes place, and the other 4,650,000 to be held in reserve for possible issuance in connection with acquisitions. Scott, Ryan, and Bernhardt would each purchase 120,000 shares at a price of one dollar a share, the par value. Carlson, Warren and Company would purchase 150,000 shares at a price of $8.50. The remaining 840,000 shares would be sold to the public at a price of $8.50 per share.

Carlson, Warren and Company's underwriting fee would be 5 percent of the shares sold to the public, or $357,000. Legal fees, accounting fees, and other charges associated with the issue would amount to $63,000, for a total underwriting cost of $420,000. After deducting the underwriting charges and payments to Lucas from the gross proceeds of the stock sale, the reorganized Ariel Electronics would receive funds in the amount of $105,000, which would be used for internal expansion purposes.

Table 1 Purchase Financing Proposal

Price paid to Lucas			
(12 × $687,500 earnings)			$8,250,000
Authorized shares		6,000,000	
Initially issued shares		1,350,000	
Initial Distribution of Shares			
Scott	120,000 shares at $1.00		120,000
Ryan	120,000 shares at $1.00		120,000
Bernhardt	120,000 shares at $1.00		120,000
Carlson, Warren and Co.	150,000 shares at $8.50		1,275,000
Public stockholders	840,000 shares at $8.50		7,140,000
	1,350,000		$8,775,000
Underwriting costs: 5% of $7,140,000	$ 357,000		
Legal fees, and so on, associated with issue	63,000		420,000
			$8,355,000
Payment to Lucas			8,250,000
Net funds to Ariel Electronics, Inc.			$ 105,000

As a part of the initial agreement, Scott, Ryan, and Bernhardt each would be given options to purchase an additional 80,000 shares at a price of $8.50 per share. Carlson, Warren and Company would be given an option to purchase an additional 100,000 shares at $8.50 a share.

Questions

1. What is the total underwriting charge, expressed as a percentage of the funds raised by the underwriter? Does this charge seem reasonable in the light of published statistics on the cost of floating new issues of common stock?
2. Suppose that the three men estimate the following probabilities for the firm's stock price one year from now:

Price	Probability
$ 3.50	0.05
7.00	0.10
12.50	0.35
13.90	0.35
19.40	0.10
22.90	0.05

Assuming Carlson, Warren and Company exercises its options at the expected stock prices, calculate the following ratio (ignore time-discount effects):

$$\frac{\text{total return to Carlson, Warren and Company}}{\text{funds raised by underwriter}}$$

Disregard Carlson, Warren and Company's profit on the 150,000 shares it bought outright at the initial offering. Comment on the ratio.
3. Are Scott, Ryan, and Bernhardt purchasing their stock at a "fair" price? Should the prospectus disclose the fact that they would buy their stock at one dollar per share while the public stockholders would buy their stock at $8.50 per share?
4. Would it be reasonable for Carlson, Warren and Company to purchase its initial 150,000 shares at a price of one dollar?
5. Do you foresee any problems of control for Scott, Ryan, and Bernhardt?
6. Would the expectation of an exceptionally great need for investment funds next year be a relevant consideration when deciding upon the amount of funds to be raised now?

Case 19: *Rights Offerings*

Fairchild Industries

Fairchild Industries is one of the largest manufacturers of mobile homes in the nation. Organized in 1932, the company experienced a steady rate of growth in the post-World War II period, when its market consisted primarily of vacationers, companies needing trailers for use at construction sites, and residents of areas where temporary housing was required. However, in the 1960s and 1970s more and more mobile homes were produced for use as permanent residences, particularly for retired persons and young married couples, while sales of units for vacation homes remained strong.

In 1980 and 1981, the demand for mobile homes increased even faster than in the past. The tight money and high interest rates that prevailed during these years hit the housing industry harder than most other sectors of the economy, and, as a result, the construction of conventional housing units was drastically curtailed. The reduction in housing construction, combined with the increase of new families as the members of the post-World War II "baby boom" married, produced a serious housing shortage. The scarcity of conventional homes and apartments stimulated the sale of mobile homes, which are much less expensive than the average house or apartment, and which can be financed through normal bank channels even when customary sources of mortgage funds have dried up. In addition, the introduction of the "triple wide" mobile home has proved to be a great impetus to sales in recent years. Finally, the mobile home industry was helped by the passage of an amendment to the National Housing Act which allowed the Federal Housing Administration to insure loans on mobile homes for as long as 12 years at a fixed interest rate.

To meet the increased demand, Fairchild Industries is undertaking a major capital expansion program. Approximately $45 million in new capital, over and above an expected $7.5 million of retained earnings, is required for the years 1982 and 1983. Of this $45 million, $22.5 million has already been borrowed from a group of five insurance companies on a long-term basis. The loan agreement, which has already been finalized, calls for Fairchild to raise an additional $22.5 million through the sale of common stock.

Fairchild's board of directors is considering alternative ways to raise the $22.5 million in new equity funds. The firm's investment banker, Sampson Brothers, has informed the board members of the following possibilities:

1. Fairchild can sell shares of stock directly to the public, not to stockholders, at a price of $48 per share. The company would net $45.50 per share, with $2.50 per share going to the investment bankers as a commission. The current market price of the stock is $49, but the investment bankers feel that the price will decline temporarily to $48 as a result of the new shares coming on the market. The investment bankers will, of course, promote the new issue in an effort to stimulate demand.
2. The company can sell shares to its stockholders at a price of $45 per share. An oversubscription plan giving stockholders the right to any stock not taken in the primary rights offering would be employed. Sampson Brothers would guarantee the sale of the issue, and the commission would be $1.50 per share for every share subscribed to by stockholders, and $3.50 per share for any shares left unsubscribed after the oversubscription, which would be purchased by Sampson Brothers. In other words, if its stockholders subscribed to the full amount of the rights offering, Fairchild would receive $45 per share less a $1.50 commission, or a total of $43.50 per share. The proceeds of any unsubscribed shares would be $45 minus $3.50 commission or $41.50 per share.
3. Fairchild can sell stock through a rights offering at a price of $40 per share. Under this agreement, the underwriting cost would be $0.75 for each share subscribed to, and $3.50 for each unsubscribed share purchased by the investment banker.
4. Shares can be sold to current stockholders at a price of $25 per share. Under this arrangement, underwriting costs would be $0.25 per share for each share subscribed to by stockholders, and $3.50 per share for each share taken by the investment banker.
5. Shares can be sold to current stockholders at $5 per share. The assistance of investment bankers would not be necessary under this proposal, as the company could be quite sure that all shares offered would be taken.

After reviewing the proposals for the distribution of the new common stock issue, the six members of Fairchild's board of directors had conflicting opinions as to the best alternative.

Brice and Kent Fairchild, the oldest members of the board and the original founders of Fairchild Industries, thought that Proposal 2 was the best because a rights offering at a high subscription price would result in the least amount of dilution in earnings per share while still giving loyal stockholders an opportunity to maintain their equity positions at a discount. They both opposed Proposal 1 because it would dilute proportional ownership and give voting power to outsiders. Brice Fairchild stated, "If we sell directly to the public, we will be going against the interests of the current stockholders. Furthermore, to choose any other alternative would cause serious dilution of the market price of the stock, which is a testament to our success." Kent Fairchild was not as strongly opposed as Brice to Proposals 3 and 4, but he did agree with Brice that dilution in earnings per share could hurt the company's hard-earned reputation.

Disagreeing with both of the Fairchilds was Bill Arena, president of City National Bank, Fairchild Industries' primary bank. Arena argued, "Proposal 1 is the most favorable because it will allow for greater distribution of the stock throughout the market." He believed that this would expose the firm to a wider range of knowledgeable investors who would buy Fairchild Industries stock with genuine interest in the operations and objectives of the company. Arena also noted that selling the new issue at a minimal discount would alleviate any significant depressing effect on the current market price, and that, based on rights offerings in related industries, 60 percent of the stockholders would be expected to sell their rights to outsiders anyway.

Mary Brouske represented the interest of an influential group of local professional business people who own a large block of Fairchild stock. She stated to the board, "Proposal 1 is clearly against the position of my constituents, since present stockholders should have the right to maintain their proportionate holdings in the company with as little dilution as possible." Brouske also opposed Proposal 2 because of the high risk of unfavorable market price fluctuations. If the market price of the stock were to drop below $45 per share, the flotation costs of the issue would go up dramatically. Brouske contended that Proposal 3 is the best alternative because it provides an adequate margin of safety against downward market price fluctuations, protects the stockholders from excessive equity dilution entailed in Proposals 4 and 5, and gives an appealing purchase discount.

Jorge Christy, a representative of many small stockholders, argued that Proposal 5 is the only fair alternative. He said, "If a shareholder is given a privileged rights offering, he is almost forced to contribute additional capital or to accept an equity dilution as a consequence." He thought that the privilege of maintaining a proportionate share of the company is an important factor in upholding stockholder loyalty and argued that Proposals 2 and 3 cater to a small percentage of stockholders who may have immediate funds available for reinvestment, while leaving the larger percentage of stockholders no choice but to sell their rights. A subscription price of five dollars per share would appeal to a wider range of stockholders, and Fairchild Industries could be assured that all shares offered would be taken. Not only would this enhance stockholder relations, but it would also eliminate the need for investment banking services. "I do realize the stock split effect of this proposal," Christy said, "but I believe the anticipated increase in future earnings will put the price of our stock within a more favorable trading range."

After listening to the various arguments, Monk Robbins, board chairman, tentatively concluded that Proposal 4 is the best alternative, since it appears to contain favorable aspects of each proposal. In his view, Proposal 1 fails to consider the importance of stockholder loyalty, while Proposal 5 goes to the opposite extreme and neglects the hard-earned reputation of Fairchild Industries' stock price. He also argued against Proposal 2 by pointing up that the high risk of unfavorable market fluctuations, due to the small discount margin, could result in high flotation expenses. Proposal 3 has a reasonable safety margin between the subscription price and the market price of the stock, but he felt that the ex-rights price per share would be above the optimum trading range. Proposal 4 would, however, put the stock in a popular trading range; a subscription price of $25 would ensure a successful offering at a low flotation cost, and the resulting ex-rights price would appeal to a wider range of investors.

As the time for the board's adjournment approached, Monk Robbins asked Steve Smythe, financial vice-president, to prepare a report recommending which, if any, of the alternatives should be accepted. Tables 1 and 2 provide some of the data Smythe needs as he works on the report.

Table 1   Balance Sheet

Year Ended December 31, 1981 (in millions)

Cash and marketable securities	$ 5.25	
Accounts receivable	34.30	
Inventories	36.90	
Total current assets		$ 76.45
Fixed assets (net)	$65.00	
Total assets		$141.45
Accounts payable	$14.65	
Bank loans	20.85	
Total current liabilities		$ 35.50
Long-term debt		$ 30.00
Capital stock (4 million shares outstanding)	$20.00	
Retained earnings	55.95	
Total common equity		$ 75.95
Total claims on assets		$141.45

Table 2   Selected Financial Data

	1979	1980	1981
Total earnings after taxes (in millions)	$ 7.30	$ 7.875	$ 8.60
Total dividends paid (in millions)	1.125	1.625	2.125
Market price per share (year ended)	37.75	42.625	48.50

Questions

1. How many additional shares of stock would be sold under each of the proposals submitted by Sampson Brothers? Assume all shares are subscribed. (Round shares to nearest 1,000.)

2. How many rights will be required to purchase one new share under each of the four rights proposals?

3. What is the market value of each right under each of the proposals? Do you think that the average stockholder would bother to either exercise his rights or sell them at these prices? Use the rights formula to answer this question.

4. What is the price per share immediately after issue of the new shares under each of the four proposals? Use the rights formula to answer this question.

5. Selling stock through a rights offering with the subscription price set below the current market price has an effect that is similar to that of a stock split or stock dividend. What is the percentage of the stock dividend that would have to be declared to have the same effect—that is, produce the same final price per share—as each of the proposals for rights offerings?

6. Assume that the company increases its total assets by $22.5 million in net proceeds by issuing common stock at the start of 1982 (all other sources of funds, such as debt or retained earnings, are ignored for this calculation), and that the company earns 10 percent after interest and taxes on its beginning assets in 1982. Spelled out in more detail, this implies that: (a) the company earns 10 percent after interest and taxes on total assets in 1982; (b) the company obtained only $22.5 million of new equity financing during 1982; that is, the debt financing is deferred until 1983; (c) new outside capital is fully employed during the entire year of 1982; (d) additions to retained earnings in 1982 are not employed until 1983; and (e) that current liabilities remain at their 1981 level. (Note: The company's stock issue was sold to the market for more than $22.5 million, but the investment bankers retained the difference to cover flotation charges. Therefore capital stock increases by exactly $22.5 million.) What will the rate of return on net worth, earnings per share, and the price of the stock (assuming a price-earnings ratio of 20) be in 1982 under each of the alternative methods? Do not use the formula to answer this question.

7. Why do the price-per-share figures in Question 6 differ from those found in Question 4? Which seems more realistic?

8. What are the maximum and minimum flotation costs under each of the proposals? Assume that the probability of the subscription percentage may be estimated by using the following probabilities for maximum and minimum flotation costs:

Proposal	1	2	3	4	5
Probability of no rights being exercised	—	0.30	0.20	0.10	0.00
Probability of 100% of the rights being exercised	—	0.70	0.80	0.90	1.00

   What are the expected flotation costs as a percentage of gross funds raised under each proposal? What specific condition might cause the maximum cost to be incurred?

9. What effects do you think a rights offering as opposed to an offering to the general public would have on "stockholder loyalty" to the company?

10. Make a summary appraisal of each proposal and decide which method of financing Smythe should recommend to the board of directors.

Case 20: *Decision to Go Public*

Sequoia Timber Corporation

Sequoia Timber Corporation was organized in 1945 by Stanley Rhodes to exploit the growing demand for California redwood lumber products. The company was successful from the start, and it has been growing steadily and showing a profit in every year since its founding.

Stanley Rhodes, the founder, owned 100 percent of the company's common stock until his retirement in 1974 at the age of 70. He then sold 25 percent of the shares to Alan Turner, his assistant, who took over active management of the firm. Rhodes retained the remaining 75 percent of the stock. In the eight years that Turner has been running the company, Sequoia Timber has experienced the fastest rate of growth and most profitable operations in its 37-year history. Sequoia Timber continues to operate solely in the lumber products business although it has recently, under Turner's supervision, expanded to serve all of the West Coast region. Its 1981 income statement and balance sheet are shown in Tables 1 and 2.

Stanley Rhodes suffered a severe stroke in July 1981. Although he survived the attack, his health was badly impaired, and it became obvious to both Rhodes and his attorney that some serious estate planning should be done. On the basis of very rough calculations, Rhodes's attorney estimates that his estate will have a value of between $10 and $15 million. The tax on an estate of this size is close to $5 million. Since most of Stanley Rhodes's estate is represented by his common stock in Sequoia Timber Corporation, two important problems are likely to arise. First, since Sequoia Timber is a closed corporation, there could be a problem in determining the value of the stock, hence the value of Rhodes's estate. The inheritance tax appraisers might set an unreasonably high value on the stock, but, in the absence of a quoted marked price, it might be difficult to dispute this price. The second problem has to do with obtaining the cash with which to pay the estate tax. Rhodes does have some liquid assets, but since most of his assets are represented by his stock in Sequoia Timber, it would be quite difficult to raise $5 million for payment of the tax. Even though

Table 1 Income Statement

Year Ended December 31, 1981

Sales		$15,500,000
Cost of Goods Sold		9,725,000
General and Administrative Expenses		1,150,000
Interest: Notes	$ 25,000	
Bonds	600,000	625,000
Profits before Taxes		$ 4,000,000
State and Federal Income Taxes		2,000,000
Profits after Taxes		$ 2,000,000
Preferred Dividends		200,000
Net Income for Common Stock		$ 1,800,000
Dividends		$ 750,000
Additions to Retained Earnings		1,050,000

Table 2 Balance Sheet

Year Ended December 31, 1981 (in thousands)

Cash and Marketable Securities	$ 695		Accounts Payable	$ 355
Accounts Receivable	2,085		Notes Payable	265
Inventories	4,120		Other Current Liabilities	170
Total Current Assets	$ 6,900		Total Current Liabilities	$ 790
Plant and Equipment (Net)	$ 7,100		Long-Term Debt (6%)	$10,000
Timber Reserves (Cost)	12,000		Preferred Stock (8%)	5,000
			Common Stock ($1 par)	1,000
Total Assets	$26,000		Retained Earnings	9,210
			Total Claims	$26,000

there are provisions in the Internal Revenue Code to reduce the consequences of insufficient liquidity at the time of death, there is some chance that Rhodes's estate might not qualify for them. Even if they were allowed, though, Rhodes believed that the valuation problem should be viewed as the primary problem.

Because of this, David Mills, Rhodes's attorney, suggests that consideration be given to having Sequoia Timber go public. If the company were publicly owned, the price would be quoted, and an objective valuation could be placed on the estate.[1] Further, Rhodes could sell some of his shares when Sequoia

---

1. The value of the estate, in essence, is set on the date of death. Rhodes's value would be measured by the price of the stock on the date he dies multiplied by the number of shares of stock he owns.

Timber goes public, thus raising some cash that could be invested in liquid assets to prepare for his eventual death. Even if Rhodes does not sell sufficient shares to raise the full amount of cash necessary to meet his estate tax liability, either because of an immediate capital gains tax liability or for some other reason, it will, when he eventually dies, be easier to liquidate enough of his stock to pay the inheritance tax if the company is already publicly owned.

Alan Turner, who is now president of Sequoia Timber, is also in favor of having the company go public. In the first place, Turner would like to increase the liquidity of his own 25 percent ownership in the business. Second, Turner has been considering the possibility of granting stock options to certain key employees, and these options would be better received if the stock were publicly owned and actively traded. Finally, Turner has for some time felt that Sequoia Timber should undergo a major expansion program, and to do so, additional equity capital would be required. This additional equity could be raised at the time the company goes public.

Turner has scheduled a meeting with investment bankers from Harrell, Hunt, Billings & Co. to discuss going public. To give them an idea of Sequoia Timber's financial position, Turner has asked Emily Buchanan, the company's treasurer, to prepare a summary of the company's sales, earnings, and dividend records for the past decade (Table 3). Buchanan was also instructed to obtain any other information that might aid in establishing a fair market price for Sequoia Timber's common stock. She has compiled the statistics presented in Table 4. Carolina-Pacific and Airhauser Lumber Companies are more similar to Sequoia Timber than are any other companies whose stocks are traded in the public market. However, they are considerably larger than Sequoia Timber, Airhauser being about 5 times, and Carolina-Pacific about 20

Table 3   Sales, Earnings Per Share, and Dividends, 1971–1981

Year	Sales[a]	Earnings Per Share	Dividends Per Share
1981	$15,500.0	$1.80	$0.75
1980	14,625.5	1.65	0.75
1979	13,117.5	1.55	0.75
1978	8,490.0	0.84	0.62
1977	12,832.5	1.51	0.62
1976	10,582.5	1.24	0.50
1975	9,455.0	1.07	0.42
1974	7,835.0	0.91	0.35
1973	9,455.0	1.01	0.35
1972	6,890.0	0.75	0.35
1971	7,195.0	0.84	0.35

a. Sales are given in thousands of dollars.

Table 4   Carolina-Pacific and Airhauser Lumber Companies

	Carolina-Pacific	Airhauser
Earnings per share: 1981	$0.99	$ 1.46
Earnings per share: 1976	0.71	1.10
Dividends per share: 1981	0.75	1.15
Dividends per share: 1976	0.54	0.86
Book value per share: 1981	6.37	10.12
Market price per share:		
December 31, 1981	12.00	17.00
Total assets	$525 million	$127 million

times the size of Sequoia Timber (size is measured by assets). In addition, both of these companies have diversified into non-lumber-related areas.

Questions

1. To aid in making the final valuation, calculate the following items:
   a. annual growth rate of earnings and dividends of the three companies for the years 1976 through 1981 (Hint: use only the data for 1976 and 1981 for Sequoia Timber);
   b. market value/book value ratios for Airhauser and Carolina-Pacific;
   c. dividend payout ratios (dividends per share to earnings per share) for the three companies;
   d. price-earnings ratios for Carolina-Pacific and Airhauser; and
   e. the cost of equity capital based on the "riskless rate plus risk premium equation":

   $$[k = R_F + \rho]$$

   for Airhauser and Carolina-Pacific. (This riskless rate, R_F, is equal to 8.5 percent, while the risk premiums associated with Carolina-Pacific and Airhauser are 5.0 and 4.5 percent, respectively.)
2. Sequoia Timber's common stock value can be estimated in a number of ways. Develop a range of values for the stock using the items in Question 1.
3. Both Airhauser and Carolina-Pacific are listed and actively traded on the New York Stock Exchange. Of what bearing is this information on the determination of a fair market value for Sequoia Timber's common stock?
4. On the basis of the data you have developed, which particular values seem most appropriate and which least appropriate to the problem at hand? Why?

5. Can you see why the estate tax is frequently given as one of the dominant reasons for privately held companies going public? Explain.
6. What bearing would it have on your analysis if you learned Sequoia Timber's beta coefficient was 2.0, while that of the other two firms was about 1.0?

Case 21: *Stocks versus Bonds*

Chicago Intertype Corporation

"You've seen it happen again and again. The historic leader in a product area goes to sleep at the switch, and an upstart rival moves in on the strength of a technological development or a marketing change," stated Roland Moore, president of Chicago Intertype Corporation, to the board of directors. "We are continually being snipped at by smaller but faster-moving competitors. Thus, we must carry out the plant modernization immediately to begin production of our new line."

Chicago Intertype was formed in 1950 in the Chicago area and had dominated the typesetting industry ever since with their largest single product, the Linographic Typer. This "hot lead" machine was an innovation in the market and Chicago Intertype owes a large measure of its success to the development of the Linographic Typer.

A threat to their hot lead machines surfaced with the development of "cold type" computer typesetting systems which recently began hitting the market. Newspapers and magazines have shown a keen interest in switching to cold type machines because they are cheaper and easier to operate. Chicago Intertype observed this trend early and proceeded to develop and test its own version of the cold type computer typesetter, tentatively named Lino II.

The board agreed with Moore that Chicago Intertype must not hesitate and should begin plant remodeling immediately so they could start production as soon as possible. To commence this construction Chicago Intertype will need approximately $34 million of new capital to cover not only the remodeling of existing plants but also to purchase new equipment and materials and to initiate Lino II's marketing program. Historically, Chicago Intertype has always obtained equity funds in the form of retained earnings. Short-term debt in modest amounts had been used on occasion, but no interest-bearing short-term debt is currently outstanding. The company borrowed $16 million at 7.5 percent in 1967, and no additional long-term funds have been acquired since that date in order to keep the level of long-term debt constant (see Tables 1 and 2).

Elizabeth Lancaster, vice-president and controller, must recommend a method of financing the required $34 million to the board of directors. In discussions with the firm's investment bankers, Lancaster has learned that the funds may be obtained by three alternative methods:

1. The company can sell common stock to net $32 per share. Since the current price of the stock of $37 per share, the flotation cost of $5 per share is involved. The sale would be made through investment bankers to the

---

Table 1   Year Ended December 31, 1981 (in millions)

Current Assets	$104	
Fixed Assets	160	
Total Assets		$264
Current Liabilities (Accruals and Payables)	$ 40	
Long-Term Debt (7.5 percent)	16	
Common Stock ($1 par, 10 million shares out)	10	
Retained Earnings	198	
Total Liabilities and Net Worth		$264

Table 2   Year Ended December 31, 1981 (in millions)

Sales	$254.0	
Cost of Goods Sold[a]	188.0	
Gross Profit		$66.0
General and Administrative Expenses	$ 9.9	
Lease Payment on Equipment[b]	2.4	
Earnings before Interest		$ 53.7
Interest Charges	$ 1.2	
Earnings before Tax		$ 52.5
Tax (48 percent, marginal rate federal and state)	$ 25.2	
Net Income		$ 27.3
Dividends	$ 6.8	
Addition to Retained Earnings		$ 20.5

a. Includes depreciation charges of $16 million.
b. Five-year lease for equipment.

general public; that is, the sale of common stock would not be through a rights offering. The possibility of a rights offering was considered, but Lancaster agreed with the investment bankers that the firm's currently outstanding common stock is not distributed widely enough to ensure the success of such an offering. The stock is traded over-the-counter, but at some future time the company will probably apply for listing on the American Stock Exchange.

2. The company can privately sell 25-year, 16 percent bonds to a group of life insurance companies. The bonds would have a sinking fund calling for the retirement, by a lottery method, of 4 percent of the original amount of the bond issue each year. Covenants under the bond agreement would also stipulate that dividends be paid only out of earnings subsequent to the bond issue; that is, the retained earnings of the company at present could not be used to pay dividends on the common stock. The bond agreement would also require that the current ratio be maintained at a level of 2 to 1, and the bonds would not be callable for a period of ten years, after which the usual call premium would be invoked. No flotation cost would be incurred.

3. The third alternative available to the company is to sell 6 percent cumulative preferred stock. The issue would not be callable and would not have a sinking fund. The price of the preferred would be $33 per share, the annual dividends $6 per share, and the stock would be sold to net Chicago Intertype $30 per share.

In preliminary discussions with Joseph Harris, chairman of the board and the company's major stockholder, Lancaster learned that he favors the sale of bonds. Harris believes that inflation will continue for some years to come, so by borrowing now, the company will be able to repay its loans with "cheap" dollars. In addition, the chairman notes that the firm's price-earnings ratio at present is relatively low, making the sale of common stock unappealing. Finally, he notes that while his personal holdings are not sufficient to give him absolute control of the company, his shares, together with those of members of his family and the other directors, give management control of just over 50 percent of the outstanding stock. If additional shares are sold, management's absolute control will be endangered, and the company might be subjected to the possibility of a takeover by one of the major conglomerate companies. Finally, Harris notes that the after-tax cost of the bonds is relatively low and that the covenants should not prove onerous to the company.

Lancaster also discussed the financing alternatives with Jason McCord, a long-term director and chairman of Chicago Intertype's finance committee as well as president of McCord & Company, an investment banking firm. McCord disagrees with Harris and urges Lancaster to give consideration to the common stock option. McCord argues, first, that the company's sales have experienced some sharp downturns in the past and that similar downturns in the future would endanger the viability of the firm. As Table 3 shows, sales declined sharply on three occasions: in 1974, when the company faced a decrease in demand due to a fall in the magazine market; in 1977, when the company was involved in a long, drawn-out labor dispute; and in 1979, when a fire closed down much of the company's manufacturing facilities for a substantial part of the year. McCord has pointed out to Lancaster that the danger of a major strike is still present and that the economy in general is in a tenuous position with some economists predicting an even deeper recession. If interest rates should decrease as the Federal Reserve acts to stimulate the economy, now is not the time to issue debt.

McCord also disagrees with Harris regarding the terms of the bond agreement. He observes that the dividend provision might require the company to forego paying cash dividends in any one year and that the combined cash drain on the firm, resulting from the required payment of the interest plus the sinking fund, would be very serious in the event of a severe drop in sales. He further notes that the interest rate on the bonds would be 16 percent and that the company could not call the bonds for ten years.

McCord then points out one final factor to Lancaster: the company's stock is currently traded over-the-counter, although the management group would like to obtain an American Stock Exchange listing. When the company made a tentative application for listing it was denied on the grounds that: (1) a large percentage of the stock is owned by management and members of the Harris family, so that the floating supply would not be sufficient to meet American Stock Exchange requirements; and (2) the floating supply of stock does not have the broad geographic distribution required by the American Stock Exchange. McCord emphasizes that if stock is sold through investment bankers,

Table 3   Selected Information (in millions)

Year	Sales	Profit After Taxes	Dividends Per Share	Earnings Per Share	Price of Stock
1981	$254	$27.3	1.68	$2.73	$37
1980	229	21.2	1.27	2.12	36
1979	136	(4.1)	—	(0.41)	25
1978	187	19.3	0.77	1.93	33
1977	136	7.6	0.60	0.76	23
1976	190	14.2	0.30	1.42	25
1975	175	12.4	0.30	1.24	19
1974	99	(5.9)	—	(0.59)	24
1973	155	10.1	0.30	1.01	23
1972	142	8.0	0.30	0.80	22

the distribution will be sufficiently broad and the number of shares outstanding sufficiently large to qualify Chicago Intertype Corporation for listing.

Lancaster herself wonders if the preferred stock alternative might not overcome Harris's objection to common stock and McCord's objections to bonds, thus representing the best financing choice.

Questions

1. Assuming that the new funds earn the same rate of return currently being earned on the firm's assets (earnings before interest and taxes/total assets), what would earnings per share be for 1982 under each of the three financing methods? Assume that the new outside funds are employed during the whole year of 1982, the sinking fund payment for 1982 is ignored, and retained earnings for 1982 are not employed until 1983.

2. Calculate the debt ratio at year end 1982 under each alternative method of financing. Assume that 1982 current liabilities remain at their current level and additions to retained earnings for 1982 total $18 million. Compare Chicago Intertype Corporation figures with the industry averages as given in Table 4. These figures should be discussed in your answer to Question 6.

4. Calculate the before-tax times-interest-earned coverage for 1982 under each of the financing alternatives. Then compare Chicago Intertype Corporation's coverage ratios with the industry average. These figures should be discussed in your answer to Question 6.

3. Calculate the fixed charge coverage under each of the three alternatives for the year 1982. Ignore the sinking fund payment in the debt alternative. Then compare your results with the industry average. Calculate the debt service coverage ratio (the fixed charge coverage ratio including the sinking fund payment) for the bond alternative. What effect will the sinking fund covenant have on Chicago Intertype Corporation's ability to meet its other fixed charges? These figures should be discussed in your answer to Question 6.

5. Assume that after the new capital is raised, fixed operating charges are $24 million (not including depreciation) and the ratio of variable cost to sales

---

Table 4   Industry Ratios

Debt/Total Assets 35%
Times-Interest-Earned 8.5X
Fixed Charge Coverage 5.0X
Profit After Taxes/Sales 6%
Profit After Tax/Total Assets 8%
Profit After Tax/Net Worth 12%
Price/Earnings 18X

stays the same. How much would sales have to drop before the equity financing would be preferable to debt in terms of EPS? (Hint: calculate the level of sales at which EPS will be equal under bond or stock financing.)

6. Discuss the pros and cons of each of the financing methods that Lancaster is considering. How does stock exchange membership affect the decision? Which method would you recommend to the board? Fully justify your recommendation.

Case 22: Stocks versus Bonds

Stratton Electronics, Inc.

In the early seventies, International Circuit Corporation (I.C.C.), a major producer of circuitry for computer hardware, saw an opportunity for diversifying its product line into the rapidly growing market for hand-held calculators. I.C.C. spent approximately twelve million dollars developing a small calculator that could produce hard line copy (i.e., printed output) in the spring of 1975, and employed a Boston marketing research firm to determine the optimum marketing strategy for the product. To the horror and amazement of I.C.C., the marketing experts' conclusion was that the market segment interested in such a product was virtually nonexistent, and, due to the intense competition developing in this market, they questioned the overall fiscal viability of such an undertaking. Taken aback by this unanticipated conclusion, management decided to drop the product before full-scale production began and any more costs were incurred.

Carole Stratton, director of this new division, had more faith in the product than in the marketing research team and its conclusions. She pointed out that the survey used as a basis for their conclusions was conducted by telephone to individual homes between 9:00-11:00 a.m. on weekday mornings in two suburbs outside of Miami. Over 80 percent of the participants were housewives who showed little, if any, interest in a product designed mainly for business people, students, and engineers. A Miami-based investment banking firm agreed with Stratton and helped to form a syndicate of investors who put up $10 million to purchase all of I.C.C.'s rights to the calculator and to establish a manufacturing facility for Stratton Electronics, Inc.

Operations started in the winter of 1976. During the remainder of that year sales totaled $12,600,000 with a profit before tax of $798,000 (see Table 1). Stratton's faith in the product proved to be well founded as sales grew rapidly until 1982 when they were $39,230,000 and profits were $3,591,000 (see Table 2). The price of the company's stock, which was traded over-the-counter from

Table 1 Selected Information (in thousands)

Year	Sales	Profit after Tax	EPS	Stock Price
1982	$39,230	$3,591	$0.36	$10.60
1981	35,860	3,064	0.31	7.13
1980	33,210	2,558	0.26	5.20
1979	27,930	2,109	0.21	4.41
1978	21,750	1,398	0.14	3.05
1977	15,507	989	0.10	1.80
1976	12,600	798	0.08	1.50

Table 2 Year Ended December 31, 1982 (in thousands)

Sales	$39,230
Cost of Goods Sold[a]	28,970
Gross Profit	$10,260
General and Administrative Expenses	1,560
Earnings Before Interest	$ 8,700
Interest Charges	2,400
Earnings Before Taxes	$ 6,300
Taxes (43 percent effective rate)	2,709
Net Income	$ 3,581
Dividends	$ 898
Addition to Retained Earnings	$ 2,693

a. Includes depreciation of $3.96 million.

1976 through 1979, is currently listed at $10.60 per share and it earned $0.36 per share in 1982.

Not only did a strong market segment exist for the original hard copy calculator introduced by Stratton Electronics, there were indications of even greater future opportunities in more specialized calculators. To begin full-scale production of the latest addition to their product line, a hand-held calculator which could convert over 500 common phrases into six different languages and display the answer both as an LED readout and verbally using a voice synthesizer, Stratton needed approximately $10 million for the necessary asset expansion.

Stratton Electronics had met its financial requirements in the past through the use of retained earnings and long-term debt. Because of a shortage of funds, however, Stratton's primary bank, Miami National, has advised the company that its present 15 million dollar line of credit cannot be increased.

After researching the various possibilities, George Collins, the financial vice-president, has decided that there are three viable alternatives available to the company: (1) sale of a long-term debt issue that would be purchased by the Florida Mutual Life Insurance Company; (2) sale of common stock; or (3) sale of preferred stock. The terms under which these sources would be made available are as follows:

1. Common stock can be sold to net Stratton Electronics $9.60 per share after brokerage costs of $1.00 per share.
2. The company can sell preferred stock with a par value of $100 that would pay a $15 annual dividend. Preferred stock would be sold to the public at par and would incur brokerage costs of four dollars per share.[1]
3. Stratton can sell $10 million of notes to the Florida Mutual Life Insurance Company. The notes would be fully amortized over the next 20 years and would bear an interest rate of 14 percent. Key provisions of this loan agreement require that the company: (1) maintain a current ratio of 2.5 to 1.0; (2) pay cash dividends only out of cash generated after the loan agreement is signed; and (3) engage in no additional long-term debt financing without the agreement of the Florida Mutual Life Insurance Company. The notes would be callable, but at a call premium of 17 percent.

When the senior officers met to discuss these three alternatives, Sergio Torres, executive vice-president, spoke in favor of the common stock financing, pointing out that relative to other firms in the industry the company's capital structure is already overloaded with debt (see Tables 3 and 4).

Stratton, however, disagreed, observing that the company's sales and profit projections suggest that earnings will continue to increase at a substantial rate over the next several years. Especially if certain new developments now in the research and development stage bear fruit, the actual rate of increase would be significant. Based on new project development, Stratton projected that earnings would be as high as $0.64 per share by 1984. Assuming the price-earnings ratio stayed at its current level, this would mean that stock should be selling at $19.20 per share in one year. Stratton opposed selling stock for $10.60 per share that would soon be worth $19.20 per share.

Lyle Spalding, sales manager, informed Stratton that a major competitor was also planning to begin production of a similar language conversion calculator and to promote it heavily with an aggressive sales team and advertising program. If this is true, sales and profit margins would suffer drastically until other markets were developed and prices were stabilized.

Walter Johanson, vice-president of production, backed Torres's position and also indicated that the cost of establishing production for the new language

---

1. The preferred stock would not be callable for five years after which it could be called at $111.00 per share.

Table 3   Year Ended December 31, 1982 (in thousands)

Current Assets	$19,000
Fixed Assets	33,000
Total Assets	$52,000
Current Liabilities (Accruals and Accounts Payable)	$ 9,000
Long-Term Debt (12 percent)	20,000
Common Stock ($1.80 par)	18,000
Retained Earnings	5,000
Total Liabilities and Net Worth	$52,000

Table 4   Industry Ratios

Debt/Total Assets	50%
Times-Interest-Earned	8X
Times Fixed Charges Covered	6X
Profit after Taxes/Sales	9%
Profit after Tax/Total Assets	9%
Profit after Tax/Net Worth	14%
Price/Earnings	40X

converter might be higher than anticipated, thus temporarily causing profits to drop below projected levels. Because of the uncertainties surrounding this new product, both Johanson and Spalding recommended the common stock alternative.

Collins suggested that a compromise in the form of preferred stock might be the optimum decision. Spalding, Johanson, and Stratton all thought this was worth looking into, but after the meeting Collins himself questioned the cost of such a proposal. His primary concern was that the after-tax cost of preferred stock would be substantially higher than the after-tax cost of debt, and the company would still be locked into coverage of a fixed payment.

Questions

1. Assuming that the new funds earn the same rate of return currently earned on the firm's assets (earnings before interest and taxes/total assets), what would earnings per share be with each alternative? Assume that the new outside funds are employed during the whole year of 1983, but that 1983 additions to retained earnings are not employed until 1984. What would earnings per share available to common stockholders be?

2. Calculate the debt ratio at year end 1983 with each of the alternatives. Assume current liabilities increase as a percentage of sales, profit margins and the dividend pay out ratio both remain constant, and predicted sales for 1983 are $41,600,000. Note that the assumed increase in retained earnings derived from sales in 1983 differs from the amount of earnings calculated in Question 1.

3. Calculate the before-tax times-interest-earned ratio for the year 1983 for each alternative.

4. Calculate the debt service coverage ratio[2] for the bond, common stock, and preferred stock alternatives. What effect does inclusion of the "sinking fund" component of the amortization payment have on Stratton Electronic's ability to meet its other fixed charges? (Note: You can use dividends in lieu of the sinking fund payment for the stock alternatives.)

5. Assume that: (a) annual fixed costs will rise to $6 million after the new capital is acquired; and (b) the ratio of variable costs to sales is 74 percent. How much must sales increase before bond financing becomes preferable to equity in terms of EPS? (Hint: Calculate the level of sales at which EPS will be equal under the two alternatives.)

6. Discuss the pros and cons of the financing methods that Collins is considering. Incorporate comparisons of Stratton's financial position with the industry averages in your analysis. Which method should Collins recommend to the board? Fully justify your recommendation.

2.

$$\text{Debt service coverage} = \frac{\dfrac{\text{profit before}}{\text{taxes}} + \dfrac{\text{interest}}{\text{charges}} + \dfrac{\text{lease}}{\text{payments}}}{\dfrac{\text{interest}}{\text{charges}} + \dfrac{\text{lease}}{\text{obligations}} + \dfrac{\text{before-tax sinking}}{\text{fund requirement}}}$$

$$\text{Before-tax sinking fund requirement} = \frac{\text{sinking fund payment}}{1 - \text{tax rate}}$$

Case 23: *Lease versus Loan*

Franklin Foto Finishing

As part of their overall plant modernization and cost reduction program, Franklin Foto Finishing has decided to install a new automated system to control the pouring and mixing of chemicals in the various "baths" used in film processing. This equipment would improve quality by virtually eliminating costly spills and improperly mixed "baths"; it would also reduce the steep labor costs incurred when mixing and pouring is done manually. In the capital budgeting analysis done prior to the decision to proceed with the new system, the IRR of the project was found to be 29 percent versus a required return of 18 percent. The company uses an after-tax cost-of-capital of 16 percent for relatively low risk projects and 20 percent for projects with above average risk, so this project passed with flying colors.

The pouring system has an invoice price of $100,000 including delivery and installation charges. The net financing required for the system, if Franklin borrows the funds, would be the purchase price less the applicable investment tax credit of 10 percent. The funds needed could be borrowed from the bank on a four-year amortized loan at a 15 percent interest rate. The manufacturer will maintain and service the mixer, in the event that it is purchased, for a charge of $8,000 per year. Franklin uses the method for calculating depreciation specified by the Accelerated Cost Recovery System (ACRS) for a five-year asset, and its effective tax rate is 40 percent.

Lucas Automation, Inc., maker of the equipment, has offered to lease the pouring system to Franklin Foto Finishing for $27,100 upon delivery and installation plus four additional annual lease payments of $27,100. Actually, the pouring system has an expected life of approximately eight years, at which time it should have a zero market value. However, Franklin estimates that the system will have a resale value equal to its book value at the end of the fourth year. Franklin plans to completely automate the processing line in four years by installing a continuous development system. Since the continuous development process will have its own integral pouring system, Franklin has no interest in either leasing or owning the proposed pouring system for more than four years. The lease includes a service contract under which the equipment will be maintained in good working order.

Marie Franklin, president and founder of the photo lab, has always made the final decisions on such lease versus purchase options. The actual calculation of the relevant data, however, is the task of her assistant, Roland Gunther. Traditionally, Franklin's method of evaluating such a decision has been to calculate the present value cost of lease payments versus the present value of total charges if the equipment is purchased. However, in a recent decision concerning a matter similar to the one presently being considered, Franklin and Gunther got into a heated discussion about the appropriate discount rate to use in determining the present value costs of leasing and of purchasing. The following points of view were expressed:

1. Franklin argued that the discount rate should be the firm's average cost of capital. A lease versus purchase decision is, in effect, a capital budgeting decision, and as such, should be evaluated at the firm's cost-of-capital. In other words, one method or the other will provide a cash saving in any year. The dollars saved using the most advantageous method will be invested to yield the firm's cost-of-capital. Therefore, the average cost-of-capital is the appropriate discount rate to use in evaluating leasing versus purchasing.
2. Gunther, on the other hand, felt that the cash flows generated in a lease versus purchase situation are more certain than are the cash flows generated by the firm's average projects. Consequently, these cash flows should be discounted at a lower rate because of their lower risk. At the present time the firm's cost of debt reflects the lowest risk rate to Franklin Foto Finishing. Therefore, 15 percent should be used as the discount rate in the lease versus purchase decision.

To settle the debate over the previous decision, Franklin and Gunther asked their accountants to review the situation and advise them on which discount rate was appropriate. This led to an even more confused situation as their accountants, Paula and Alan Ross, could not agree between themselves as to the appropriate discount rate. Alan, on the one hand, agreed with Franklin that the discount rate should be the average cost of capital, but on the grounds that leasing is simply an alternative to other means of financing. Since leasing is a substitute for "financing," which is a mix of debt and equity, leasing saves the cost of other financing; this cost is the firm's average cost of capital. Paula, on the other hand, felt that none of the discount rates mentioned so far adequately accounted for the tax effects inherent in any capital budgeting decision and suggested the use of an after-tax cost of debt.

In the last lease-versus-purchase decision, the average cost-of-capital (18 percent) was used, but now Franklin is uncertain about the validity of this procedure. She is inclined toward Gunther's alternative, but she wonders if it would be appropriate to use a low risk discount rate for evaluating all cash flows in the analysis. Franklin is particularly concerned about the risk of the differential cash flows on the lease versus loan decision, as compared to the risk of the expected salvage value. While the firm is almost certain of the flows required under the lease or loan, the salvage value is relatively uncertain, having a distribution of possible outcomes that makes its risk comparable to that of the average risk project undertaken by the firm.

Questions

1. Set up a worksheet and calculate the comparative cost of leasing versus buying the new pouring equipment. (Note: The equipment must be depreciated over 5 years by the ACRS provisions. This method is a modified version of 150 percent declining balance depreciation and the following depreciation rates are specified by the IRS: Year 1, 15 percent; year 2, 22 percent; year 3, 21 percent; year 4, 21 percent; year 5, 21 percent. Also assume that if the decision is made to purchase the machine, it will be sold for its book value at the start of year 5 rather than at the end of year 4. Otherwise, the year 4 depreciation could not be taken.)
2. Justify the discount rate or rates that you use in the calculation process.
3. Assume that Franklin Foto Finishing leased the equipment and that the value of the leased property ($100,000) was a substantial sum of money in relation to Franklin's total assets. What problems might this cause for outside financial analysts, and how might such analysts solve the problem?
4. Should Franklin Foto Finishing lease or buy?
5. In some instances, it might be possible for a leasing company to offer a contract with a cost less than the debt cost that the firm would incur if it were to attempt to finance the purchase. If the equipment represented a significant addition to the firm's assets, could this affect its overall cost of capital?
6. Now assume that Franklin will definitely use the equipment for its full 8-year life. However, it can only lease the equipment for 4 years. Assume further that, if the equipment is leased, Franklin will have to buy the equipment from the lessor at its market value in year four. This expected year four market value is still equal to the book value in that year; however, the actual value could be close to zero or so high that to buy it would cause severe financial stress for Franklin. How would this modification change your analysis of the lease-versus-purchase decision? (Hint: You only need to move the residual value from one column to another, and then think about the rate at which to discount the residual and the effect of this discount rate on the decision.)

7. Suppose Franklin had been operating at a loss and therefore had tax loss carryforwards which caused the company to project: (1) that it would be unable to use the investment tax credit; and (2) that its income tax rate would be zero for the next few years. How would these changes alter the analysis and your recommendation?

Case 24: *Sale and Leaseback*

Pringle, Inc.

Irwin Schaeffer, financial vice-president of Pringle, Inc., a locally owned and operated department store, has just learned that a group of real estate developers is planning a major new residential and industrial subdivision in the rapidly growing northeast section of the city; they plan to build a large shopping center to service both present and expected northeast area residents. The developers are anxious to have a major department store in the shopping center, and they have offered Pringle a chance to open a new facility there. If Pringle does not exercise this option to branch into the new center, the developers plan to hold discussions with several national department stores, including Gloomingdales, Kurdines, and Gracey's. Given the expansionist mood in the department store industry, Schaeffer is quite certain that one of the national chains will move into the new shopping center if Pringle does not.

After reviewing statistics on his company's sales and profits over the past 12 years (Table 1), Schaeffer notes that sales increased by roughly 5 percent per year from 1971 to 1977, while profits increased similarly. In late 1977, however, a national department store chain opened a branch in a major new westside shopping center. As the population on the west side of town grew, and as the new store gained experience in determining the type of goods desired, completed its personnel training program, and began to enjoy the full effect of a heavy advertising budget, it completely arrested Pringle's growth. Between 1979 and 1981, it caused an actual decline in Pringle's sales and an even sharper decline in profits. By 1982, however, population growth in the community was sufficient to offset the impact of the new store, and Pringle had a small increase in both sales and profits.

As Schaeffer sees it, Pringle's profitability can be increased to its pre-1978 level if the new store is opened. The downtown facility is already making a comeback, and the new store, which would be opened in about 1986, would be very well situated. Further, a new facility should not make a material inroad in sales of the downtown store because population growth in the area should be

Table 1   Sales and Profits[a]

Year	Sales	Net Profit after Taxes[b]
1971	$27,144,000	$597,090
1972	28,392,000	624,624
1973	29,718,000	687,960
1974	31,122,000	712,530
1975	32,175,000	748,800
1976	33,813,000	786,240
1977	35,334,000	821,340
1978	36,036,000	794,300
1979	36,270,000	704,340
1980	35,802,000	631,800
1981	35,217,000	526,500
1982	35,431,500	538,200

a. Depreciation charges during the period shown were $121,875 a year for furniture, fixtures, and equipment, and $276,250 a year for the buildings.

b. Tax Rate = 40 percent.

sufficient to provide an adequate market for both of these facilities, as well as for the westside competitor. In fact, the profit margins should be improved somewhat after the proposed new store opens because of purchasing and administrative economies of scale. Then too, Schaeffer thinks Pringle's risk position would be reduced somewhat if it opens the new store, as the company would be protected to some extent against a decline in the downtown area. So, all factors considered, Schaeffer is very much in favor of opening the new facility.

Although the new development is still several years away, Schaeffer must make plans for financing the venture if Pringle is to open a new store. The recent trend in sales and profits will not help, and the balance sheet (Table 2) for 1982 also presents some problems. Pringle's debt ratio, 53.4 percent as compared to 62.8 percent for the average department store, is good, but the company's liquidity position is quite weak. Schaeffer calculates the current ratio at 1.23 as opposed to an industry average of 2.6. Because of Pringle's liquidity position, the bank is unwilling to extend any additional credit. As a result, Schaeffer has been unable to keep his accounts payable current. Of the $4.22 million accounts payable as of December 31, 1982, approximately $2.275 million are past due. Pringle has been unable to take any trade discounts, and its reputation as a slow payer is causing the firm some difficulty. Schaeffer is quite sure that this reputation will present a serious problem if he attempts to raise funds to finance the new store. He must, then, clear up the liquidity problem before he attempts to obtain new financing.

Table 2   Balance Sheet

Year Ended December 31, 1982

Cash	$ 455,000	
Accounts Receivable	2,112,500	
Inventories	5,378,750	
Total Current Assets		$ 7,946,250
Furniture, Fixtures and Equipment (Cost $2,860,000 less depreciation $1,462,500)	$1,397,500	
Buildings (Cost $6,906,250 less depreciation $3,315,000)	3,591,250	
Land	325,000	
Total Assets		$13,260,000
Accounts Payable	$4,225,000	
Notes Payable	2,210,000	
Total Current Liabilities		$ 6,435,000
Mortgage on Land and Buildings (7%)	$ 650,000	
Net Worth	6,175,000	
Total Liabilities and Net Worth		$13,260,000

	Pringle	Industry Average
Current Ratio	1.23X	2.6X
Debt Ratio	53.4%	62.8%

In his discussions with a local investment banker, Schaeffer has learned that he could increase the mortgage on the company's present fixed assets to $3.25 million. This would require paying off the present 7 percent mortgage loan and taking on a new $3.25 million loan at 14 percent. Alternatively, Pringle could sell the land and buildings (but retain title to the furniture, fixtures, and equipment) to a wealthy industrialist. The stated purchase price that the industrialist would pay Pringle would be $325,000 for the land and $2,925,000 for the buildings. These sums approximate the existing market values of the two components. Pringle would immediately lease the assets back on a ten-year lease for a rental of $575,200 per year. An option to renew the lease for an additional 10 years on terms to be negotiated at the expiration of this lease was included.

A quick calculation of the interest rate implicit in the lease payment showed Schaeffer that the rate built into the lease was only 12 percent. When he asked the investment banker why Pringle would be able to obtain a 12 percent lease in a period when mortgage money was going for 14 percent, the banker informed him that the industrialist, who is in a 50 percent tax bracket and able to depreciate the building against his own income, thought that the tax advantages would be sufficient to permit him to make the lease at 12 percent.

Questions

1. How much will Pringle, Inc. net if it:
   a. takes the sale and leaseback; or
   b. increases the size of its mortgage? Assume that Pringle has no other capital gains or losses, either in this year or carried forward.
2. Will either, or both, of the two financing plans permit Pringle to become current in its accounts payable?
3. The lease payments on a $3.25 million sale and leaseback will amount to $575,200 per year for ten years (all of this is a tax deduction). The payments on a ten-year mortgage will amount to $623,069 per year, consisting of $455,000 interest and $168,069 repayment of principle for the first year (see Table 3). Calculate the nominal, or implicit, rate of interest, disregarding capital gains or losses, on each of these two instruments. (Hint: use the annuity tables to get the before-tax interest rate.)
4. The investment banker gave the treatment of depreciation by the investor who would make the sale and leaseback as the reason for the differential in effective interest rates in Question 3. Can you think of any additional factor that might account for the differences in the two rates?
5. Corporate lessees usually calculate the effective interest rate by estimating the residual values of the asset. In this case, if they assume a residual value of $2,073,057 for the land and building at the end of ten years, the formula for the effective rate of interest (r) would be:

Table 3   Loan Repayment Schedule

Year	Total Payment	Interest	Repayment of Principal	Remaining Balance
1	$623,069	$455,000	$168,069	$3,081,931
2	623,069	431,470	191,599	2,890,332
3	623,069	404,646	218,423	2,671,909
4	623,069	374,067	249,002	2,422,907
5	623,069	339,207	283,862	2,139,045
6	623,069	299,466	323,603	1,815,442
7	623,069	254,162	368,907	1,446,535
8	623,069	202,515	420,554	1,025,981
9	623,069	143,637	479,432	546,549
10	623,069	76,520	546,549	-0-

$$\$325,000 = \sum_{t=1}^{10} \frac{\$575,200}{(1+r)^t} + \frac{\$2,073,057}{(1+r)^{10}}.$$

Solve this equation for the effective rate of interest (r). How will the effective rate of interest change if the residual value is larger or smaller?

6. **a.** If the lease had been in effect during 1982, what would the profit have been?

   b. What would the profit have been had the larger mortgage loan been in effect? (Hint: work backward to build up pro forma earnings before interest and taxes for 1982, and then use this figure to answer the question.)

7. Which of the two alternative financing methods, if either, should Schaeffer recommend to his store's board of directors?

Case 25: *Leveraged Lease;*
Multiple Rates of Return

North American Airlines

In the spring of 1979, North American Airlines (NAA) sought $500 million to finance the purchase of a new fleet of fuel-efficient jets. The aircraft manufacturer suggested that NAA consider a leasing arrangement, and the manufacturer volunteered to help NAA set up a meeting with a leading New York bank. NAA indicated, however, that it preferred to deal with its regular bank, the Security World Bank, and asked Security World about the possibility of financing the aircraft through a leasing arrangement. The bank was short of funds as a result of the Federal Reserve System's restrictive monetary policy. However, Security World Bank recently arranged several "leveraged leases" in cooperation with the Viking Insurance Company, and Susie Aiken, the loan officer handling the NAA account, thought such an arrangement might be suitable for NAA. In these leveraged leases, Security World Bank serves as the owner-lessor, but the bank borrows most of the funds needed to purchase the equipment from the insurance company.

The leveraged lease concept, which is analyzed as a capital budgeting problem by the bank-lessor, seems to make sense in this specific instance. Security World Bank is itself in a 40 percent tax bracket; NAA is in a loss position, so it pays no income taxes; and Viking Insurance Company has an effective tax rate of 30 percent. Because the value of a tax shelter depends on the recipient's tax rate, to the extent that the tax shelter involved in the $500 million aircraft purchase can be transferred from NAA, with a zero tax rate, to Security World Bank, in the 40 percent bracket, the lease arrangement can be favorable to both parties. The tax shelters include: (1) the investment tax credit, (2) accelerated depreciation on the planes, and (3) interest payments on any loan involved in the purchase of the aircraft. The investment tax credit amounts to eight percent, and, because of its loss position, NAA would be unable to utilize the credit should it purchase the aircraft directly.

Depreciation will be calculated by the double-declining-balance method. The life used to compute depreciation for income tax purposes is 10 years, and the expected salvage value, for tax purposes, is zero. However, Aiken and others in the bank think that the aircraft will actually be worth approximately $10 million at the end of 10 years. Thus, even though no salvage is recognized in the depreciation computation, the expected residual value is $10 million before taxes, or $6 million after taxes. (The appropriate tax rate, assuming that the airplanes can, in fact, be sold for $10 million, is the tax rate on ordinary income, not the capital gains tax rate, because the sale will represent a recapture of depreciation.) The depreciation schedule, calculated on the basis of these assumptions, is shown in Table 1. (Notice that no values are shown for years 2 and 8; these are to be calculated as part of the case assignment.)

When Aiken met with officials of the Viking Insurance Company, she learned that Security World Bank's leasing subsidiary could borrow 85 percent of the funds needed to make the purchase, or $425 million, at a rate of 9 percent on the declining balance. The loan would be amortized over a 10-year period. The loan repayment schedule, with blanks for years 2 and 8, is shown in Table 2.

The cash flows received by the bank in each year, shown in Table 3, are determined as follows:

For year 0:

$$-\left(\begin{array}{c}\text{payment}\\\text{for aircraft}\end{array}\right) + \left(\begin{array}{c}\text{loan principal}\\\text{amount received}\end{array}\right) + \left(\begin{array}{c}\text{investment}\\\text{tax credit}\end{array}\right)$$

Initial cash outlay $= -\$500 + \$425 + \$40 = -\$35$ million

---

Table 1   Aircraft Depreciation Schedule (in millions)

Year	Depreciation	Remaining Balance
1	$100	$400
2		
3	64	256
4	51	205
5	41	164
6	33[a]	131
7	33	98
8		
9	33	32
10	32	—

a. Straight-line depreciation on the $164 million undepreciated balance exceeds DDB depreciation in year 6 and thereafter, so in year 6 it would pay to switch to straight line.

Table 2 Loan Repayment Schedule (in millions)

Year	Total Payment	Interest	Repayment of Principal	Remaining Balance
1	$ 66.20	$38.25	$27.95	$397.05
2				
3	66.20	33.00	33.20	333.30
4	66.20	30.00	36.20	297.20
5	66.20	26.75	39.45	257.75
6	66.20	23.20	43.00	214.75
7	66.20	19.35	46.85	167.90
8				
9	66.20	10.50	55.70	61.10
10	66.20	5.10	61.10	—
	$662.00			

For years 1–9, illustrated for year 1:

Net cash flow$_t$ = CF_t = lease payment received − taxes − loan payment

= lease payment received − tax rate
(lease payment − depreciation − interest on the loan)
− loan payment

$$CF_1 = \$64.75 - 0.4(\$64.75 - \$100 - \$38.25) - \$66.2 = \$27.95$$

The lease payments are based on a $500 million cost, 10-year amortization schedule, and a 5 percent interest rate; that is, the annual lease payment is the amount which would amortize a $500 million loan over a 10-year period at a 5 percent rate of interest. Cash flows to the bank for other years are calculated in Table 3; the missing items are to be filled in as part of the case assignment. The Security World Bank's lease terms are approximately the same as those being offered by New York banks.

The bank's senior loan committee must approve any credit in excess of $5 million, so Aiken must now decide whether to seek permission from the committee to make a formal lease offer to NAA. For most loans and other credit arrangements, the loan committee wants to know the details of the credit worthiness of the borrower (or lessee) and the rate of return on the loan (or lease). Since the bank already has a complete credit file on NAA, Aiken must now concentrate on the profitability of the lease to the bank.

Table 3   Calculation of Cash Flows to the Bank for the Years 0 Through 10

CF_0	$= -\$500 + 425 + 40$	$= -\$35.00$
CF_1	$= \$64.75 - 0.4(64.75 - 100 - 38.25) - 66.20$	
	$= \$64.75 - (-29.40) - 66.20$	$= +\ 27.95$
CF_2	$= \$64.75 - 0.4(64.75 - 80 - 35.75) - 66.20$	
	$= \$64.75 - (-20.40) - 66.20$	$= +\ 18.95$
CF_3	$=$	
CF_4	$=$	
CF_5	$= \$64.75 - 0.4(64.75 - 41.00 - 26.75) - 66.20$	
	$= \$64.75 - (-1.20) - 66.20$	$= -\ \ \ 0.25$
CF_6	$= \$64.75 - 0.4(64.75 - 33.00 - 23.2) - 66.20$	
	$= \$64.75 - (3.40) - 66.20$	$= -\ \ \ 4.85$
CF_7	$= \$64.75 - 0.4(64.75 - 33.00 - 19.35) - 66.20$	
	$= \$64.75 - (4.75) - 66.20$	$= -\ \ \ 6.40$
CF_8	$= \$64.75 - 0.4(64.75 - 33.00 - 15.10) - 66.20$	
	$= \$64.75 - (6.65) - 66.20$	$= -\ \ \ 8.10$
CF_9	$= \$64.75 - 0.4(64.75 - 33.00 - 10.50) - 66.20$	
	$= \$64.75 - (8.50) - 66.20$	$= -\ \ \ 9.95$
CF_{10}	$= \$64.75 - 0.4(64.75 - 32.00 - 5.10) - 66.20 + 6.00$	
	$= \$64.75 - (11.05) - 66.20 + 6.00$	$= -\ \ \ 6.50^a$

a. Notice the additional $6.0 million in CF_{10}; this is the after-tax residual value, or the after-tax sales price of the aircraft, expected in ten years.

Questions

1. Show how the following items are calculated: (a) the lease payment of $64.75 million, and (b) the loan payment of $66.20 million.
2. Fill in the missing items in Tables 1, 2, and 3.
3. Explain why cash flows to the bank are first positive and then become negative in later years.
4. Calculate and graph the present value profile of the bank's investment in the lease. Proceed by determining the NPV's to the bank at the following costs of capital: (a) 0 percent; (b) 10 percent, and (c) 50 percent. Other NPV's at different discount rates are: 15 percent, $2.4 million; 70 percent, − $9.655 million; and 90 percent, − $13.275 million. Next, graph the present-value profile and discuss why the profile takes this shape.
5. If the senior loan committee asked what rate of return (IRR) the bank could expect on the investment in the lease, what would you tell them?
6. Assume that the bank's cost of capital is 4 percent (the total cost of interest paid on time deposits times $[1.0 - \text{tax rate}] = 6\% \times 0.6 \approx 4\%$.) Should it make the lease under the terms set? Should it make the lease if its after-tax cost of capital is 10 percent?

7. Suppose you calculate that the bank should not make the lease under the terms that were set. Suggest some modifications in the terms of the lease that would make the lease acceptable to the bank.

8. The Security World Bank can borrow from Viking Insurance Company at a 9 percent rate to finance 85 percent of the purchase price of the planes. Do you think the insurance company would lend $425 million to NAA on the same terms? Explain. If NAA borrowed $425 million, what would its initial cash outlay be?

Note: the instructor may want to make Question 9 optional.

9. Discuss the nature of the cost of capital to a bank with capital coming largely from: (a) demand deposits; (b) time deposits; and (c) equity capital. If this lease is "about as risky as the average loan," and if the after-tax rate of return on the average loan is 5 percent, would it be reasonable to use 5 percent as the risk-adjusted cost of capital for the lease?

Case 26: *Financing with Convertibles*

Kennesaw Edison Power & Light

Kennesaw Edison Power & Light, whose balance sheet is given in Table 1, provides electric service to a large region of the eastern U.S. To meet projected demand in the coming years, the company has contracted for the construction of a coal-fired power plant that will cost approximately $325 million. All planning for the plant has been completed, construction approval has been obtained from the Environmental Protection Agency and the state regulatory commissions, and contracts for the actual construction have been signed. The construction period will last approximately five years, with required payments of $65 million per year, for a total construction cost of $325 million.

Norman Robinson, KEP&L's treasurer, has just returned from a meeting with the company's principal underwriter, Selby, Lucas, Rossiter and Co. At the meeting, alternative ways of raising the $65.0 million required for the first year were discussed. The underwriter suggested that common stock, first mortgage bonds, convertible debentures, or nonconvertible preferred stock could be used; the approximate terms under which such securities could be issued are the following:

1. Common stock sold to the public at $17.50 to net KEP&L $16.15 per share after a $1.35 underwriting charge;
2. First mortgage bonds with an effective interest cost to the company of 14 percent;
3. 10 percent, $1,000 par value debentures, convertible into 50 shares of common stock, maturing in 25 years and callable after two years at an initial call premium of $80 per bond, with the premium declining by $3.48 per year after year 2;
4. 12 percent, $1,000 par value debentures, convertible into 40 shares of common stock, maturing in 25 years and callable after two years at an initial call premium of $90 per bond, with the premium declining by $3.91 per year after year 2;

Table 1 Balance Sheet (in millions)

Assets

Fixed Assets		
Plant and Equipment (Net)		$585.00
Current Assets		
Cash	6.50	
Accounts Receivable	16.25	
Materials and Supplies	42.25	
Total Current Assets		65.00
Total Assets		$650.00

Claims on Assets

Common Stock	$ 97.50	
Retained Earnings	162.50	
Total Common Equity		$260.00
Long-Term Debt	$325.00	
Total Long-Term Funds		$585.00
Current Liabilities		
Notes Payable	$ 48.75	
Accounts Payable	16.25	
Total Current Liabilities		$ 65.00
Total Claims on Assets		$650.00

5. 10 percent preferred stock, $100 par value, sold to net KEP&L $58.50 per share.

Robinson immediately rejected the use of preferred stock, as KEP&L's board of directors has a long-standing policy against the use of these securities on the grounds that preferred dividends really amount to a non-deductible interest payment. Thus, the effective choice is between common stock, mortgage bonds, and convertible bonds. KEP&L, like most utilities, has been facing some difficult financial problems. Because of inflation in general, and the rise in oil prices in particular, the cost of providing electricity has increased dramatically in recent years. Prices for electricity, however, have not increased as rapidly as costs; electricity rate increases must be approved by the Public Service Commission, and the commission has delayed authorizing rate increases. The combination of "regulatory lag" and rising costs has depressed KEP&L's earnings. This, in turn, has depressed the price of the stock and also lowered the bond interest coverage, which has caused the bonds to be downgraded from Aaa to Aa. Three years ago KEP&L's stock sold for $34 per share, which was 30 percent over its book value at that time. Today the stock is selling for $17.50 per share, which is only 65 percent of the current book value. If new stock is sold at a price below book value, this will necessarily dilute book value per share. Since the company is authorized to earn a specified rate of return on the book value of equity, reducing book value per share implies that the authorized earnings per share will also be diluted. Thus KEP&L is reluctant to sell new common stock at the present time.

KEP&L's debt-to-total-capital ratio is currently 60 percent, and the times-interest-earned ratio is only 2.8. Robinson makes some quick calculations and sees that, if $65.0 million of long-term debt is sold, the debt ratio will rise to approximately 64 percent and the interest coverage ratio will drop to 2.5. Without a substantial rate increase, and none is likely within the next year, this deterioration in KEP&L's financial position would undoubtedly cause the bonds to be downgraded again. Thus, mortgage financing does not look very promising.

In view of the difficult situation in the stock and bond markets, a convertible issue seems relatively attractive. Robinson recalls that Elizabeth Peters, a commercial banker and long-time member of KEP&L's board of directors, has argued against the use of convertibles, stating that such "gimmick financing" should be saved for a rainy day. Robinson's own conclusion is that, as far as KEP&L is concerned, the rainy day has come. He thinks that the best policy might be to simply stand pat and raise no additional capital until things improve, but this is not a feasible choice. The company must continue its construction program if projected demands for power are to be met. Thus the $65.0 million must be raised, regardless of conditions in the stock and bond markets.

Robinson's next task is to conduct a more detailed analysis of the financing choices, reach a conclusion, then prepare a report for presentation to the board of directors. This report must: (1) describe the conditions in the various markets; (2) provide details on the financing alternatives that are presently available; (3) develop pro forma financial statements assuming different financial plans are utilized; and (4) calculate the firm's weighted average cost of capital under the various alternatives.

The projected financial statements are generated by KEP&L's computerized corporate model, and the average cost of capital is calculated as follows:

$$k_a = w_d k_d (1 - t) + w_s (k_r \text{ or } k_e).$$

Here w_d is the weight assigned to debt,
    k_d is the cost of new debt,
     t is the marginal tax rate,
    w_s is the weight assigned to equity,
    k_r is the cost of retained earnings, and
    k_e is the cost of new common stock.

If convertibles are used, the corporate model will have to be modified in two ways. First, assumptions will have to be made regarding when the bonds will be converted to common stock. Second, the cost of capital equation will have to be modified by adding another term, $w_c(k_c)$, where w_c is the percent of capital obtained from convertibles and k_c is the cost of convertible capital.

The current capital structure, which calls for 60 percent debt and 40 percent common equity, was established on the basis of a study prepared by Robinson and others on the financial staff. The data upon which this conclusion was reached are shown in Table 2 and graphed in Figure 1. It is clear from the figure that Robinson and his staff feel the cost of capital would rise significantly if KEP&L deviates very much from the current 60 percent debt ratio, especially if the debt ratio is increased. This projected cost of capital increase

Table 2   Assumed Cost of Capital Schedules

Effect of Leverage on the Cost of Debt		
Leverage (Debt/Assets)	**Interest Rate**	**After-Tax Cost of Debt**
0.0%	12.0%	6.00%
10.0	12.1	6.05
20.0	12.2	6.10
30.0	12.3	6.15
40.0	12.7	6.35
50.0	13.2	6.60
60.0	14.0	7.00
70.0	18.0	9.00

Effect of Leverage on Required Rates of Return on Equity		
Leverage (Debt/Assets)	**Cost of Retained Earnings[a]**	**Cost of New Common Stock[b]**
0.0%	15.00%	15.80%
10.0	15.10	15.90
20.0	15.15	16.00
30.0	15.20	16.10
40.0	15.30	16.20
50.0	15.90	16.85
60.0	17.00	18.00
70.0	23.00	24.50

a. k_r with 60% debt $= R_F + P = 11\% + 6\% = k_S = D/P + g = 12\% + 5\% = 17\%$.

b. k_e with 60% debt $= \dfrac{D/P}{1-F} + g = \dfrac{12\%}{1-0.077} + 5\% = 18\%$.

Figure 1   Cost of Capital Schedules

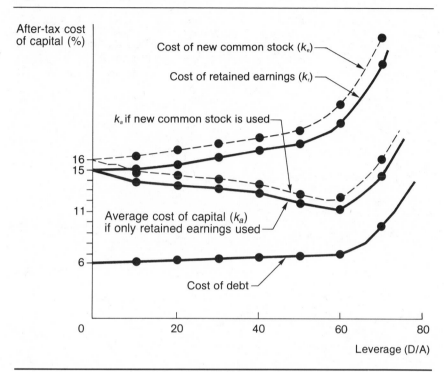

occurs primarily because Robinson feels quite strongly that the mortgage bonds would be downgraded if a sizable amount of new mortgage debt is issued without enough additional equity to maintain the 60 percent debt ratio.

If convertibles are used, they will be debentures and subordinated to the first mortgage bonds. Thus, using debentures will actually strengthen the mortgage bonds by: (1) raising the total assets that support these bonds; and (2) increasing the interest coverage on the mortgage bonds. The convertibles, on the other hand, will definitely be weaker than the mortgage bonds. Robinson and the investment bankers project that the convertible bonds, if used, will be rated Baa as compared to the Aa rating of the first mortgage bonds. Robinson also notes that Standard & Poor's and other rating services give "pure bond values" for outstanding convertible bonds. These bond values are calculated by discounting future coupon interest payments, plus the maturity value of the bond, back to the present at an interest rate appropriate for straight bonds of the same degree of risk as the convertible in question. At the present time, Baa bonds are yielding approximately 15 percent; thus the "bond value" of any KEP&L convertible bond will be calculated using a 15 percent discount rate.

Table 3 Conversion and Bond Values for 12% Convertible Bonds

Year	Conversion Value*	Bond Value*	Call Price*	Maturity Value
0	$ 700	$ 806	$1,090	$1,000
5	893	812	1,078	1,000
10				
15	1,455	849	1,039	1,000
20	1,857	899	1,020	1,000
25	2,370	1,000	1,000	1,000

*The equations used to calculate the values in this table are the following:

a. Conversion value $= C_t + P_o(1 + g)^t R$

where t = years since issue date
P_0 = initial stock price
g = growth rate in stock price
R = conversion ratio.

Example for year 5: $C_5 = \$17.50(1 + 0.05)^5\ 40$
$C_5 = 22.33(40)$
$C_5 = \$893$

b. Bond value $= B_t = \sum\limits_{j=1}^{T} \dfrac{I}{(1 + k_d)^j} + \dfrac{M''}{(1 + k_d)^T}$

where T = number of years remaining until maturity
j = time subscript from 1 to T
k_d = market rate of interest of equivalent risk, nonconvertible debt issue

I = dollars of interest paid each year
M'' = maturity value.

Example for year 5: $B_5 = \sum\limits_{j=1}^{20} \dfrac{\$120}{(1 + 0.15)^j} + \dfrac{\$1,000}{(1 + 0.15)^{20}}$
$B_5 = \$120(6.2593) + \$1000(0.0611)$
$B_5 = \$812$

c. The bond is not callable for the first two years. After year 2, the call premium is reduced by a constant amount each year to result in a zero call premium at maturity; that is, the premium is reduced by $1/23(\$90) = \$3.91$ per year.

Example for year 5: original call price = $1,090.
Call price in year 5 = $1,090 − 3(3.91) = $1,078.27 = $1,078.

Questions

1. Robinson plans to include a graphic model of the 12 percent convertible bond issue as one exhibit in his report to the directors. Complete Table 3,

---

Figure 2   Graphic Model of a Convertible Bond, 12.0% Issue

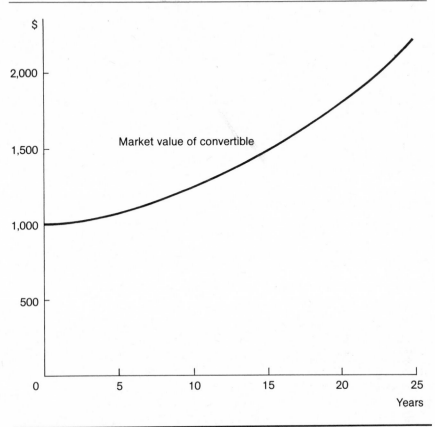

---

and then complete Figure 2 on the basis of the data calculated in Table 3. In your calculations, assume that the price of the common stock is $17.50 at present, and is expected to increase at a rate of 5 percent per year.

2. If all projections in Figure 2 are realized, and if Robinson calls the convertible issue when the conversion value of the bond is 30 percent above the bond's par value, in what year will the bond be called for conversion? (Hint: Set C_t = par value $\times$ 1.3, and find the t that forces equality.)

3. Regardless of your answer to Question 2, assume that $N = 12$. What is the after-tax component cost of the 12 percent convertible issue? k_c for the 10 percent issue is: 8.00 percent, as developed in the following illustration:

Procedure for Finding k_c, Using 10% Coupon Bond

Given the equation

$$M = \sum_{t=1}^{N} \frac{I(1-T)}{(1+k_c)^t} + \frac{P_n R}{(1+k_c)^N},$$

where M = market value of bond = $1,000
N = number of years to conversion = 12
I = interest in dollars = $100
T = tax rate = 0.5
P_n = expected market price of stock at end of period N = $31.43
R = conversion ratio = 50.

$$\$1,000 = \sum_{t=1}^{12} \frac{\$100(1-0.5)}{(1+k_c)^t} + \frac{\$31.43(50)}{(1+k_c)^N}$$
$$= \$50.00(\text{PVIFA for 12 years @ } k_c\%)$$
$$+ \$1,571.37(\text{PVIF for 12 years @ } k_c\%)$$

Try 8%: $50.00(7.5361) + $1,571.37(0.3971) = $376.81
 + $623.99 = $1,000.80. Therefore, $k_c \approx 8\%$

4. Calculate the before-tax rate of return an investor can expect to receive on the 12 percent convertible issue. Is this rate of return reasonable? Why or why not? How does the investor's return compare with the company's cost on the same issue? What accounts for the difference?

5. Calculate KEP&L's average cost of capital assuming that the company raises the $65.0 million by either: (a) a $26 million issue of common stock plus $39 million of first mortgage bonds; or (b) the 12 percent convertible issue. Develop weights from the company's balance sheet, adjusted on a pro forma basis, to reflect the addition of $65.0 million of convertibles. For the cost of equity in (a), use the cost of new common stock; in (b) use the cost of retained earnings. Although the capital structure will necessarily be changed if convertibles are used, assume that the cost of mortgage bonds and common stock will not change; that is, in (b) use the cost of mortgage bonds and common stock that is associated with the original capital structure, k_d = 14% and k_r = 17%. (Note: k_a = 10.72% if the 10% convertibles are used.)

6. A market value of the convertible line is shown in Figure 2. In year 10 the expected market value of the bond is given as $1,250. Suppose that an investor buys ten bonds at $1,250 and that the next day the company calls the bonds for conversion. How much will the investor gain or lose? Does

this suggest that the indicated market value line is inconsistent with the other data and should be redrawn? Explain.

7. List the advantages and disadvantages of the financing alternatives available to KEP&L. Given this information, which alternative should KEP&L accept? Why?

Case 27: *Convertibles*

Benson Petroleum Corporation

Rebecca Hauser, age 37, just had a shattering experience. On the evening of Thursday, December 13, 1980, she calculated her net worth to be $95,380. With the exception of $3,500 equity in her home, her investments were in relatively safe, she thought, convertible bonds. But on Friday, December 14, after losing $40,000 in one day, Hauser is not so sure about the safety of her portfolio.

Hauser's market holdings are shown in Table 1. On the Thursday in question, she owned the convertible debentures of three companies, with the bulk of her holdings in Benson Petroleum Corporation. Her original cost was $125,000, but the market value of the convertibles had increased to $261,880 by December 13. When the market value of securities increases, a holder of those securities may borrow additional funds to purchase new securities. Since she had followed this practice, by the Thursday in question the total borrowing in her margin account was $170,000.[1] Her net ownership was thus $91,880, up from an original investment of about $30,000.

Hauser is a vice-president and loan officer of the Flagstaff National Bank, the principal bank of Benson Petroleum. Although she does not handle the Benson account, she had studied the firm's history, present situation, and prospects carefully, and she had gone over her review with the loan officer who does manage the account. On the basis of this analysis, Hauser invested the inheritance she had received eight months earlier in Benson Petroleum convertibles. She felt that while the company's common stock was relatively risky, the convertibles offered an assured 8½ percent yield with the possibility of a substantial capital gain.

---

1. The Federal Reserve Board imposes limits on borrowing against certain listed securities. Prior to 1969 there were no limits on convertibles such as those imposed on common stocks. After 1969, margin requirements were imposed on the bonds of certain corporations. None of the companies whose convertibles Hauser held fell in this category, and her broker permitted her to borrow up to 70 percent of the market value of her holdings.

Table 1   Rebecca Hauser's Portfolio

December 13, 1980	Original Cost	Present Value	Borrowing[a]	Net Worth
Benson Petroleum Corporation	$100,000	$200,000	(Totals only. They do not apply to individual securities.)	
Nazareth Steel Corporation	7,000	45,500		
Transnational Implement Corp.	18,000	16,380		
	$125,000	$261,880	$170,000	$91,880
December 14, 1980				
Benson Petroleum Corporation	$100,000	$160,000	(Totals only. They do not apply to individual securities.)	
Nazareth Steel Corporation	7,000	45,500		
Transnational Implement Corp.	18,000	16,380		
	$125,000	$221,880	$170,000	$51,880

a. Borrowed against the total value of the portfolio, not against individual securities.

Shortly after Hauser purchased the Benson Petroleum bonds, the company announced discovery of a substantial oil strike in Central Utah. As a result, the price of the stock doubled, moving from $16 to $32, and the convertible bonds also doubled in price. On November 30, Benson Petroleum announced that it was making an offer to the shareholders of Big Sky Investment Corporation to buy Big Sky stock at $80 per share. Since Big Sky Investment was selling at approximately $60 per share on the New York Stock Exchange at the time of the offer, there was every reason to believe that most Big Sky stockholders would tender their stock to Benson Petroleum. Hauser learned from the loan officer handling Benson Petroleum that approximately $120 million was necessary to complete the transaction. The bank had stipulated, however, that Benson Petroleum must call its convertible bond issue to bring the debt ratio down to an acceptable level prior to finalizing the new loan. The bank was obviously afraid that some unforeseen event would occur that might cause the price of Benson Petroleum's stock to decline, and was anxious to see the convertibles converted into common stock before making the substantial new loan.

Although Hauser had known all of the above the previous week, she had decided not to sell her Benson Petroleum convertibles. She reasoned that because Big Sky Investment was actually worth substantially more than the $80 per share offered by Benson Petroleum, the proposed merger, when it took place, would cause Benson Petroleum's common stock to rise still more, pulling the price of the convertible bonds up with it.

On Friday, December 14, Benson Petroleum called the convertible debenture issue. The price of the debentures fell from $2000 per bond to $1,600 per bond, and Hauser's net worth dropped from $95,380 to $55,380, a loss of $40,000. Upset by these circumstances, Hauser decided to reexamine her entire portfolio. As a first step, she compiled the information shown in Table 2 for each of the three convertible issues she holds.

Table 2   Information on Portfolio

Benson Petroleum Corporation
On February 25, 1980, bought at par one hundred $1,000 bonds, 8½ percent, convertible into 50 shares of stock (conversion price: $20 per share). The bonds mature in 2002. Market price of stock at time of bond issue: $16 per share. On December 13, 1980, the market price of the stock was $32, and the market value of the bonds was $2,000. Benson Petroleum stock pays a $2.50 dividend. The bonds are callable at a price of $1,085.

Nazareth Steel Corporation
On May 12, 1976, bought at par seven $1,000 bonds, 9 percent, convertible into 40 shares of stock (conversion price: $25 per share). The bonds mature in 1998. Market price of stock at time of bond issue: $20 per share. On December 13, 1980, the market price of the stock was $150, and the market price of the bonds was $6,500. The stock pays an $8 dividend. Originally there were $15 million par value of convertibles outstanding. Now all except $600,000 have been converted voluntarily. The conversion price rises to $30 on January 1, 1981, and to $35 on January 1, 1988. These bonds cannot be called prior to January 1, 1981, at which time they are callable at a price of $1,090.

Transnational Implement Corporation
On January 10, 1976, bought at par eighteen $1,000 bonds, 10 percent, convertible into 40 shares of stock (conversion price: $25). Market price of stock at time of bond issue: $20 per share. On December 13, 1980, the market price of the stock was $12 per share. The stock pays no dividends, and the prospects for the stock are not good. The market price of the bonds, which mature in 1990, is $800, providing a yield to maturity (interest from 1980 through 1990, plus capital gain from $800 to par value of $1,000) of 13.8 percent. Transnational Implement recently sold a $20 million issue of subordinated debentures (nonconvertible) to yield investors 15 percent. These bonds have the same degree of risk of default as the convertibles. The convertibles have a call price of $1,050, and they can be called immediately.

Question

What portfolio changes, if any, should Rebecca Hauser make? In answering this question, (a) compare the December 1980 market value of each bond with its conversion value and call price, and (b) compare current interest yields on the bonds with dividend yields on the related stocks for each of the convertible issues.

Part **4:** Financial Structure, Dividend Policy, and the Cost of Capital

Case 28: *Financial Leverage*

Medical Innovations Corporation

Over the past five years, Medical Innovations, a company that began in 1969 as a piece of balsa wood in its founder's palm, has averaged a solid return on equity of 33 percent and an equally spectacular 40 percent average annual increase in earnings per share. George Thomas, president and chief executive officer of Medical Innovations, was described by his senior vice-president, Deborah Russell, as a "restless Yankee tinkerer with a wealth of curiosity, but without a college education, who used to hang around the local patent broker's office." One day as Thomas was idly fingering a long neglected invention, he began to see how he could make the object into a commercial success. The idea was for a disposable cartridge of staples inside a reusable staple gun that could be used as a replacement for hand-sewn sutures in abdominal surgery. After Thomas developed a prototype made from balsa wood in the basement of his home, two surgery professors at the Mayo Clinic offered to test the stapler. With the enthusiasm of the surgeons, Thomas was able to gain the financial and managerial resources of Russell, and Medical Innovations was launched.

Although the stapler product line saw 45 percent growth throughout the seventies (with only 15 percent of its market tapped), Thomas aggressively widened the product line with inventions and innovations made in conjunction with surgeons and other medical personnel.

In late 1982, Medical Innovations finished the final design, testing, and production plans for a new and revolutionary nonevasive method to monitor arterial blood gases. It was developed by a team of surgeons to measure blood electrolytes quickly during surgery, but the process would be extremely useful not only in the operating room, but in private physicians' offices as well. This application would eliminate the need for doctors to send blood samples to laboratories when checking for levels of various gases (oxygen, carbon dioxide, etc.). Just how receptive the market will be to the device is uncertain, since Medical Innovations does not know whether physicians in private practice will be attracted by the long-run cost savings of such a device, especially when they would be investing their own private funds. The major hospitals, on the other hand, have already inquired as to when the device will be available for sale.

Despite the uncertainty over the ultimate market for the monitoring device (reflected in Table 1), Thomas and Russell plan to go ahead with full scale production. Further, they have decided that since a plant expansion is necessary for production of the new device, the firm should expand now to meet future growth requirements as private physicians slowly enter the demand side of the market. The projected total capital outlays plus additional working capital needed involves a $13 million increase in total assets during 1983.[1]

Thomas and Russell are now faced with two major decisions: (1) which of two available production methods should be used; and (2) how the necessary expansion should be financed.

The monitoring device can be produced by either of two methods. Plan A calls for using a minimum amount of fully automated equipment and for purchasing, rather than manufacturing, major components. Under Plan A fixed costs will be $3.5 million per year, while variable costs will be $150 per device. Plan B calls for more operating leverage: fixed costs will be $11 million, but variable costs will be $105 per device. Regardless of the production method employed, the estimated sales price is $200 per monitoring device.

To finance this expansion, Medical Innovations has the alternatives of using bonds, common stock, or some combination of the two. George Thomas and Deborah Russell will have to make the final decision. In a recent directors' meeting, two views were presented, and Thomas and Russell are now trying to decide on the relative merits of these two positions.

Lane Silberman, a director and chairman of the board of J. C. Silberman & Co., the investment banking firm that has handled Medical Innovations' long-term financing needs, strongly recommends that the company choose debt financing at this time. Silberman believes that inflation is likely to be persistent in the nation's economy and that "debt" incurred now can be repaid in future years with "cheap dollars." Silberman also indicates that his discussions with the company's stockholders (and Silberman's firm has many customers who own Medical Innovations stock) suggest that the investing public is currently interested in companies whose securities are more highly leveraged rather than in conservative firms. He notes that most investors hold diversified portfolios, which minimizes their risks on any one stock; this increases their willingness to assume more risk on any individual security.

Lauren Pallin, vice-president of finance, takes the opposite point of view, arguing that the firm's risk will be increased considerably if it sells additional

---

1. Some of the requirements for funds could be met by retained earnings, but disregard this factor. Assume that the $13 million increase must be met entirely with outside funds, and that it will be raised either by selling bonds, by selling stock, or by using a mix of these two types of securities. Current liabilities will stay at their 1982 level (see Tables 2 and 3).

Table 1   Sales Estimates for New Monitoring Device

Probability	Sales in Units
0.1	80,000
0.2	110,000
0.4	150,000
0.2	190,000
0.1	220,000

Table 2   Income Statement

Year Ended December 31
(in thousands)

	1982	1981
Sales	$40,000	$32,000
Total Costs (excluding interest)	24,440	20,899
Earnings Before Interest and Tax	$15,560	$11,101
Debt Interest (9 percent)	900	630
Earnings Before Tax	$14,660	$10,471
Tax (48 percent)	7,037	5,026
Net Income	$ 7,623	$ 5,445

Table 3   Balance Sheet

Year Ended December 31
(in thousands)

	1982	1981
Current Assets	$13,500	$12,850
Net Fixed Assets	14,500	8,950
Other Assets	7,000	5,200
Total Assets	$35,000	$27,000
Current Liabilities	$ 6,480	$ 4,500
Long-Term Debt (9 percent)	10,000	7,000
Common Stock, $2.50 par	5,000	5,000
Retained Earnings	13,520	10,500
Total Claims	$35,000	$27,000

debt at this time. Pallin maintains that although the sales forecasts are favorable, if the cost of the new process is higher than anticipated, or if sales fall below the anticipated level, the company could be in serious trouble. Pallin also notes that the company's commercial bankers have frequently mentioned the debt ratio as a measure of corporate strength.[2] She adds that investors' aversion to risk generally results in lower stock prices for companies with high debt ratios. Finally, Pallin stresses that if the company uses additional common stock now, its financial position will be strong. Should demand exceed expectations, causing new facilities to be required in the near future, the company would be in an excellent position to sell the debt at a later date. Although it is not in her report, Thomas recalls that Pallin believes interest rates are high at the present time and, if the company defers debt financing, it may be able to obtain debt at a lower cost in the near future.

The currently outstanding long-term debt carries a 9 percent interest rate. Because the general level of interest rates is higher now than it was when the old debt was issued, the new debt would carry a higher rate. There is a provision in the contract for the presently outstanding debt which states that it must be retired (without penalty) before new long-term debt is issued if the new debt has a higher rate of interest. At the directors' meeting, Pallin indicated that this provision would present no problem because the company would be able to sell enough new debt to provide funds for the expansion and also to pay off the old debt. Another clause in the debt contract states that there is a 20 percent prepayment penalty for repaying the debt ahead of schedule unless it is refunded with higher cost debt. Thus, Medical Innovations is essentially prevented from reducing its long-term debt below ten million dollars.

When Thomas and Russell pressed Silberman and Pallin for information on how increasing the debt ratio would affect the price-earnings ratio, there was some disagreement. Pallin felt that the current price-earnings ratio of 6.5 would decline, while Silberman felt that because investors would not be averse to Medical Innovations' use of more debt, the current P/E would not change.

To aid them in making their final decision, Thomas and Russell asked Pallin to prepare a report for presentation at the next directors' meeting. Pallin asks you, her assistant, to help her with the report by providing her with the answers to the following questions.

Questions

1. Which production method should Medical Innovations choose? In answering this question, calculate the break-even point and expected EBIT under each plan, then analyze the riskiness of Plans A and B. (Hint:

---

2. The industry average debt ratio is 50 percent, and the average times-interest-earned is 8X.

the break-even point can be determined graphically or by use of the equation

$$Q = F/(P - V),$$

where Q equals break-even volume, F equals fixed costs, V equals variable cost per unit, and P equals selling price per unit.)

2. Regardless of your conclusion to Question 1, assume that Medical Innovations decides on Plan A. A $13 million increase in total assets will be required to implement the plan. Debt is available according to the following schedule:

Amount Borrowed	Interest Rate
$ 7.01 to $11 million	14.00%
11.01 to 14 million	14.75
14.01 to 17 million	15.50
17.01 to 20 million	16.50
20.01 to 23 million	18.50

(Remember that the $10 million long-term debt must also be retired if Medical Innovations chooses to use additional debt.)

The matter of the P/E ratio concerned Pallin, who asked you to consult with other investment bankers for their opinions. Based on these conversations, you conclude that the following schedule is applicable:

Debt/Assets	P/E
up to 30%	6.5
30.1–36%	5.5
36.1–45%	5.0
45.1–50%	4.5

The debt/asset ratios shown here do not include current liabilities; they relate only to long-term debt. If short-term debt were included, these data would be somewhat different.

To maximize the price of the firm's stock, what capital structure should you recommend? Assume a 35 percent growth rate on 1982 EBIT from existing operations, and combine this 1983 projected EBIT with the expected incremental EBIT assuming Plan A is carried out. Use a 48 percent tax rate in your calculations. Also assume that debt is available only in three million dollar increments, and that any funds not raised by debt will be raised by selling common stock at a price of $25 per share less a

$5 per share flotation cost. Hint: You can calculate expected EBIT and work only with this figure to generate expected EPS. Also, you can use this equation to simplify calculations:

$$\text{EPS} = [(\text{EBIT} - I) \cdot (1 - t)] / \text{shares}.$$

3. At the expected level of sales, and with your target debt/assets ratio, what is Medical Innovations' times-interest-earned?
4. Suppose the debt is in the form of a 20-year term loan. What will the annual amortization payment be? Use this to calculate the debt service coverage for 1983.[3]
5. What is Medical Innovations' expected rate of return on common equity? (The expected rate of return on equity is equal to the expected net income available to common divided by total common equity.)
6. Assume that Medical Innovations pays out all earnings as dividends and has a zero growth rate, and that investors are aware of this. What value for K_s is implied by the data used in this case?
7. How would the decision be influenced if: (a) Thomas's and Russell's entire net worth is tied up in the company; or (b) they hold diversified portfolios in addition to Medical Innovations stock?
8. If the board as a whole, not including Thomas and Russell, had control of the stock, would it matter whether management's compensation consisted entirely of a fixed salary or a substantial element in the form of stock options?
9. No mention of the Capital Asset Pricing Model (CAPM) was made in the case because the CAPM was not considered in the decision. Explain how the CAPM concepts might have been employed in the analysis. Be sure to discuss how operating leverage and financial leverage would affect the firm's beta coefficient, hence the firm's cost of capital and value.
10. What decision would you recommend? In answering this question play the role of Lauren Pallin, assume that Thomas and Russell each own 35 percent of the outstanding stock, or 70 percent together, and that this represents essentially all of their personal net worth.

---

3. Debt Service Coverage $= \text{EBIT}/[\text{interest} + (\text{principal})/(1 - t)]$.

Case 29: *Optimum Capital Structure*

Page Solarlite, Inc.

Tampa, Florida, architect Jennifer Page observed the increasing popularity of building designs utilizing skylights over open indoor spaces. She knew, however, that the high cost of custom-made skylights made them an extravagance that few could afford, especially with recently rising construction costs. To capitalize on this growing market, in her spare time Page developed and patented an economical prefabricated skylight which could be mass produced and sold at a profit to the producer.

Once the design was finalized, the durability testing completed, and the sales potential of the skylights estimated, Jennifer Page and her younger brother, Andrew, decided to form a company to produce and market the product. Andrew, a recent MBA graduate from the University of Florida, was to oversee the actual production process, and he was also to handle financial arrangements. Jennifer, in turn, was to supervise quality control and be in charge of distribution through various contractors and architectural firms. Because of the predicted population and housing growth in the Sunbelt area, local banks and insurance companies indicated a willingness to supply the Pages with debt capital. Equity could be raised through a stock sale to local investors at a price of $10 per share.

A local attorney advised the Pages that now, before any value was created and before raising any outside capital, the business should be incorporated. He further suggested that there be 10 million authorized shares with a $0.10 par value. It would not be necessary to issue the full 10 million shares initially—only as many as were actually needed could be issued. The Pages decided that the best course of action was to issue a yet-to-be determined number of shares to themselves at a share price of $0.10 each, or $X in total, to assign a value of $1.00 to the patent, and to utilize the cash account as the offsetting entry. These actions would produce the initial balance sheet (see Table 1).

Before the corporate charter can be filed, it is necessary to determine the number of shares Jennifer and Andrew can issue to themselves at $0.10 each; if

Table 1 Pro Forma Balance Sheet

Cash	$ X − 1	Accounts Payable	$ 0
Accounts Receivable	0	Notes Payable	0
Inventory	0	Other Current Liabilities	0
Plant and Equipment	0	Long-Term Debt	0
Patents	1	Common Stock ($0.10 par)	X
Total Assets	$ X	Total Liabilities and Net Worth	$X

they sell themselves too many, outside investors will not be willing to buy sufficient stock at $10 per share to meet the firm's financial requirements. Thus, a realistic business plan is required to set forth information about the production processes, the market, and financing arrangements for additional capital.

The Pages are planning to distribute the skylights through all types of contractors and architects. They project a selling price of $500 per unit, which is a large cost reduction as compared to custom-made skylights. This low price, coupled with the recent trend toward innovative interior designs, will provide a solid basis for sales.

Although some sales will be made in the home improvement and renovation markets, the primary demand will be from new construction. Due to the cyclical nature of this industry, as well as the recent uncertainty in the economy as a whole, Jennifer and Andrew have estimated full-operation sales for three scenarios—optimistic, expected, and pessimistic. Andrew interprets the most likely value as the mathematical expected value of a normal probability distribution, and the pessimistic and optimistic values as being two standard deviations above and below the expected value.

After an in-depth study, Jennifer identified two alternative production processes that could be employed, and she asked Andrew to help her select the one to implement. Plan A holds down initial investment and fixed costs; it involves the use of a minimum amount of highly automated equipment, combined with purchasing major components from local suppliers rather than

Table 2 Distribution of Sales

Scenario	Sales in Units	Sales in $
Pessimistic	52,200	26,100,000
Most Likely	67,500	33,750,000
Optimistic	82,800	41,400,000

manufacturing components. Under this plan, annual fixed costs are estimated to be $5,095,000, while variable costs would be $390 per unit produced. The second alternative, Plan B, involves more operating leverage: fixed costs would be $11,979,500 per year, and variable costs $275 per unit. The selling price will be set at $500 regardless of the production process, and neither of the estimated fixed costs includes any interest charges. Total capital requirements for current and fixed assets, plus operating funds during the start-up period, are estimated to be $11.0 million under Plan A and $15.0 million under Plan B. Assume that these investment requirements are known with certainty.

Questions

1. Which production plan should Andrew Page choose? To answer this question, calculate the break-even point and the expected EBIT under each plan, as well as the level of EBIT at the different sales levels. Then use this information to help analyze the riskiness and relative rates of return of Plans A and B. Also, calculate ROIs for each project, and the sales level at which $ROI_A = ROI_B$. It should be noted that the information given to this point in the case will not be sufficient to enable you to reach a definite conclusion regarding Plans A and B. You can, however, think about the issues.

2. Regardless of your conclusion in Question 1, assume that Andrew decided to go with Plan B, and that the total capital required by Page Solarlite is $15 million to put this plan into effect.[1] Andrew contracted various commercial banks, investment bankers, and other potential sources of outside capital. Based on his notes from these meetings, he constructed the following schedule for the cost of debt (these rates apply to all the debt raised to finance Plan B):

Table 3   Debt Schedule

Amount Borrowed	Interest Rate on All Debt
up to $ 3 million	11.00%
$ 3.1 to $ 5 million	11.25%
$ 5.1 to $ 7 million	11.70%
$ 7.1 to $ 9 million	12.50%
$ 9.1 to $11 million	13.95%
$11.1 to $13 million	16.75%
$13.1 to $15 million	21.75%

---

1. Before the asset decision can be finalized, Andrew would need to perform the same analysis for Plan A as he is going through here for Plan B. Only with information on both the operating cost structure of the production process and the associated optimum financial structure for each alternative can a rational decision be made.

It is clear to Andrew that some equity will be required; all of the capital requirements cannot be financed by debt. The investment banker had suggested that an initial price of $10 per share should maximize the appeal and thus the marketability of the stock. Most of the issue would likely be subscribed locally in the Tampa area, and the consensus is that for Plan B, the following cost of equity schedule, stated as a function of the amount of debt employed, is a reasonable estimate:

Table 4   Cost of Equity Schedule

Debt (Millions)	Cost of Equity
$ 0.0	11.12%
$ 3.0	11.25%
$ 5.0	11.50%
$ 7.0	12.10%
$ 9.0	13.25%
$11.0	15.25%
$13.0	19.75%
$15.0	26.75%

The investment banker indicated that if no debt is used, and the Pages finance only with common stock, 1.5 million shares can be sold at the $10 price to raise the $15 million of capital required for Plan B. If debt financing is used, stock will be sold at $10 per share, but fewer shares will have to be issued to raise the required $15 million.

Andrew is interested in choosing the financing plan that will cause him and Jennifer to have the greatest personal net worth, where net worth is defined as follows:

Net Worth = Value of Stock × Number of Shares for the Pages.

The price is to be set at $10, so you need to find the maximum number of shares that the founders can issue to themselves and still have investors be willing to pay $10 per share while raising the required equity. To simplify the calculations, assume that the capital requirements are net of any cash received on the sale of the stock at $0.10 per share to the Pages. Thus, you may ignore this amount and presume for calculation purposes that the Pages pay nothing for their stock. Assume a tax rate of 48 percent, and complete the following table.

Table 5 Value Calculations

Debt	K_d	K_e	Firm Value	Shares the Pages Can Issue to Themselves
$ 0	11.00%	11.12%	$15,001,439	144
$ 3,000,000	11.00%	11.25%	$16,302,756	130,276
$ 5,000,000	11.25%	11.50%		
$ 7,000,000	11.70%	12.10%		
$ 9,000,000	12.50%	13.25%		
$11,000,000	13.95%	15.25%		
$13,000,000	16.75%	19.75%	$15,713,215	71,322
$15,000,000	21.75%	26.75%	$14,894,056	Negative

Hints: (1) You can base your analysis on expected EBIT, calculated at the expected level of sales. This requires fewer calculations than would be involved if you calculated values at each of the three sales levels. (2) If the Pages use no debt, they will sell 1.5 million shares at a price of $10 each (disregarding the shares they themselves will receive). If they do use debt, they will sell fewer shares. In setting up your analysis, first analyze the situation at zero debt, then analyze the leverage situations. The value of the firm, and the shares the Pages can keep, will change at each debt level.

3. From the standpoint of the times-interest-earned ratio, how safe does the company look? Explain. (Note: The average manufacturing firm has a TIE ratio to about 6 × .)

4. Suppose the debt is in the form of a 20-year term loan. What will the annual amortization payment be (interest plus principal)? Use this to calculate Page Solarlite's debt service coverage ratio. (For simplification, the debt service coverage ratio here is defined as EBIT/[Interest Charges + Before = Tax Principal Repayment].) Does this ratio indicate that the company is in a safe position? Explain. (Note: The average manufacturing firm has a coverage ratio of about 4 × .)

5. Suppose this were *your* company. What level of debt would you choose? Would your choice be influenced by your other assets; that is, would it matter whether your entire net worth was invested in the company versus a situation where you owned about $1 million of other securities?

Case 30A: *Operating Leverage*

American Telephone and Electronics Company, Part I

In late 1981, the process of deregulating major segments of the telecommunications industry was well underway. In particular, the Congress, the Justice Department, and the Federal Communications Commission had all taken important steps to increase competition in long distance calling, in the provision of telephone hardware, and in the offering of data processing services. In those areas, competition is to set prices. However, traditional regulation by utility commissions is to be maintained on local telephone service. As a part of the deregulation process, and to ensure that costs properly attributable to their competitive activities are not charged to local telephone customers ("cross-subsidization"), AT&T, General Telephone and Electronics, and other telephone companies are being required to set up separate corporations to handle competitive and regulated offerings.[1]

American Telephone and Electronics (AT&E) has been studying the question of whether or not to make a major investment and to set up a new subsidiary to manufacture, distribute, and service "Masterphones," which are small but very sophisticated computer terminals that can serve each of these functions: (1) as a regular telephone, (2) as an answering service/call forwarding device, (3) as a video receiver for news and advertising information similar to a combination of the yellow pages and cable TV, and (4) through a tie-in with a central computer, as an extremely powerful "home computer." The

---

1. The deregulation process was thrown into some confusion when, on January 8, 1982, a settlement was signed in the long-standing antitrust case against AT&T. In exchange for keeping long-distance service, Bell Telephone Laboratories, Inc., Yellow Pages, and Western Electric Co., its manufacturing subsidiary, under the corporate umbrella, AT&T agreed to spin off all of its telephone operating companies. Many questions still remain concerning the ramifications of the settlement and the extent to which the courts, the FCC, and Congress will intervene in setting the final terms, but the competitors to AT&T are still faced with the problem of structuring their own operations so as to be in the best strategic position to compete effectively in the environment of the future—whatever that turns out to be.

new terminals would have a sales price of $3,000. The subsidiary's fixed operating costs per year, including both amortization of developmental costs and maintenance of the data processing system, would be approximately $1.5 billion. An initial investment of approximately $3 billion would be required to set up manufacturing plants, develop the required software, and get the system operational. Variable production/distribution/servicing costs are estimated at $1,000 per unit in the projected output range. The proposed new company's effective tax rate would be 40 percent.

Because of the risks involved, management's tentative plans call for raising the entire $3 billion as common equity. AT&E would supply $1.5 billion of the equity, with the remainder being raised by selling stock to the public. Thus, if AT&E were to go ahead with the project, it would own a half interest in a new, all-equity-financed subsidiary.

The AT&E Board of Directors, like those of most very large companies, consists of two groups. First, there are "inside directors," headed by the chairman, vice-chairman, and president, who are full-time employees of the corporation and who comprise the top management of the firm. Second, there are the "outside directors" who provide different perspectives to management and who represent various constituents, especially various groups of stockholders. AT&E's outside directors include an investment banker, two commercial bankers, the presidents or chairmen of five NYSE listed companies, and the presidents of a large life insurance company, a major foundation, and a major university (this latter director is a former finance professor).

The role of the outside directors, all of whom are very competent and very independent individuals, is to help management make better decisions regarding major corporate policies, including strategic decisions such as whether or not to move into new ventures such as Masterphones. In order to maintain a degree of independence, and to avoid unconsciously biasing the outsiders' views, the corporation has provided the outside directors with a budget to hire outside consultants to assist these directors in making appraisals of various proposed corporate actions. Obviously, the consultants must have access to all corporate information, but they are permitted—and even encouraged—to play the role of devil's advocate in the decision process.

AT&E's management has recommended to the board of directors that the Masterphone project, as outlined above, be accepted. However, because of the magnitude of the project and its importance to the corporation, the outside directors have concluded that they should consider it carefully before authorizing management to go forward. Therefore, they have employed the firm of Elson & Graber to make an appraisal of the project to see whether it has any obvious flaws. Elson & Graber is not expected to conduct a complete analysis, or to make a definite go or no-go recommendation. Rather, their task is to help the outside directors "ask the right questions of the management" and to ensure that these questions are answered properly before the final decision is reached.

One of the outside directors, Ed Jemmings, the former finance professor who is now a university president, has been appointed by the other outside directors to work with John Kose, the Elson & Graber partner in charge of the project. Together, they have developed the following set of questions, and you, as a junior member of the consulting firm and Kose's assistant, must supply "first approximation" answers to them.

Questions

1. What is the break-even sales volume?
2. What would the new company's rate of return on equity (ROE) be if sales ran at an annual level of (1) 1,000,000 units, (2) 750,000 units, or (3) 1,250,000 units?
3. Based on discussions with the AT&E marketing staff, you learn that the company has assigned a probability of 0.1 to sales of 750,000 units, 0.3 to sales of 1,000,000 units, and 0.6 to sales of 1,250,000 units. Measuring risk by the standard deviation of ROE (even though the distribution is not normal), how risky is this project? Is it realistic to assign a zero probability to losses? Assume, for purposes of this question, that σ_{ROE} for the average industrial firm is 7 percent, and that the coefficient of variation of ROE is generally in the 0.5 to 0.6 range.
4. Assume, as a rough approximation, that you can estimate the cost of common equity to an unlevered firm as follows:

$$k_s = R_F + a_1(\text{beta}) + a_2(\sigma_{ROE}).$$

Assume also (1) that the Treasury bond rate is currently 11 percent, (2) that for this type of business beta is 1.0, and (3) that Elson & Graber's own in-house empirical studies indicate that $a_1 = 2.0$ and $a_2 = 0.3$, so

$$k_s = 11\% + 2.0(1.0) + 0.3(\sigma_{ROE}). \quad 6.708$$

Does it appear feasible, in terms of its effects on AT&E's stockholders, to set up the new subsidiary to produce Masterphones?
5. Can you think of anything not discussed in the facts of the case that should be considered before finalizing the go or no-go decision?

Case **30B:** *Operating and Financial Leverage*

American Telephone and Electronics Company, Part II

As noted in Part I of the case, AT&E has been studying the question of whether or not to set up a new subsidiary to manufacture, distribute, and service "Masterphones," which are small but very sophisticated computer terminals that can serve each of these functions: (1) as a regular telephone; (2) as an answering service/call forwarding device, (3) as a video receiver for news and advertising information similar to a combination of the yellow pages and cable TV, and (4) through a tie-in with a central computer, as an extremely powerful "home computer." Because of the risks involved, management's tentative plans call for raising the entire $3 billion initial investment as common equity. AT&E would supply $1.5 billion of the equity, with the remainder being raised by selling stock to the public. Thus, if AT&E were to go ahead with the project, it would own a half interest in a new, all-equity-financed subsidiary.

AT&E's management has recommended to the board of directors that the Masterphone project, as outlined above, be accepted. However, because of the magnitude of the project and its importance to the corporation, the outside directors have concluded that they should consider it carefully before authorizing management to go forward. Therefore, they have employed the firm of Elson & Graber to make an appraisal of the project to see whether it has any obvious flaws. Elson & Graber is not expected to conduct a complete analysis, or to make a definite go or no-go recommendation. Rather, their task is to help the outside directors "ask the right questions of the management" and to ensure that these questions are answered properly before the final decision is reached.

One of the outside directors, Ed Jemmings, a former finance professor who is now a university president, has been appointed by the outside directors to work with John Kose, the Elson & Graber partner in charge of the project. In Part I of the case, Jemmings and Kose investigated some of the operating leverage characteristics of the proposed subsidiary. They must now turn their attention to the question of how the new subsidiary should be financed.

AT&E's management has stated that it thinks an all-equity capital structure is best because of the risks inherent in a new company producing a new product. However, Jemmings and Kose note that most electronics manufacturers, including those which produce telephone and data processing equipment, use fairly large amounts of debt, with the target debt/assets ratio generally being in the range of 20 to 40 percent. Further, the investment banker on the AT&E board, Michael Kernan, estimates that if the new subsidiary raises up to 20 percent of its required capital (or $600 million) as debt, this debt would be rated Aaa and would carry an interest rate of 12 percent. If the debt/assets ratio were increased to as much as 40 percent, the bonds would be rated Baa and would have an interest rate of 14 percent under current market conditions. At a debt/assets ratio between these extremes, the bond ratings—and consequently interest rates—would take an intermediate position.

The new subsidiary's cost of equity will be higher if it uses debt than if it does not. Based on Elson & Graber's in-house research, it appears that the cost of equity equation used in Part I of the case would still apply, but the values for σ_{ROE} and beta would both change, causing k_s to change. This equation is

$$k_s = R_F + a_1(\text{beta}) + a_2(\sigma_{ROE}).$$

Assume for this analysis that (1) the Treasury bond rate is currently 11 percent, and (2) Elson & Graber's own in-house empirical studies indicate that $a_1 = 2.0$ and $a_2 = 0.3$. For the zero debt situation, the value for σ_{ROE}, 6.71 percent, was calculated in Part I and the estimated beta without leverage was given as I.O. New values for these factors are required if the new subsidiary uses debt. As a first approximation, assume that a leveraged firm's beta can be estimated as follows:

$$b_L = b_U[1 + (1 - t)(\text{Debt/Equity})],$$

where b_L and b_U are the betas of leveraged and unleveraged firms; t is the corporate tax rate, and debt and equity are measured at book value.[1] Therefore, if AT&E uses 20 percent debt financing, then as an approximation,

$$b_L = 1.0[1 + (0.6)(0.25)] = 1.15.$$

At 40 percent financing, the subsidiary's estimated beta would be 1.40.

1. This equation is based on a theoretical model developed by Professor Robert Hamada ("The Effect of the Firm's Capital Structure on the Systematic Risk of Common Stocks," *Journal of Finance*, May 1972). Hamada's equation actually measures debt and equity at market rather than book value, but for a new firm these values are likely to be similar though not identical.

To help them focus on the key issues, Jemmings and Kose ask you to focus your analysis on the following questions.

Questions

1. What would the net income (and EPS) breakeven point be if the subsidiary were financed with (1) 20 percent debt or (2) 40 percent debt, i.e., at what levels of unit sales would net income (and EPS) equal zero under each capital structure? Assume that (1) the subsidiary's fixed operating costs per year, including both amortization of developmental costs and maintenance of the data processing system, are expected to be $1.5 billion, (2) variable production/distribution/servicing costs are estimated at $1,000 per unit in the projected output range, (3) the sales price will be $3,000 per unit, and (4) the proposed company's effective tax rate is 40 percent.

2. What would expected ROE and σ_{ROE} be at each of the three debt levels (zero, 20 percent, and 40 percent)? Assume that the company has assigned a probability of 0.1 to sales of 750,000 units, 0.3 to sales of 1,000,000 units, and 0.6 to sales of 1,250,000 units.

3. What would the subsidiary's total market value, and total equity value, be if it were financed (1) by equity only, (2) with $600,000,000 of debt, plus equity, or (3) with $1,200,000,000 of debt, plus equity? Work with the expected EBIT, plus information developed earlier, and use these formulas:

$$V = D + \frac{(EBIT - k_dD)(1 - t)}{k_s}, \text{ and}$$
$$S = V - D.$$

Here V is the total market value of the firm, D is total debt, and S is the total stock value.

4. Jemmings and Kose have told you to assume (1) that AT&E wants to own 50 percent of the equity of the subsidiary irrespective of how much debt is used, (2) that the new subsidiary's initial stock will be sold to the public at $20 per share, and (3) that AT&E can legally purchase its stock at a price other than $20, providing the public knows of AT&E's purchase price but is still willing to pay $20 per share. The $20 price is somewhat arbitrary, but the investment banker member of AT&E's board has informed Jemmings and Kose that in his opinion $20 is the best price at which to bring out a new issue in order to maximize the total value of the firm. A low price such as $1, or a high price such as $1,000, could be set, but the conventional price is in the $15 to $25 range.

    a. How many shares should the new subsidiary have to issue at each of the three capital structures? (Hint: Recognize that $P_0 = \$20 = S/N$, and

$N = (V - D)/P_0 = S/P_0$. Here S is the total market value of the stock and N is the number of shares outstanding.)

    b. What would AT&E's initial gain or loss be at each capital structure?

    c. Does it seem fair to permit AT&E to buy stock at a price which is different from that paid by the general public?

5. What would the expected earnings per share, the coefficient of variation of EPS, and the expected P/E ratio be under the three financing plans?

6. What is the probability that the subsidiary would be unable to cover its interest charges, assuming it uses 40 percent debt?

7. We typically think of a firm's stock price as first rising as it begins to use financial leverage, then hitting a peak, and finally declining if it goes on to use excessive levels of debt. In this case, the price is assumed to be constant at $20 per share. Reconcile the typical view of leverage with the situation in this case.

8. Using the MM-with tax model, what would the subsidiary's total value and equity value be at 20 percent and 40 percent debt? [Note: The basic equation is $V_L = V_U + tD$.]

9. What would the value be at the three debt levels using Miller's formula?

$$V_L = V_U + \left[1 - \frac{(1 - t_c)(1 - t_{pS})}{(1 - t_{pD})}\right] D.$$

Here t_c = corporate tax rate, t_{pS} = personal tax rate on stock income (average dividends and capital gains), and t_{pD} = tax rate on interest income from debt. Assume that the personal tax rate on interest is t_{pD} = 45 percent, the tax rate on stock income (dividends and capital gains) is t_{pS} = 25 percent, and the corporate tax rate is t_c = 40 percent.

10. Give an explanation for the differences in value using the three models.

11. Obviously, the final decision will be based on much more detailed analysis than has been done here, but, based on the information at hand, should the outside directors recommend that AT&E proceed with the project, and, if so, how should it be financed?

Case **31**: *Valuation*

Hamner Courts

Ralph Jordan is 47 years old and has just retired after 20 years in the athletic department of the Saugatuck High School. He started his career with the school as a business instructor and part-time coach, but he enjoyed the athletic work so much that he soon devoted all his time to it. After 12 years of coaching, Jordan was made the school's athletic director, a position which he held for the past 5 years.

During his time as coach and athletic director, Jordan made a number of contacts in the sports world in eastern Michigan and gained knowledge, not only of the sports themselves, but also of how to expertly manage sporting facilities, how to control operating costs, and how to identify sports that are growing in popularity. As Jordan sees it, handball and racketball are two such boom sports. Having been the Michigan Masters State Handball Champion for the past five years, Jordan not only knows the sport and its participants well, he also has firsthand knowledge of the growing interest in the sport and the limited court space available. With the cold winters and hot summers of southern Michigan, it is impossible to play handball or racketball outside for more than four months a year. Most indoor courts are private clubs which are quite expensive and require the handball and racketball players to also help cover the costs of other facilities in which they might not be interested (such as tennis courts, swimming pools, and social areas).

During his career, Jordan has accumulated a net worth of approximately $325,000, of which $40,000 is on deposit in a savings and loan association and $285,000 is invested in a portfolio of high quality common stocks. Jordan also has a pension which provides him with payments of approximately $1,000 per month. Enjoying excellent health, Jordan has no intention of "being put out to pasture" and, in fact, was motivated to retire from academia in part by an opportunity to own and manage the small indoor court area where he plays handball.

Hamner Courts was established in 1969 by one of the early promoters of the sport, Craig Hamner, who operated the courts until his death in late 1977. Hamner's widow has been running the courts from 1977 to the present time, but the profits of the business have been much lower under her management than they were under her husband's. Her principal problems have been: (1) a tendency to be too lenient in granting and extending credit; and (2) not enough time to manage adequately both the courts and the small pro shop area. As a result, investments in accounts receivable and equipment inventories have been excessive, and losses on accounts receivable have reduced the court's profitability. Mrs. Hamner is reluctant to give up the courts, but her own health is failing, and she feels that if she receives a good offer, she should sell out.

Having been a member of Hamner Courts from the earliest days, Jordan believes that although the courts hold a great deal of promise, Mrs. Hamner is simply not running them properly. With his experience not only in handball but in general sports management as well, Jordan feels that he would be able to do considerably better. Further, Jordan's wife is eager to participate in the new venture by managing the pro shop. Although the small size of Hamner Courts was one of the original attractions for Jordan (he feels that he could easily manage the courts with his wife's assistance), he also realizes that the size means limited growth potential in terms of overall revenues.

When they discussed a possible price, Mrs. Hamner indicated that she was willing to sell the courts for $265,000, but that she would withdraw the $15,000 now held in cash before turning over the courts to Jordan.

Table 1 shows the balance sheet for Hamner Courts as of December 31, 1982, and Table 2 shows the sales and profits before taxes for the 10-year period from 1973 through 1982. On the basis of a physical examination, Jordan concluded that both the building and the inventories shown on the balance sheet were fairly valued. Further, the courts were in good shape and no

Table 1   Balance Sheet

Year Ended December 31, 1982

Cash	$ 15,000	Accounts Payable	$ 16,800
Accounts Receivable	20,000	Other Currrent	2,800
Inventories	40,000	Total Liabilities	$ 19,600
Building	190,000	Common Stock Plus	
Total Assets	$265,000	Earned in Surplus	245,400
		Total Liabilities and Net Worth	$265,000

Table 2 Sales and Profits before Taxes 1973–1982

Year	Revenue	Profit Before Taxes[a]
1973	$186,750	$18,900
1974	193,500	18,900
1975	202,500	19,800
1976	209,250	20,500
1977	186,900	21,350
1978	170,000	8,400
1979	208,000	8,600
1980	216,000	8,790
1981	220,000	8,950
1982	215,000	9,100

a. Mrs. Hamner's tax rate is about 15 percent.

improvements to the building or to the courts themselves would be necessary. He was somewhat more skeptical about the accounts receivable. Mrs. Hamner has been allowing extended terms for payment of some court time in an effort to keep the courts full, and a number of the accounts appear to be past due.

Questions

1. If Jordan purchases Hamner Courts, what will his total investment be? Be sure to include any additional investment outlays that will be required over and above the purchase price. For purposes of the question, assume that the purchase price will be $265,000 (see Table 3).
2. If Jordan asked you to make "high," "low," and "most likely" estimates of annual profits after he assumes control, what would your estimates be? Assume that: (a) Jordan will set up the courts as a corporation; but (b) he will elect to be taxed as a proprietorship (that is, he elects to be taxed under Subchapter S of the Internal Revenue Code); (c) the tax rate on the courts'

Table 3 Standard Statistics on Small Handball/Racketball Courts

Cash	4%	Accounts Payable		12%
Accounts Receivable	5	Bank Loans		25
Inventories	11	Total Current		37%
Total Current	20%	Long-Term Debt		15
Building	80	Common Stock		48
Total	100%	Total		100%

income will be 25 percent; and (d) Jordan will withdraw all profits for personal expenditures instead of reinvesting a part of the earnings in the business.

3. Using the before-tax profit estimates that you obtained in Question 2, develop a range of prices Jordan might pay for the courts. Include maximum, minimum, and most reasonable.

4. What is the minimum price that Mrs. Hamner should accept for the courts?

5. If Mrs. Hamner holds out for $265,000, should Jordan purchase the courts?

Case 32: *Cost of Capital*

Nature's Bounty, Inc.

Nature's Bounty is a leading food chain with outlets throughout the United States. It serves low calorie food in cafeteria style, on either an eat-in or take-out basis. Fast service is maintained by having a limited menu, an efficient restaurant layout, and an assembly line "production" of each menu item. Nature's Bounty has captured a substantial percentage of the fast food market from the industry leader, a hamburger chain, through its emphasis on the fact that fast food does not necessarily have to be fattening or unhealthy.

Nature's Bounty was started as a small, family-owned, stand-up lunch counter in an indoor shopping mall in Madison, Wisconsin. Its popularity grew, and operations were soon expanded throughout the upper Midwest. As the large potential market became apparent, Nature's Bounty acquired a professional corporate staff to fulfill increasingly sophisticated needs in the area of finance, operations, and general management. The success of Nature's Bounty was due in a large part to the hard work and foresight of the founder, Herman Baer, and his policy of hiring only competent employees, paying them well, and demanding first-rate performance.

Nature's Bounty was operated as a closely held, family-owned corporation until 1970, when approximately 20 percent of the outstanding stock was sold to the public by Herman Baer, Jr. Since this original public offering, members of the family have disposed of an additional 50 percent of the stock. In 1979, 70 percent of the shares were owned by outsiders, while 30 percent was still held by the Baer family.

The firm was managed by members of the Baer family until 1979, when Herman Baer, Jr. retired from active participation. Since no other member of the family was interested in or qualified to assume a dominant role in management, Jayne Harder, a C.P.A. who was then senior vice-president of another leading fast food chain, was brought in as president and chief executive officer. Harder considered the Baer management team—the people in operations, marketing, personnel, and so on—excellent, so she did not institute any major

191

personnel changes upon her takeover. But she did bring in Sam Proctor, a 28-year-old M.B.A. who had been her assistant at McConnell's. Proctor's primary responsibility was to seek out weaknesses in Nature's Bounty's operations and then to devise methods for correcting them.

One of the first things Proctor noticed was the rather haphazard manner in which capital investment decisions were reached. For the most part, capital budgeting decisions seemed to be made by David Bushnell, financial vice-president, without any systematic analysis. Apparently, Bushnell simply approved all requests for capital expenditures as they were made by the different district managers. However, Bushnell did periodically review the rate of return on investment in the different districts, and if the return for a given district was seriously below that of the firm as a whole, the district manager was notified that his results were below average. As a result of this procedure, managers with below-standard returns tended not to make substantial requests for expansion funds until their district's returns were brought up to the average for the firm.

It was apparent to Proctor that this informal procedure tended to cause available funds to be allocated to districts with the highest return on investment. He also noted that during years when expansion had been more rapid than normal, such as 1975 and 1976, Bushnell had requested information on the payback period for the larger capital expenditure proposals. He had rejected several proposals on the grounds that (1) the firm was short of funds for additional capital expenditures, and (2) the paybacks on the rejected projects were relatively long compared to those on certain other alternatives.

In early 1979 Proctor wrote a memorandum to president Harder, sending copies to the other major executives of the firm (the executive committee), in which he suggested that the capital budgeting process be formalized. Specifically, Proctor recommended that the firm adopt the net present value approach, under which projects would first be ranked in accordance with their net present values, and then all projects with positive net present values would be accepted.

The proposal was enthusiastically endorsed by Harder, but Proctor detected a certain amount of skepticism about it on the part of the other senior officers, especially Bushnell. Although Bushnell seemed to endorse the principle of using a present value approach to making capital budgeting decisions, he was uncertain about the firm's ability to find an appropriate discount rate, or cost of capital, to use in the capital budgeting process.

Nevertheless, in May 1979 Proctor was directed by the executive committee to develop a cost of capital for the firm to use in evaluating 1980 capital investment projects. As a first step in this task, he obtained the projected December 31, 1979 balance sheet (Table 1) as well as information on sales and earnings for the past ten years (Table 2). In addition, Proctor had discussions

---

Table 1   Balance Sheet

**Projection for December 31, 1979
(Millions of Dollars)**

Cash and marketable securities ..	$ 19	Accounts payable[a]	$ 8
Accounts receivable	94	Bank notes payable (9%)	80
Inventories	120	Total current liabilities	$ 88
Total current assets	$233		
		Long-term debt[b]	$120
		Preferred stock[c]	45
		Common stock[d]	55
Net fixed assets	$172	Retained earnings	97
Total assets	$405	Total claims	$405

---

a. Accounts payable are exceptionally low because the firm follows the practice of paying cash on delivery in return for substantial purchase discounts.
b. The bonds outstanding have a par value of $1,000, a remaining life of 15 years, and a coupon rate of 9 percent. The current rate of interest for bonds with Nature's Bounty's rating is 10 percent per year. The bonds pay annual interest.
c. The preferred stock currently sells at its par value of $100 per share.
d. There are 10 million shares outstanding and the stock currently sells at a price of $24 per share.

Table 2   Sales and Earnings

Year	Sales (millions)	Earnings After Taxes Available to Common Stock (millions)[a]	Earnings Per Share of Common Stock
1979	$1,152	$31.25	$3.13
1978	959	28.80	2.88
1977	848	25.40	2.54
1976	800	24.88	2.49
1975	716	21.46	2.15
1974	668	20.04	2.00
1973	608	18.24	1.82
1972	560	16.80	1.68
1971	524	15.77	1.58
1970	476	14.76	1.48
1969	413	12.10	1.21

---

a. The firm's marginal tax rate is 48 percent.

---

with several investment bankers and security analysts for major brokerage firms to learn something about investor expectations for the company and the costs that would be incurred by the firm if it attempted to obtain additional outside capital. Proctor received the impression from the security analysts that investors do not expect Nature's Bounty to continue to enjoy the same rate of growth it has had for the past ten years. In fact, most of the analysts seem to be estimating the company's future growth to be only one half the rate experienced during the last decade. The analysts, however, do expect the firm to continue paying out about 60 percent of the earnings available to common in the form of cash dividends. At the last annual meeting, Harder had in fact announced that the policy of paying out at least 60 percent of earnings would be maintained. Harder also stated that if expansion needs did not meet the required 40 percent retention rate, the payout ratio would be increased.

After a careful analysis of the existing financial structure, Proctor determined that the mix of debt, common stock, and preferred stock that was optimum (i.e., produced the lowest average cost of capital) was the one that the company presently employed. The proportions of this mix had been relatively stable over the past five years, and they were used to construct the projected December 31, 1979 balance sheet.

Proctor also asked the investment banks and Nature's Bounty's commercial bankers what the firm's cost of various types of capital would be, assuming that the present capital structure is maintained. His study yielded the following conclusions:

Debt

Up to and including $4 million of new debt, the company can use loans and commercial paper, both of which currently have an interest rate of 10 percent.

From $4.01 to $10.0 million of new debt, the company can issue mortgage bonds with an Aa rating and an interest cost to the company of 12 percent on this increment of debt.

From $10.1 to $14.0 million of new debt, the company can issue subordinated debentures with a Baa rating that would carry an interest rate of 13 percent on this increment of debt.

Over $14 million of new debt would require the company to issue subordinated convertible debentures. The after-tax cost of these convertibles to the company is estimated to be 11 percent on this increment of debt.

Preferred

The company's preferred stock, which has no maturity since it is a perpetual issue, pays a $9 annual dividend on its $100 par value and is currently selling at par. Additional preferred stock in the amount of $2 million can be sold to provide investors with the same yield as is available on the current preferred stock, but flotation costs would amount to $4 per share. If the company were to sell a preferred stock issue paying a $9 annual dividend, investors would pay $100 per share, the flotation costs would be $4 per share, and the company would net $96 per share.

From $2.1 to $3.0 million of preferred stock, the after-tax, after-flotation cost would be 10.5 percent for this increment of preferred stock.

For over $3 million of preferred stock, the after-tax, after-flotation cost would be 13 percent for this increment.

Common

Up to $2.5 million of new common can be sold at the current market price, $24 per share, less a $3 per share flotation cost.

Over $2.5 million of new common stock can be sold at $24 per share, less a $5 per share flotation cost.

President Harder asked Proctor to estimate the company's investment opportunity schedule and to interface this schedule with the cost of capital schedule to give the board of directors an idea of the amount of funds likely to be required during the 1980 budget year. After thinking about how he would develop the investment opportunity schedule, Proctor concluded that the best approach would be to ask the operating officers to estimate the number of capital projects that would have positive net present values at various cost of capital hurdle rates. However, given the current state of knowledge in the company, Proctor recognized that it would be impossible for the division heads and district managers to respond meaningfully to this request. Accordingly, he decided to investigate, on a case study basis, only major projects, and to do this on a face-to-face basis with each division and district manager.

Proctor therefore went to each operating manager and explained what he wanted to accomplish. Each manager indicated to Proctor the major projects under consideration by the division or district and the estimated costs and cash flows that would result if these projects were implemented. Proctor also requested information on minor projects (relatively small replacement decisions and the like) and concluded that their total was so small that they could be ignored without seriously affecting his results. The major projects, together with their costs and estimated annual cash flows, are shown in Table 3. Note that the projects are not divisible; each must be accepted or rejected in its entirety.

To aid Proctor in preparing his report, you are asked to answer the following questions.

Table 3 Investment Opportunities
(Millions of Dollars)

Project Identification	Cost of Project	Estimated Annual Cash Inflows	Estimated Life (Years)	Estimated Internal Rate of Return on Project
A	$ 7.0	$1.03	15	12%
B	4.0	0.81	9	
C	5.0	1.05	6	7%
D	10.0	1.54	12	
E	9.0	2.00	10	18%
F	3.0	0.60	10	15%
G	4.0	0.95	5	6%
H	6.0	1.13	8	

Note: These projects are indivisible in the sense that each must be accepted or rejected in its entirety; that is, no partial projects may be taken on.

Questions

1. Determine Nature's Bounty's existing market value capital structure, disregarding the minor amount of accounts payable, which constitute "free" capital. Also, lump notes payable in with long-term debt. Round to the nearest percentage point.

2. Assuming that Nature's Bounty maintains this optimum market value capital structure, calculate the breaking points in the MCC schedule. Recall that the company is projecting $31.25 million of earnings available to common and a 60 percent dividend payout ratio.

3. Now calculate MCC $= K_a$ in the interval between each of the breaking points, and graph the MCC schedule in its step-function form. In your calculations, use 60 percent of estimated 1979 earnings per share as your value of D_1, and use the current price as P_0. To reduce the calculations, you may take as given $K_a = 9.4$ percent in the first interval, $K_a = 9.9$ percent in the second interval, and $K_a = 13.2$ percent in the last interval. Note: the marginal tax rate is 48 percent.

4. Estimate to the closest whole percentage point the missing internal rates of return in Table 3, and then use the information developed thus far in the case to decide which projects should be accepted and which should be rejected. Illustrate your solution technique with a graph, and conclude your answer to this question with a discussion of the accept-reject decision on the marginal project.

5. Note that all of your calculations are done as of the summer of 1979; yet, actions such as selling securities and investing in assets will occur during

1980. What would happen if (a) more or fewer "good" projects are actually available than Proctor now anticipated, or (b) conditions in the capital markets change so as to raise or lower your MCC curve? How should the company react to such changes? That is, what instructions should corporate headquarters issue to the operating personnel charged with acquiring assets if and when actual conditions differ from those expected during the budgeting period?

6. Do you think Proctor is likely to be more confident about his ex ante (or estimated) MCC or his ex ante IOS schedule? Explain.

7. Are any assumptions implicit in your analysis to this point about the riskiness of the various projects with respect to: (a) each other; and (b) the firm's existing assets? If these assumptions are not valid, can you indicate how the analysis could be modified?

8. Depreciation has not been considered explicitly in the case. Suppose you were informed that the company is expected to generate cash flows from depreciation in the amount of $20 million during 1980. How would this affect your analysis?

9. The case indicated that "free capital" could be ignored. Suppose the company actually had a large amount of accruals, accounts payable, and accrued taxes, and anticipated a substantial increase in these items during 1980. How would this affect your analysis?

10. In the MCC calculations, no distinction was made between short-term notes payable and long-term debt. Is this treatment appropriate? If not, how should short-term debt be treated?

11. Suppose you learned that members of the Baer family controlled a large amount of the firm's stock (60 percent) and also were in the 75 percent tax bracket (state plus federal) for dividends. How might this influence the analysis?

12. Use the CAPM equation to determine Nature's Bounty's cost of equity at its existing capital structure. Assume that the firm's beta coefficient is 1.2, the risk-free rate is 7.5 percent, and the average market return is 12.3 percent. How does this value compare with your calculations in Question 3? Which, if either, do you believe to be more nearly correct? Why?

Case **33A:** *Integrated Case on Capital Budgeting and Cost of Capital*

National Telecommunications Corporation, Part I

National Telecommunications is a diversified, independent telephone company serving parts of several states. Originally operating only to provide telephone service, National engaged in a diversification campaign in the mid-1960s when it acquired several large manufacturers of industrial and consumer electronics equipment. Other acquisitions were made in the late 1970s and early 1980s when the company expanded into the data services market. As National is presently structured, there is a central headquarters staff and three operating divisions: telephone operations, manufacturing activities, and data services.

Although the divisions are decentralized in many respects, the finance function is handled at the corporate level; Ronald Akers, the financial vice-president, has the overall responsibility for both treasury and controllship functions. All external funds are obtained by the corporate treasurer, Diane Reeves, then allocated to the separate divisions as required. Akers's budget director, Max Willocks, has direct control over the budget system, including the capital budget, which is used to control and coordinate the various divisions.

The budgeting process works as follows. First, divisional vice-presidents construct budgets for the coming year, then submit these budgets to the corporate planning staff by August 15. During the period between August 16 to September 1, the corporate planning staff reviews the divisional budgets and meets individually with the divisional budget officers to clarify points and perhaps recommend modifications. During September, the consolidated budget data are analyzed, and pro forma earnings are generated using a computer corporate planning model. Next, on approximately October 1, the top corporate and divisional officers, together with their staffs, hold a joint meeting to discuss the overall corporate plan for the coming year.

Prior to 1970, the budget was processed "by hand," but since the system is quite complex, Akers decided that the budgeting process should be computerized. Accordingly, Akers's staff developed an integrated corporate computer model that utilizes projected revenue, cost, production, and financial data to generate pro forma balance sheets and income statements for each division, as well as consolidated statements for the entire company. Use of the model began in 1970, and increasingly complex versions of it have been implemented since that time.

At each October 1 meeting at least three sets of pro forma data are generated and discussed: one assuming a strong national economy, one assuming a weak economy, and one assuming a "normal" economy. All the assumptions underlying the pro forma forecasts are discussed at length during this meeting, and questions such as these are asked: Will the manufacturing division's expansion of the consumer electronic products facility begin operations as scheduled next July 15, and what effect would a delay have on the division's profitability? Should the data services division go ahead with its expansion plans? A key labor contract is up for renewal next May 1; what effect would a strike or an unexpectedly high settlement have on the telephone modernization and service improvement project? Will the requests for rate increases now pending before several public utility commissions be granted in full, reduced somewhat, or denied totally? And, if the increases are granted but the higher prices result in substantially reduced demand, what effect would this have? The corporate model is used to determine just how sensitive operations are to factors such as these, and frequently plans are altered as a result of the analysis.

Once the budget for the coming year has been established, it is used for control purposes during the year. Actual results, on a monthly basis, are compared with the forecasted figures, and any significant deviations must be explained by the operating officers in charge of the relevant divisions. In this way, deviations can be detected early, and appropriate adjustments can be made to meet the changing situation.

Until the mid-1970s, there was never a question of a capital shortage. National generates large amounts of funds internally (depreciation, retained earnings, and deferred taxes), and it had ready access to the capital markets for debt and external equity capital. During the late 1970s the company's credit rating dropped, limiting the availability of outside capital, and at the same time the divisions' demands for capital were abnormally high because of inflation and rising product demand. Thus, corporate headquarters was compelled to impose capital rationing. During 1974, the first year of severe capital rationing, funds were apportioned on the basis of "need," and all available funds were used in the regulated utility part of the business. Profitability was simply not considered. However, to avoid being squeezed out, after 1974, division executives began to work harder to "prove" that they needed capital, and the executive committee began to make allocations on the basis of a percentage of previous years' budgets. However, difficulties were encountered when capital was allocated in this manner. In 1978, for example, it turned out that the telephone division's least profitable projects had negative expected rates of return, yet were allocated capital, whereas the data services division was forced, under the capital rationing system, to reject projects with expected returns of 25 percent. This, together with the fact that the company was not earning a high enough return to adequately cover debt service, persuaded management to restructure the capital budgeting process to give greater weight to profitability.

The main problem facing National and other regulated utilities is an erosion of profits caused by inflation. Regulated utilities are supposed to be allowed to earn a "fair rate of return." Most utilities provide an essential service under a franchise agreement that makes the company the sole supplier of the service in its territory; in the absence of regulation, the companies would be able to earn excessive profits. Thus, regulators (1) determine the amount of investment the company has made in facilities to serve the public, which in general is close to the amount of capital investors have supplied; (2) determine a "fair rate of return," which is based on the cost of capital; and (3) set prices that result in profits just high enough to provide the "fair return."

Under normal conditions, commissions establish a "target rate of return" equal to the fair rate, and, implicitly or explicitly, establish upper and lower bounds around this target. Actual rates of return naturally vary somewhat from year to year depending on business conditions and other random factors, and it would not be feasible to hold a rate case hearing every time the actual rate of return varied from the target. Thus, the upper and lower control limits are set, and rate case hearings are held only if the actual rate exceeds these bounds. Figure 1(a) shows this situation under inflationary conditions, where costs are constantly being driven up. As operating costs rise, both profits and the realized rate of return on investment decline. When the lower control limit is reached, rates are raised, causing the realized rate of return to rise to the target level. However, continued inflation causes the cycle to be repeated, and rates of return are again eroded. The net result of this condition is that the rate of return over a period of time will, on average, fall below the target level.

Figure 1(b) shows the nature and effects of regulatory lags. At point A the actual rate of return penetrates the lower control limit, prompting the company to seek a rate hearing, which occurs at point B. At point C an order is issued permitting the company to raise rates, and the rate increase takes effect at point D. As shown here, the actual rate of return at point D does not return to the target level. The cost figures generally used in the point B rate cases are those of the most recent past year. If inflation continues, by the time the new rates take effect the cost figures are outdated—they are too low. Hence, the calculated telephone rates are too low to boost the rate of return on investment to the target level. It would, of course, be possible for regulatory authorities to anticipate price increases (in utility parlance, this is called using a "forward test year") and this would lessen the impact of regulatory lag. However, the

Figure 1   Typical Rate of Return Pattern Under Inflationary Conditions
                (a) No Regulatory Lag, and (b) With Regulatory Lag

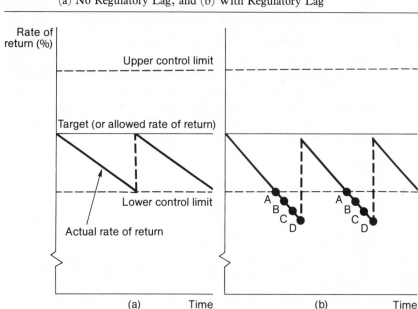

past test year is used in most jurisdictions, including National's, and this has a negative effect on utility profits under inflationary conditions.[1]

Another problem faced by National and other utility companies is the fact that they have, during the past few years, experienced a rising cost of capital. Controversy exists over the actual measurements of the cost of capital, but because of the general increase in interest rates, no one seriously questions the fact that the cost of capital has risen in recent years. However, because of regulatory lags, the target rate of return has generally been set below the actual cost of capital. Figure 2 illustrates this situation. From T_0 to T_1, the cost of capital is both stable and equal to the allowed rate of return. At T_1, the cost of capital begins to rise, and during the interval from T_1 to T_2, the rate of return shortfall widens. At T_2, a rate case hearing is held, and the allowed rate of return is adjusted upward. However, the continuing increase in the cost of capital causes the cycle to be repeated, and over the entire period the actual rate of return averages less than the cost of capital.

1. We should note that forward test years are being used by some commissions, and that other procedures that lessen regulatory lag are beginning to be employed by regulatory agencies. The automatic fuel adjustment clause, which permits certain electric utilities to raise prices automatically when fuel costs rise, is an example, but it does not help telephone utilities.

Figure 2   Illustration of Rising Cost of Capital Combined
with Lagging Changes in the Allowed Rate of Return

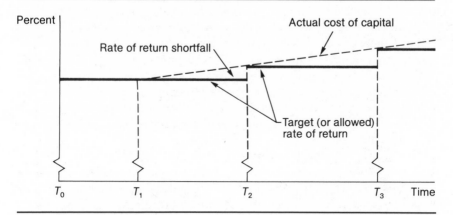

The combined effects of rising cost of capital, inflation, and regulatory lags are
shown in Figure 3. Here we see that the company's average realized rate of
return is substantially below its cost of capital. National's "allowed rate of
return on common equity" as prescribed, on average, by its public utility

Figure 3   Combined Effect of Rising Costs, Rising Cost-of-Capital,
and Regulatory Lag

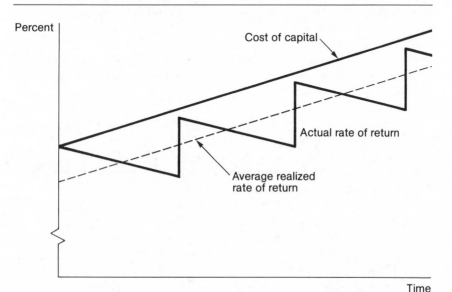

commissions during 1981, was 14.3 percent, but the company only earned 12.3 percent. Further, the true cost of equity is above 14.3, so the gap between the actual rate of return and the cost of equity capital was over 2 percentage points. A similar situation has pertained during each year since 1973.

When choosing among competing investment projects, National formerly selected those projects whose future costs, when discounted at the cost of capital, were lowest. Future costs, or "revenue requirements" as they are generally called, include the following items: (1) labor, repair parts, and other operating costs; (2) depreciation; (3) property taxes; (4) income taxes; and (5) a return on the capital invested in the project. The sum of these cost items, all discounted at the current (marginal) cost of new capital, is the present value of revenue requirements.

Most utility investment is required, or mandatory, in the sense that it is necessary to provide service to new or existing customers. Sales revenues from such projects were, in the past, simply disregarded on the grounds that they would be the same (and equal to revenue requirements for the project) regardless of which mutually exclusive project was chosen. In other words, National might have projected a requirement to serve an additional 25,000 customers in a rapidly growing rural area, then set about deciding how to provide this added capacity. The method selected would have been the method that had the lowest present value of future revenue requirements.

Until the mid-1970s, this method of project selection was satisfactory for National and other telephone companies, as they could be reasonably sure that revenues would match requirements; if revenues were insufficient, the company would simply request and receive a rate increase. In 1979, however, National decided to abandon the PV-of-revenue-requirements method whenever data could be obtained on revenues as well as on revenue requirements. The PV-of-revenue-requirements method was based on the assumption that timely rate increases would bring revenues up to revenue requirements, but the combination of inflation and regulatory lags had invalidated this assumption. Thus, National began using the NPV method. Note that public utility theory assumes that customers' payments will exactly equal revenue requirements; hence, the annual revenue requirement is really the expected annual cash flow from a project. Also, note that if revenues are exactly equal to revenue requirements, as utility theory assumes they will be, the NPV of any project (or at least the NPV of the total investment required to provide a class of service) will be zero.

In applying the NPV method, National works as follows. First, investment projects are put into one of two categories, (1) mandatory and (2) discretionary, which involves new service or cost-saving investments associated with providing existing services.[2] Next, NPVs are calculated, using existing rate

---

2. A great deal of difficulty is sometimes encountered in classifying projects. For example, when the telephone division has to add capacity to meet population expansion, it can

schedules and projected operating and capital costs. For discretionary projects, the rule is to accept if NPV > zero, and to choose among competing projects the one with the highest NPV. For mandatory projects, National chooses the alternative with the highest positive (or least negative) NPV. Some quite large equipment replacement projects that were originally in the mandatory category showed negative NPVs. The magnitude of the projected losses caused management to reconsider the situation, and several projects were changed to discretionary and postponed. These decisions meant lowering the reliability of the system and delaying the introduction of direct long-distance dialing to a large number of National's customers. However, management felt compelled to take these steps because declining stock prices and rising interest rates were making it extremely difficult to attract capital, and to invest in projects that were almost sure to reduce profitability even more (as is implied by a negative NPV) would further imperil the company's financial integrity.[3]

The decision to switch from the minimum-PV-of-cost to the NPV method represented a fundamental change, and it had to be approved by the board of directors. To secure this approval, Akers used Figures 1, 2, and 3 above to illustrate what was happening and the reasons that he felt a change was needed, and he used Figure 4 to illustrate National's situation in 1981. Each potential project's NPV was calculated on the basis of a series of cost of capital figures.[4] The dollar volume of mandatory projects that had NPV > zero at different discount rates was determined and plotted on Figure 4; for example, point X indicates that $20 million of mandatory projects would have NPV > zero when evaluated at a 13 percent cost of capital. The area designated A represents "profitable" mandatory projects, B represents unprofitable mandatory projects, and C represents profitable discretionary projects.[5] Area B exceeded the

---

simply add new switching systems, or it can replace old, relatively inefficient electromechanical switching systems with new, more efficient electronically controlled switching systems and obtain the increased capacity in the same physical space. In considering a combined expansion-modernization decision, is it mandatory or discretionary? No really satisfactory classification scheme has been worked out. But if, because of lags or other factors, the projects do not appear to be profitable in the NPV sense, then National will opt for the one with the least negative NPV. This usually means "expand only—do not modernize."

3. Consolidated Edison's problems reinforced this decision. In 1974 Con Ed (the New York electric company) was literally unable to obtain the capital to meet its construction budget, and the company had to be bailed out by the state. The price of its stock fell from $17 to $6 within a few weeks. Many other utilities have encountered similar, though less dramatic, problems.

4. National's computer system generated these NPVs.

5. One might think that an unregulated firm would have no mandatory investments, but this is not the case. Pollution control equipment, for example, may be regarded as a zero (or negative) return mandatory project.

Figure 4   Capital Budgeting with Mandatory and
Discretionary Investments

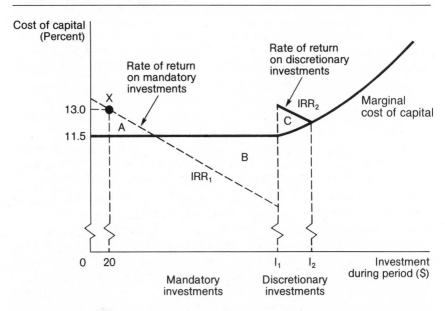

sum of areas A and C; this indicated to Akers and the others that National's
capital investment program was, in a sense, costing stockholders money.[6]

Beginning in 1978, the corporate budgeting staff, which works directly
under Akers, began going through the following process:

1. The capital budgeting director, Max Willocks, obtained from Diane
   Reeves, the corporate treasurer, an estimate of National's cost of capital for
   the coming year. The treasurer supplies this estimate by June of the year
   preceding the budget period. To estimate the cost of capital, the treasurer
   is required to project (1) depreciation; (2) the level of retained earnings; (3)
   the interest rate on new debt issues; and (4) both the cost of equity capital
   and the terms under which new issues of common stock could be sold.
   Naturally, if either national economic conditions or the firm's own profit
   position change radically between June 1 and the time that funds are

6. By definition, the NPV of a project is the amount the project is supposed to add to the
   market value of the company. A negative NPV means that taking on the project reduces
   the value of the company. Since National's capital projects, on balance, had negative
   NPVs, this meant that the value of the firm was reduced by its investment program.
   Thus, it would appear that the way to maximize the welfare of the stockholders would be
   to minimize investment.

actually raised, then the cost of capital estimates will be wrong. The projected, or ex ante, marginal cost of capital (MCC) schedule for 1982 is plotted in Figure 5.

2. Capital budgeting director Willocks also obtains from each division estimates of (1) the total amount of "mandatory" investments required for the next year, regardless of their NPVs; and (2) the most probable level of discretionary capital expenditures assuming a cost of capital of 20 percent, 19.5 percent, 19 percent, and so on down to 9 percent, in increments of 0.5 percentage points. Estimated levels of expenditures plotted against the specified rates of return represent the expected investment opportunity schedule for each division. Further, if the estimated expenditures of each division at each cost of capital level are totaled, these aggregates, when plotted against the rates of return, represent the total corporate IOS schedule. Figure 5 shows the estimated investment opportunity schedule for the total corporation.

Figure 5   Cost of Capital and Investment Opportunity Schedules

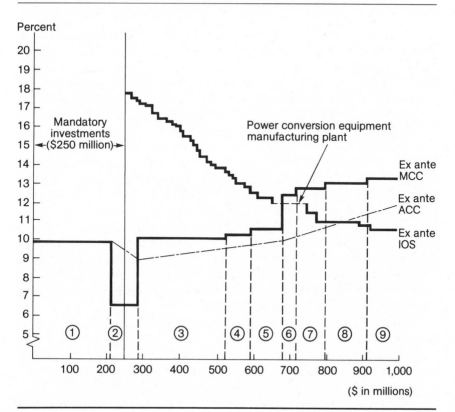

The number and size of projects determines the width of each "step," which, in turn, represents the aggregate cost of projects in that block. National's total number of potential capital projects is quite large, typically about 5,000 projects per year, and many are small in relation to the total capital budget. By going to smaller intervals in the discount rate (i.e., 0.1 to 0.01), some segments of the IOS would become virtually continuous. Other segments, however, would always be discontinuous. Thus, at the limit, the IOS schedule would be a discontinuous curve with some continuous sections.

3. When the cost of capital schedule obtained from the treasurer is plotted on the same graph as the IOS schedule, the firm's optimum capital budget, and the cost of capital at this level, is determined by the intersection of the two schedules. Assuming that the estimated IOS schedule and the estimated cost of capital schedule are in fact correct, if the corporate capital budgeting director instructs the divisional capital budgeting directors to use the specified cost of capital as the discount rate when calculating NPVs, the divisions will indeed submit proposals equaling the firm's optimum capital budget.

Notice the major all or nothing project in the $650 to $750 million interval. This involves a plant for manufacturing power conversion equipment (PCE) for the telecommunications and computer industries, with an expected cost of $100 million and a 12 percent expected rate of return. This project is at the intersection of the IOS and marginal cost of capital schedules. The project is discretionary—it can be taken or rejected—and it is judged to be about as risky as National's average project. Two points should be noted about this project. First, if the PCE plant could be accepted on a small scale, then a plant costing about $30 million would be built. But since this is an all-or-nothing decision, the plant must be accepted or rejected in its entirety. Second, if the PCE plant is rejected, then the IOS beyond $750 million is simply shifted over to the $650 million, i.e., the dashed section of the IOS curve is eliminated.

National's consolidated balance sheet and income statement are shown in Tables 1 and 2, and its key financial ratios are presented in Table 3, where they are compared with industry average ratios. Management does not try to stay within industry averages for the debt ratio, times-interest-earned, or any other ratio, although the nature of utility firms' operations tends to cause firms to correspond fairly closely to one another.

National estimates its cost of capital as a weighted average of debt, preferred, and equity, using as weights the financial structure shown in Table 2. The cost of equity is estimated in two ways: (1) by using the "capital asset pricing model," where the cost of equity equals a riskless rate plus a risk premium, $k_s = R_F + P$; and (2) by using the formula, $k_s = D_1/P_0 +$ expected g. Also, the company recognizes that the cost of capital is a function of the amount of

Table 1 Consolidated Balance Sheet
December 31, 1980
(in millions)

Assets		Liabilities	
Property, Plant and Equipment		*Equity*	
Telephone	$4,674	Preferred Stock	$ 121
Less depreciation	664	Common Stock (no par value	
		100,000,000 author.	
	$4,010	59,070,000 outstanding)	1,420
Manufacturing and Data Services	3,116	Common Stock Expense ...	(8)
Less depreciation	443	Retained earnings	1,523
Net property, plant &		Total Equity	$3,056
equipment	$2,673		
		Long-Term Debt	$3,305
Investments			
Equity Securities	$ 91		
Other investments	33	*Current Liabilities*	
		Notes Payable	$ 486
Less reserve for		Accounts Payable	6
depreciation	$ 7	Accrued Taxes	2
		Other Current Liabilities ...	5
Total investments	$ 117	Total Current Liabilities	$ 499
Current Assets			
Cash	$ 75	*Reserves and Deferred Credits*	
Accounts Receivable	145	Deferred Taxes[a]	279
Material and Supplies	181	Customer Deposits	127
Other Current Assets	63	Total Reserves & Deferred	
Total Current Assets	$ 464	Credits	$ 406
Deferred Charges	$ 2	*Total Liabilities and*	
Total Assets	$7,266	*Net Worth*	$7,266

a. National uses straight-line depreciation to compute profits reported to stockholders but double-declining-balance (DDB) depreciation for income tax purposes. As shown on the income statement, in 1980 depreciation reported to stockholders was $189 million, but depreciation used for tax calculations was $268 million. Thus, taxes saved by using accelerated depreciation amounted to $39.5 million (which is 50 percent of the extra depreciation) during 1980. This $39.5 million may have to be paid at some future date, depending on the firm's continued growth. Thus a "reserve for deferred taxes" has been established; it totaled $279 million at 12/31/80, after the $39.5 million in taxes deferred for 1980 had been included.

National reports that it believes its assets decline in value on a straight-line basis, yet to take full advantage of income tax laws, which are established by Congress to stimulate investment, the company uses DDB depreciation. Thus, the $279 million deferred taxes shown on the balance sheet amounts to an interest-free loan from the federal government, and the $39.5 million deferred taxes for 1980 shown on the income statement represent the 1980 addition to this "loan."

Table 2   Consolidated Income Statement

Year Ending December 31, 1980 (in millions)

Telephone Operations
Operating Revenues .... $ 888

   Operating Expenses
     Operations   225
     Maintenance   123
     Depreciation   95

      Total Operating Expenses .... $ 443

      Net Operating Revenues .... $ 445

   Operating Taxes
     Income Tax .... $ 132
     Deferred Taxes   20
     Investment Tax Credit—Net ....   (2)

      Total Operating Taxes .... $ 150

      Net Telephone Revenues .... $ 295

Other Operations
Net Sales $1,220
Cost of Goods Sold   563
Other Expenses   152
Depreciation   94

  Net .... $ 411

Taxes .... $ 162
Deferred Taxes   20

Net Revenues .... $ 229

Earnings Available for Investors .... $ 524
Interest Charges   173

  Net Income .... $ 351
    Preferred Dividend Requirements   6

  Income Applicable to Common Stock .... $ 345

Table 2   *Continued*

Per Share of Common Stock
Earnings .... $ 5.84
Dividends 2.36

Retained Earnings
At beginning of year $1,317
Add Net Income 351
                                                              ─────
                                                              $1,668

Deduct-dividends declared
Preferred .... $ 6
Common 139
                                                              ─────
                                                              $ 145
Retained Earnings at End of Year $1,523

Table 3   Key Financial Ratios (1980)

	National	Integrated Telecommunications Company
Debt ratio[a]	56%	53.2%
Times-interest-earned	2.92X	2.91X
Return on common equity	11.3%	10.9%
Return on total capital[b]	8.73%	8.62%

a. $\text{Debt ratio} = \dfrac{\text{long-term debt} + \text{customer deposits} + \text{current liabilities}}{\text{total liabilities and net worth} - \text{deferred taxes}}$.

b. $\text{Return on total capital} = \dfrac{\text{earnings available for investors}}{\text{total capitalization}}$.

Table 4   Data Used in Cost of Capital Calculations

---

1. Riskless rate of interest estimated for 1982: $R_F = 12\%$.

2. Rate of return on a stock with beta = 1.0, or on "the market": $k_m = 15\%$.

3. National's beta coefficient as calculated for the past five years and also as reported by major investment advisory services: b = 0.90. National's beta coefficient has been stable for the last five years.

4. Stock flotations costs, including an allowance for "pressure" on shares already outstanding. Up to \$35 million of new stock sold during the year, 10% flotation cost; next \$50 million of stock sold during the year, 15% flotation cost; any additional stock, 20% flotation cost.

5. Analysts assume that National's earnings and dividends will grow in the future at the same rate as in the past. Here are some past EPS and DPS values:

   Earnings per share during 1976 \$4.07
   Dividends per share during 1976 \$1.63
   Estimated EPS during 1981 \$6.02
   Estimated DPS during 1981 \$2.44
   Estimated EPS during 1982 \$2.50 (Use this for D_1).

6. Estimated 1/1/82 stock price: \$36.42 per share (Use this for P_0).

7. 1982 additions to retained earnings are estimated to be \$225 million.

8. 1982 additions to estimated cost of debt: (a) Up to \$135 million of additional new long-term debt: 13% before tax, 6.50% after tax. The 13.0% interest rate represents a 1% premium over the 12% riskless rate, i.e., $k_d = R_F + P = 12\% + 1\% = 13\%$. This debt will be sold under an existing loan commitment to a group of life insurance companies and pension funds. (b) Next \$35 million of long-term debt: 13.5% before tax, 6.75% after tax. This debt will represent mortgage bonds permitted under indenture provisions of existing debt. (c) Next \$50 million of long-term debt: 14.5% subordinated debentures. (d) Any additional debt will have to be sold as convertibles or bonds with warrants with an estimated *after-tax* cost of 10.5%; this cost includes the dilution effect of potential conversion or warrants being exercised.

9. Deferred taxes, increases in accounts payable, and increases in accruals are regarded as being "free" capital. These funds should be taken into account when determining the weighted cost of capital, and averaged in as having a zero cost. However, for National only deferred taxes are large enough to be of consequence (\$44 million). Current liabilities are disregarded in the cost of capital calculation, but they are lumped into "debt" for purposes of determining the debt/equity mix.

Table 4 *Continued*

---

10. For purposes of analysis, National determines its cost of capital schedule in blocks, or increments, as follows:

1st Increment = Depreciation, whose cost is determined by retained earnings and the average after-tax cost of existing debt, adjusting to reflect their weights in the corporate capital structure.[a] The average after-tax cost of existing debt is given as 6.1 percent. For 1982, projected depreciation amounts to $208 million. (See Table 5 for an illustration of how the cost of depreciation is determined.)

2nd Increment = "Free capital," discussed above, plus an appropriate amount of retained earnings to maintain the existing financial structure. If sufficient retained earnings are not available, new equity must be included in this increment. (See Table 5 for an illustration of the 2nd increment cost calculation.) For 1982 projected retained earnings are $225 million, and the company must use $34.6 million of this amount in the second increment to maintain the present capital structure.

Additional increments depend on the amount of funds available at each specific cost. Since $190.4 million in retained earnings remain from the 2nd increment, the 3rd increment is determined by the $135 million of new long-term debt. See Table 5.

---

a. The use of the average after-tax cost of existing debt in this calculation has been the subject of considerable debate within the firm. The existing procedure has not been questioned sharply because the firm is operating far to the right of this first increment of capital. The marginal cost of capital that is used as the effective hurdle rate is the cost of the increment through which the IOS passes; this is the only relevant cost for capital budgeting. If National were actually operating back in the region where the IOS might cut the MCC in the first increment, then serious consideration would be given to the use of the after-tax cost of the highest cost existing debt.

Table 5 Calculations of the Cost of Capital (in Millions)

Cost of 1st Increment (Depreciation Funds)

	Amount	% of Total	Component Cost	Weighted Cost
Debt		.56	6.1%	3.42%
Retained earnings		.44	14.75	6.49
Total depreciation funds	$208			9.91%

Cost of 2nd Increment ("Free Debt" Plus Retained Earnings)

	Amount	% of Total	Component Cost	Weighted Cost
"Free capital" from deferred taxes	$44.0	.56	0%	0%
Retained earnings	34.6	.44	14.75	6.49
	$78.6			6.49%

3rd Increment

	Amount	% of Total	After-Tax Cost	Weighted Cost
New long-term debt	$135.0	.56	6.5%	3.64%
Retained earnings	106.1	.44	14.75	6.49
Total for 3rd increment	$241.1			10.13%

Notice that an additional $84.3 million of retained earnings still remain for use in additional increments. The point to remember is that every time there is a change in one of the component costs of capital, we will have a new increment, and we must calculate a new marginal cost for that increment.

For ease of calculations, we have included the preferred stock in the equity component and all current liabilities in the debt component.

capital raised during the year. The treasurer calculates the marginal cost of capital schedule (MCC). The data and assumptions used to estimate the 1980 cost of capital schedule, which is used in 1981 to help establish the 1982 capital budget, are given in Table 4. Table 5 illustrates the procedure used to calculate the cost of depreciation and the second and third increments of capital.

Audrey Keefer, an MBA with experience in financial management consulting, recently joined National as a financial analyst and assistant to vice-president Akers. Because he had some uncertainties about the validity of all phases of the process, Akers asked Keefer to review National's system and report to him on its strengths and weaknesses.

Questions

1. As shown in Figure 5, there are eight breaking points in the MCC schedule:
   a. $208 million
   b. $286.6 million
   c. $527.7 million
   d. $590.2 million
   e. $679.5 million
   f. $719.4 million
   g. $798.9 million
   h. $912.6 million

   Show how the breaking point at $719.4 million was determined.

2. The cost of capital in the various intervals between breaking points is given below. Complete the table by calculating the MCC in the intervals from $527.7 to $590.2 million, and over $912.6 million. To get a cost of retained earnings, use both $k_r = R_F + b(k_m - R_F)$ and $k_r = D_1/P_0 +$ expected g, and if these two estimates differ, average and round off to the nearest hundredth of a percentage point (e.g., 14.75 percent).

Interval	MCC
$ 0.0 – $208.0	9.9%
208.0 – 286.6	6.5
286.6 – 527.7	10.1
527.7 – 590.2	
590.2 – 679.5	10.6
679.5 – 719.4	12.4
719.4 – 798.9	12.7
798.9 – 912.6	13.0
912.6 – Beyond	

3. How much capital should National plan to raise and invest during 1982? Before finalizing your answer, consider the following points:
   a. Should the PCE plant be accepted?
   b. If the PCE plant is rejected, should any less-profitable projects be accepted?
   c. Discuss the logic behind the MCC as the hurdle rate. What would the total capital budget be if the MCC is used as the hurdle rate?
4. What would happen if the ex ante cost of capital schedule is inaccurate, i.e., if it deviates from the ex post schedule? For example, if interest rates increase during 1982 and raise the entire cost of capital schedule above the ex ante schedule before National has obtained all needed funds, but after the budget has been approved, what would this do to National's optimum capital budget, and how should National react?
5. What would happen if the ex ante IOS schedule is incorrect? For example, suppose a cost of capital is given to the divisions for use as a cutoff point, and then projects that are substantially more profitable than those originally accepted are submitted? Should all projects that meet the predetermined hurdle rate be accepted? If not, what criteria should be used to determine where cutbacks should be made? In your response, consider how projects might be rated with respect to how postponable they are, especially in view of National's status as a regulated utility.
6. What strengths can you find in the capital budgeting process outlined in this case? What weaknesses can you identify? How would you suggest overcoming these weaknesses?

Case 33B: Divisional and Project Hurdle Rates

National Telecommunications Corporation, Part II

National's financial planning process, as described in Part I, does not formally incorporate risk considerations in project selections. It works like this: a corporate hurdle rate is developed; projected cash inflows and outflows are fed into the computer; and each project's NPV, IRR, and payback is calculated. If a project's NPV is positive and large, if its IRR is well above the hurdle rate (say 3 percentage points), and if its payback is short (say four years or less), then the project will usually be accepted without much ado. On the other hand, if NPV is negative, if IRR is well below the corporate hurdle rate, and if the payback period is long (eight years or more), the project will be rejected. Projects with NPV close to zero, IRR close to MCC, and paybacks in the five-to-seven-year range are marginal, such projects are accepted or rejected depending on (1) management's confidence in the cash flow forecasts, and (2) the project's long-run, strategic effects on the firm.

Ronald Akers, financial vice-president, recognizes the problems inherent in an informal risk adjustment process. Also, his assistant, Audrey Keefer, concluded her review of National's budgeting process with a strong recommendation that project risk be given more formal consideration and that the idea of different hurdle rates for different divisions be investigated.

With the annual budget completed and no urgent problems facing him, Akers set up a committee to study the question of risk-adjusted hurdle rates. Diane Reeves, the corporate treasurer, Max Willocks, the corporate capital budgeting director, and the divisional vice-presidents were appointed to the committee, while Audrey Keefer was assigned to the committee's staff and given the task of developing a report outlining the major issues involved. In its first meeting, the committee asked Keefer to consider the following specific questions, plus any others she regarded as important:

1. Should hurdle rates be established for each division, each project line within a division, or for individual projects?

2. How should risk be measured?

3. How should capital structure, or debt capacity, be handled?

Keefer began by using her recently acquired knowledge of "betas." After several discussions, she found that National's management believed that the firm's risk, as estimated by investors, is a key determinant of its cost of equity capital. They also agreed that investors estimate risk, in large part, by relative volatility as measured by the beta coefficient. She also found that the financial staff had conducted a series of studies on the determinants of National's beta and concluded that the corporate beta is a weighted average of the betas that the three divisions, if operated as separate firms, would have. Keefer then set up the following table:

Division	% of Corporate Assets	Estimated Divisional Beta	Product × .01
Data Services	10	1.95	.195
Manufacturing	30	1.05	.315
Telephone	60	.65	.390
	100		
		weighted average corporate beta =	.900

In setting the divisional betas, Keefer (1) examined the betas for telephone, manufacturing, and service companies, and (2) looked at volatility of earnings in each division vis-à-vis both National's consolidated earnings and earnings on the standard utility indices.[1] The betas as calculated by each of these methods for each division were then averaged, and this average was used as the divisional beta. The weighted average of the divisional betas, 0.9, is quite close to the beta coefficient given for National by the various financial services (e.g., Value Line).[2]

Keefer uses these divisional betas to set basic risk-adjusted costs of capital for each division. The process works in the following manner. First, it is

---

1. It was felt that both transfer pricing and overhead allocations could possibly affect divisional earnings and assets artificially. However, discussions with the accounting staff convinced Keefer that transfer pricing was not significant for National and allocation procedures were as accurate as possible.

2. Not everyone agreed that betas are good indicators of risk for utility companies. Diane Reeves, for example, pointed out that GPU's beta over the past several years was low, indicating low risk, yet the stock declined from $17 to $6 in a few weeks in 1979. Reeves argued that the concept of betas was good, but that past betas were not reliable proxies for the future betas that investors should be using. Her argument was the same as the one against using past growth rates as estimates of expected future growth rates when conditions are in a state of flux.

recognized that the required rate of return on equity (K_r) is set in the market approximately in accordance with the following equation:

$$K_r = R_F + b(k_M - R_F).$$

Here, k_M is the return on an "average" stock, R_F is the riskless rate, and b is the stock's beta coefficient.

The beta for the average stock is 1.0, so the risk premium for an average stock is

$$P_M = 1.0(k_M - R_F) = k_M - R_F.$$

Using this formulation, the cost of equity for National is 14.7 percent:

$$\begin{aligned} K_r &= 12\% + 0.9(15\% - 12\%) \\ &= 12\% + 0.9(3\%) \\ &= 14.7\%. \end{aligned}$$

(Note: the 14.75 percent used in Part I came from averaging this 14.7 percent with the Gordon model's 14.8 percent. For simplicity we will use 14.7 percent.)

Each division's cost of equity differs from 14.7 percent depending on its own beta. The divisional costs of equity can now be determined:

Data Services

$$\begin{aligned} k_{DS} &= R_F + b_{DS}(k_M - R_F) \\ &= 12.0 + 1.95(3.0) \\ &= 17.85\%. \end{aligned}$$

Manufacturing

$$\begin{aligned} k_{MAN} &= 12.0 + 1.05(3.0) \\ &= 15.15\%. \end{aligned}$$

Telephone

$$\begin{aligned} k_{TEL} &= 12.0 + 0.65(3.0) \\ &= 13.95\%. \end{aligned}$$

Keefer felt that individual project hurdle rates, especially for large projects, or hurdle rates for investment "types" should be the ultimate objective, but as a first step she decided to try divisional rates until more specific data are available and the idea of multiple hurdle rates is more widely accepted.

The next question Keefer must consider is capital structure: should different divisions be assigned different capital structures and debt costs, or should they be assigned corporate averages? If different capital structures are to be used, how should they be derived? What interest rate should be used for debt? And how should divisional equity costs be adjusted to reflect varying capital structure?

Keefer decided to use the corporate capital structure for each division for the following reasons:

1. The average cost of capital is insensitive to capital structure over a fairly wide range of debt ratios; therefore, the issue is not as critical as it might first appear.
2. If a division is assigned a high debt ratio, its interest rate and cost of equity would rise, and this would tend to offset the use of the high debt ratio.
3. Keefer reasoned that she was already going to have a hard time persuading management to accept multiple hurdle rates, and the simpler her approach, the greater its chances of acceptance.

Keefer next calculated basic hurdle rates for each division, using the already developed equity costs, a 56 percent debt ratio, and a 6.5 percent after-tax cost of debt:

$$k_{A(DS)} = 0.56(6.5) + 0.44(17.85) = 11.49 \approx 11.5\%$$
$$k_{A(MAN)} = 0.56(6.5) + 0.44(15.15) = 10.31 \approx 10.3\%$$
$$k_{A(TEL)} = 0.56(6.5) + 0.44(13.95) = 9.78 \approx 9.8\%$$

These rates were converted to indices, using the following procedure:

1. Calculate a weighted average of divisional hurdle rates using the percentage of total assets as weights:

$$\text{Average } k_A = 0.1(11.5) + 0.3(10.3) + 0.6(9.8)$$
$$= 10.12 = 10.1\%$$

2. Develop divisional indices $= \dfrac{k_A(\text{division})}{\text{corporate average hurdle rate}}$

  (DS) $I_{(DS)} = \dfrac{11.5}{10.1} = 1.14$

  (MAN) $I_{(MAN)} = \dfrac{10.3}{10.1} = 1.02$

$$(TEL) \qquad I_{(TEL)} = \frac{9.8}{10.1} = 0.97.$$

These index numbers can be multiplied by the corporate cost of capital as developed in Part I of the case to determine each division's relevant hurdle rate. The corporate cost of capital varies depending on market conditions and the amount of money the company is raising (see Figure 5 in Part I). For example, if, because of a rise in market rates, or because of an extremely large demand for funds, National's overall k_A goes up to 16 percent, then the applicable hurdle rates for each division would be calculated as follows:

$$k_{A(DS)} = 1.14(16) = 18.24 = 18.2\%$$
$$k_{A(MAN)} = 1.02(16) = 16.32 = 16.3\%$$
$$k_{A(TEL)} = 0.97(16) = 15.52 = 15.5\%$$

When the basic rates were presented at a meeting of the ad hoc committee on hurdle rates, the people from the data services division were unhappy. Tom Abbott of DS was displeased with the high cost of capital proposed for his division, and also with the fact that a uniform capital structure of 56 percent debt was proposed. He notes that other firms offering essentially the same service as the DS division tended to use a 70 percent debt ratio, an after-tax cost of debt of 6.5 percent, and an equity cost of 18.5 percent, resulting in a hurdle rate of about 10 percent:

$$k_A = 0.7(6.5) + 0.3(18.5) = 10.10 = 10\%$$

Abbott argued that if he is forced to use a hurdle rate of 11.5 percent while other firms use 10 percent, National will lose its ability to compete in the marketplace, and even its own intracompany service would deteriorate due to both reduced new investment and loss of outside revenues to offset costs. Akers backed him up, noting that he had recently attended a conference at which a Dartmouth professor had discussed American Food's problem in setting divisional hurdle rates. Its restaurant division had 70 percent debt as compared to about 35 percent for its other divisions, and American ended up using a 70 percent debt ratio for the division. American also uses a relatively high debt ratio for its toy division. Other speakers at the conference noted that Apex Steel's equipment lease financing division also has a high debt ratio (about 80 percent debt as opposed to 33 percent for other divisions). In the cases of both American Foods and Apex Steel, the companies indicated that they could remain competitive only if they allowed the divisions cited to follow industry practice with regard to debt structures when calculating hurdle rates.

When Akers finished, Donald Maynard, vice-president for the manufacturing division, noted that both the restaurant and equipment leasing industries have been experiencing difficulties recently. With regard to American, Walker cited the following quote from the *Wall Street Journal*:

> American Foods Co. disclosed some more bad news about its earnings and received some bad news itself from a major credit service, which reduced the rating on the food processor's debentures . . . net income fell 27% while sales rose 16% . . . debentures were downgraded to Single-A-plus from double A by S&P because of the "continuing deterioration in earnings and fixed charge coverage."

Maynard then suggested that these problems might have been brought on by over expansion resulting from the use of hurdle rates that were unrealistically low. Others agreed with his point but no conclusions were reached at the meeting; the committee decided to defer action until Keefer's report was finalized.

After the meeting, Keefer had extended discussions with operating personnel regarding various ways of accounting for individual project risk. They concluded that any system would necessarily be somewhat arbitrary and imprecise. Most individual projects are parts of larger processes, and the results of a given capital project are highly sensitive to market and production conditions for the service. Still, experienced operating personnel admitted that they are more confident about some cash flows than others, and they recognize that some projects are simply riskier than others. Also, capital budgeting director Willocks reported that some operating personnel have better "track records" in forecasting cash flows than others have, and Willocks takes this fact into account in his own assessment of project risk.

For a few very large projects, generally involving entirely new technologies or services, simulation models have been developed and used to generate distributions of rates of return. Probabilities are assigned to sales prices, output quantity, and so on, and an expected rate of return and standard deviation of return are developed. However, the vast majority of capital projects are not subjected to such an analysis because management feels that the costs generally outweigh the benefits of such approaches, especially in view of the "wild guesses" that must be used for the probability data.

Keefer recommended that divisional personnel be required to classify projects into three groups: high risk, average risk, and low risk. Risky projects would be evaluated at a hurdle rate 1.15 times the divisional rate; average projects would be evaluated at the divisional rate; and for low risk projects the hurdle rate would be 0.85 times the divisional rate. When this part of the report was taken up at the ad hoc committee meeting, Akers and the others agreed that the recommended procedure was arbitrary, but they also agreed that this was similar to what was currently being done, and they could suggest no better procedure.

Keefer's final report stressed that capital budgeting must involve judgment as well as numerical data. At present, the capital budgeting process is as follows: (1) one hurdle rate is used through the entire corporation; (2) NPVs, IRR comparisons, and paybacks are calculated by the computer; and (3) these quantitative data are used, along with such qualitative factors as "what the project does for our strategic position in the market," in making the final "accept, reject, or defer" decision. Keefer's report emphasized that this general procedure should be retained, but that the quantitative inputs used in the final decision would be better if a risk-adjusted discount rate of the type she proposed is used.

Questions

1. Diane Reeves, the corporate treasurer, indicated that she did not completely understand some of the calculations, and she asked Keefer to illustrate them by showing the combined effects of the following changes:
   a. MAN's beta rises to 1.2; all other divisional betas remain the same.
   b. the riskless rate increases from 12 to 13 percent and k_M rises to 16 percent.
2. Suppose that the DS division has an exceptionally large number of projects that exceed its hurdle rate, so its growth rate substantially exceeds the corporate average. What effect would this have, over time, on National's corporate beta and MCC?
3. Suppose that, despite the higher cost of capital for risky projects (1.15 times divisional cost), the MAN division made relatively heavy investments in projects deemed to be more risky than average. What effect would this have on National's corporate beta and MCC?
4. Do you agree with Keefer on the capital structure issue? How would your thinking be affected if: (a) each division raised debt separately, i.e., divisions were set up as wholly-owned subsidiaries, which then issued debt; (b) divisions issued their own debt, but the company guaranteed divisional debt; or (c) all debt is issued by the company (which is actually the case for National)?
5. Describe briefly the key provisions in any plan for developing risk-adjusted discount rates that you would suggest yourself.
6. At its last annual meeting, a group of National's stockholders proposed that the corporate charter and bylaws be amended to preclude the sale of common stock at prices below book value. These stockholders correctly pointed out that: (a) issuing stock at prices below book value reduces book

value per share; (b) earnings per share are, under regulation, a function of book value per share; so (c) reducing book value through sale of stock at below book ultimately reduces earnings, dividends, and stock prices. Thus, they sought to prevent management from making below book stock issuances.

Management pointed out National's obligation to meet service demands as they arise, the need for investment well ahead of demand in order to meet projected demand, the need to raise capital to finance the construction program, and the need to raise some of the required capital as common stock. Ronald Akers noted that both National's bond indentures and its agreements with bankers supplying short-term credit specified a maximum debt ratio and minimum interest coverage ratios, and since the company is already close to these limits, failure to sell stock could prevent further issues of debt. This would, of course, dry up the supply of new capital and bring the construction program to a halt. If that occurred, new residents and businesses would be denied service, and the economy of the entire area (which includes most of the state) would be disrupted. Akers further underscored National's responsibility to the public, and its obligation to prevent the economic chaos that would result from a construction cutback.

The stockholders were unimpressed. They argued that the only reason for a utility's stock selling below book value is that its actual rate of return on equity is below the cost of capital. Therefore, if a company's stock does sell below book, this signifies that the Public Service Commission is not allowing the company to charge adequate prices. And, according to the spokesman for this group of stockholders, if the commission is not allowing adequate prices and rates of return, the company is under no obligation to inflict further financial hardships on the stockholders by making unprofitable investments.

Emotions ran high, and it was clear that most stockholders actually in attendance favored the resolution limiting the sale of stock. However, management had enough proxies to keep the resolution from passing. Still, it was obvious to Akers and the other officers and directors that the issue would probably come up again next year, and, in any event, the dissident stockholders did have a point.

a. Examine the following equation:

$$P = \frac{D_1}{k_r - g} = \frac{(1 - b)rB}{k_r - br} = \frac{r(1 - b)B}{k_r(1 - b)} = B.$$

Here P = stock price, D_1 = the expected dividend next year,
$\quad$ k_r = the required rate of return on equity,
$\quad$ B = book value per share,

g = expected growth rate,
b = percent of earnings retained,
r = rate of return on book equity, and
$k_r = r$.

Use the equation to explain why $P < B$ if $k_r > r$.

b. Discuss the pros and cons of the resolution to forbid the sale of stock at prices below book. Consider the question of whether management could continue the construction program, assuming the resolution is not passed, regardless of how low r gets in relation to k_r.

Case 34: *Dividend Policy*

Bellweather Oil Company

The Bellweather Oil Company (BOC) was established in 1938 by Dawson Tyler, an independent oil producer, who acquired the assets of a number of bankrupt oil companies during the Depression. Tyler recognized the growing demand for petroleum products, and under his direction the company aggressively sought new oil reserves both by acquisitions and through its own explorations. The company made two major strikes, one off the Louisiana coastline in 1960 and another in Indonesia in 1976. While BOC is not one of the giants of the industry, it is extremely well endowed with oil reserves relative to its own refining and marketing capacity. Further, most of its reserves are in politically stable areas. This excellent reserve situation has put the company in a favorable position to expand its refinery facilities and retail outlets during the 1980s.

Tyler has always operated the firm in an aggressive manner. His policies have paid off in rapid growth in sales and assets, but this rapid growth, in turn, has produced some acute financial problems. The extent of these problems is revealed in Table 1, which shows condensed balance sheets for 1962, 1972, and 1982. It can be seen from Table 1 that the debt ratio rose from 30 to 50 percent over the 20-year period, the current ratio declined from 5 to 1 to only 1.6 to 1, and the cash-to-current-liabilities ratio declined from 1.5 to 1 in 1962 to only 0.14 to 1 on December 31, 1982.

Tyler and members of his immediate family owned 75 percent of BOC stock in 1962. Because of the issuance of shares to acquire new companies, the need to sell common stock to raise funds for expansion, and gifts to charitable foundations, Tyler's ownership position had declined to only 35 percent of the outstanding stock in 1982.

The company has never paid a cash dividend, nor has it ever declared a stock dividend or had a stock split. Tyler has always taken the position that the firm needs to retain all of its earnings to help finance its expansion program, and on that basis he has followed a policy of paying no cash dividends. It is his opinion

Table 1 Condensed Balance Sheet
Year Ended December 31
(in millions)

	1962	1972	1982
Cash and marketable securities	$ 22.0	$ 38.0	$ 21.0
Accounts receivable	31.0	62.2	151.6
Inventories	20.5	31.8	65.5
Total current assets	$ 73.5	$132.0	$238.1
Fixed assets (net)	65.5	232.2	707.5
Total assets	$139.0	$364.2	$945.6
Current liabilities	$ 14.8	$ 37.7	$148.8
Long-term debt	27.0	108.0	324.0
Common equity	97.2	218.5	472.8
Total liabilities and net worth	$139.0	$364.2	$945.6
Current ratio (2.7 to 1)[a]	5 to 1	3.5 to 1	1.6 to 1
Cash to current liabilities (1 to 1)[a]	1.5 to 1	1.0 to 1	0.14 to 1
Debt ratio (28%)[a]	30%	40%	50%

a. The numbers in parentheses represent industry averages, which were stable over the
period covered.

that both stock dividends and stock splits are pointless. In his words, "They merely divide the pie into smaller slices." Tyler also thinks that stock dividends or stock splits would increase the costs to the company of processing the additional pieces of paper. Finally, since the stock is listed on the New York Stock Exchange, and since the commission, as a percentage of the transaction, is higher on large purchases of lower-priced stocks than it is on higher-priced ones, a stock split or dividend would increase stockholders' transfer costs.

At the annual stockholders' meeting in April 1982, a number of very vocal stockholders expressed disapproval of the firm's past dividend policy. One stockholder made a passionate speech in which he pointed out that while earnings in 1982 amounted to $156 per share, while the book value of equity per share (most of which was represented by retained earnings) was over $2,100, and while the president of the company's salary and other benefits for 1982 amounted to over $225,000, the stockholders received a zero dividend for the forty-first consecutive year. He also noted that publicly owned oil companies as a group had paid out about 40 percent of their earnings as dividends over the past 10 to 15 years. When other stockholders joined in the chorus, the chairman of the board, Tyler, and the president, Sidney Ives, realized that they had the makings of a stockholder revolt on their hands. Since rumors were currently circulating around Wall Street that two large conglomerates were considering making tender offers for BOC's stock, management was anxious to keep stockholders as happy as possible. Accordingly, Tyler announced to the group that not only would he call a special meeting of the board of directors within the next month to consider the dividend policy, but he would also announce the results of the meeting to stockholders in the next quarterly newsletter.

At the special directors' meeting it was immediately apparent that the directors were divided into five groups. The first group, headed by Tyler, felt that while a cash dividend would appease certain stockholders, such a dividend was out of the question. Tyler pointed to the balance sheet as dramatic proof of this position. The second group's principal spokesman was Robert McKay, an investment banker whose firm represented many small stockholders. McKay felt that a cash dividend was definitely advisable, and a sizable stock split was in order. A third group of directors agreed with McKay that a cash dividend was necessary, but they preferred a stock dividend as opposed to a stock split.

A fourth group of directors agreed that cash dividends should be paid as soon as possible, even if it meant a cutback in the company's expansion plans, and also contended that a sizable stock split or stock dividend should be declared at once. This group went even further, however, and recommended that the company announce a large stock split immediately and thereafter follow a practice of declaring quarterly stock dividends with a value approximately equal to earnings retained during the quarter. In other words, if the firm earned two dollars per share during a given quarter and paid a cash dividend of one dollar, this group would have the company declare a stock dividend of a percentage equal to one dollar divided by the market price of the stock. For example, if the stock were selling for $50 per share at the time the one dollar cash dividend was declared, a 2 percent stock dividend would be distributed.

Finally, since there was a prevailing belief among many of the stockholders that Tyler's position was a result of his desire to avoid paying income taxes on cash dividends, an offshoot of the fourth group made the additional proposal that, as an alternative to cash dividends, the firm might consider a share repurchase plan under which the distribution would take the form of a capital gain that could be realized or not realized at the discretion of the shareholder.

After an extended discussion, it became apparent that the directors were too widely split to reach a decision at that time. Another meeting was called for the following week. Wayne Smith, financial vice-president, was directed to evaluate the five positions taken at the meeting and to recommend a dividend policy to the board the following week.

Just as he began to map out his research strategy for the hurried report, Smith received a memorandum from Douglas Gould, sales manager and a member of the board. Gould supplied Smith with the figures shown in Table 2

Table 2 Selected Information

Year	Earnings Per Share (BOC)	Book Value Per Share (BOC)	Average Market Price Per Share (BOC)	Price-Earnings Ratio, Industry Average	Market Value/ Book Value Ratio, Industry Average
1982	$156	$2,182	$1,880	16X	2.5X
1977	118	1,852	1,534	19X	2.9X
1972	112	1,458	1,332	18X	2.6X
1967	102	1,242	1,212	17X	2.5X
1962	70	972	700	10X	1.2X

Period	Industry Average Annual Compound Growth Rate in Earnings
1977–1982	8%
1972–1977	7
1967–1972	6
1962–1967	7

and added a short note asking Smith to consider whether or not the firm's dividend policy and position on stock splits might have had an effect on the price of the company's stock as compared to the prices of other stocks.

Questions

1. Calculate P/E ratios, market value/book value ratios, and earnings growth rates for the Bellweather Oil Company and compare these with the industry averages given in Table 2. In your answer, consider explicitly the relative rate of return on new investment for BOC as compared to that for the industry and anything else that you think relevant. What is the significance of these comparisons?
2. Evaluate the advantages and disadvantages of having an announced dividend policy.
3. What effect does the payout policy have on the growth rate of earnings per share?
4. People on Wall Street sometimes talk about an "optimal range of stock prices," meaning a price per share range with the required rate of return for a given firm lower than it would be if the stock were not in this range. The range generally given is from $20–$60 per share. What bearing does this concept have on BOC?

5. How does the firm's debt position affect the dividend decision?
6. Evaluate each of the five positions taken by the different groups of directors. Consider the policies as they apply to BOC.
7. Recently there have been several takeovers of oil companies by other firms, most notably the acquisition of Marathon Oil by United States Steel. In light of BOC's low market value to book value ratio, the critical cash situation, and the unhappiness of the public shareholders, how vulnerable do you believe BOC to be to an attempted takeover? How might dividend policy affect this vulnerability? Do any of the five positions taken by the different groups of directors appear to be more helpful in this regard than the others?
8. Make a recommendation, and be prepared to defend it against alternative proposals, on desirable cash dividend and stock dividend and/or stock split policy for BOC. Be sure to specify how large the stock split should be if a stock split is employed, or how large the stock dividend should be if this procedure is followed.

Case 35: *Dividend Policy*

Genetic Industries, Inc.

Genetic Feeds, Inc., a leading hybridizer and producer of feed grains for cows, pigs, and chickens, was located outside Peoria, Illinois. The management of Genetic, seeing that growth potential was limited in their industry, made a decision in 1975 to diversify into totally new product lines. Genetic was generating substantial cash flows every year from profits and depreciation which could be used to buy firms in high growth, evolving industries. Also, in 1975, Genetic Feeds had a relatively small amount of debt outstanding, so management planned to use debt financing in its acquisition program.

Genetic Feeds saw a good opportunity in the newly developing market for genetic engineering services and products. The genetic engineering industry would enable Genetic Feeds to utilize its existing expertise in feed production and its present supply channels to greater advantage, and also to maintain headquarters in the Peoria area. Genetic's managers felt they could add a degree of professionalism to the industry and could further achieve a nation-wide distribution system along lines similar to those of their existing product line. With this in mind, Genetic Feeds acquired a number of small firms engaged in both pure and applied genetic research. These acquisitions strengthened the research and development capabilities of the company and positioned it to compete more effectively against all comers in the Midwest area by genetically producing new types of feeds, seeds, and other products.

At the beginning of 1975, all of the assets of the company were invested in traditional feed grain hybridization and production. By the end of 1980, however, these traditional products amounted to only 50 percent of assets, sales, and income, with the other 50 percent coming from new products directly attributable to spinoffs from recombinant DNA technology. To reflect the diversified nature of its business, the name of the company was changed in 1980 from Genetic Feeds to Genetic Industries.

The company has followed the practice of paying out 60 percent of earnings as cash dividends for the past 30 years. Accordingly, dividends have fluctuated with earnings from year to year. In each annual report the policy of paying out 60 percent of earnings has been restated, establishing a generous dividend as one of the hallmarks of Genetic Industries. Because of the firm's liberal dividend policy, Genetic's stock is owned by retired individuals, college endowment funds, income-oriented mutual funds, and other investors seeking a stable source of income. Surveys taken by the company clearly indicate that most of its present stockholders are income-seeking investors. Further, it is significant to note that not one growth-oriented mutual fund owns Genetic Industries' stock.

The directors traditionally have considered plans for the coming year at the January directors' meeting, but until 1981, dividend policy was never discussed. It was simply assumed that the policy of a payout of 60 percent would be maintained. At the meeting on January 15, 1981, however, Judy Rosenblum, the vice-president in charge of the genetic engineering division who was brought into the company when the firm she had founded merged with Genetic, stated that the dividend policy should be examined. Rosenblum reasoned that while a high dividend payout might have been a desirable policy for the company when it had poor internal growth potential, it is totally inappropriate for a firm with growth opportunities as good as those now available to Genetic. Rosenblum pointed out that capital limitations had recently forced the firm to turn down some expansion opportunities which promised relatively high rates of return. She also indicated that she and several other directors who had large holdings of the firm's stock were paying approximately 60 percent of all dividends received to state and federal governments in the form of income taxes. If, instead, the company were to retain most of its earnings, it would be reflected favorably in the price of the stock. Should she or other large stockholders desire to obtain cash, they could sell some of their shares and be taxed at the capital gains tax rate of 20 percent, rather than at the 60 percent tax rate on dividends.

Ellen Rose, secretary-treasurer of Genetic Industries, strongly supported Rosenblum's suggestion that dividends be reduced. Rose declared that the firm's current ratio had deteriorated from a level of about 5.5 in 1972 to only 1.71 in 1980, and that the debt ratio had risen from only 16.8 percent in 1972 to almost 60 percent in 1980. Rose reported a reluctance on the part of banks, insurance companies, and other lenders to continue making funds available to Genetic Industries if the debt and liquidity ratios continued to deteriorate. She offered the figures shown in Table 1 to illustrate her position.

Richard Leach, trustee of the endowment fund of a major university and a long-term member of Genetic's board of directors, took exception to the position of Rosenblum and Rose. Leach contended that the firm had followed a consistent dividend policy for many years and that present stockholders had made their purchases of the stock on the assumption that this policy would be continued. Moreover, he reported that the questionnaire sent out with the last

Table 1 Year Ended December 31, 1980
(In Millions)

	1972	1980
Current Assets	$ 47.0	$ 615.0
Fixed Assets	70.0	627.0
Total Assets	$117.0	$1,242.0
Accounts Payable	$ 1.8	$ 155.0
Notes Payable	3.9	163.8
Other Current Liabilities	2.9	41.2
Total Current Liabilities	$ 8.6	$ 360.0
Long-Term Debt: Nonconvertible	$ 11.1	$ 180.0
Long-Term Debt: Convertible	——	215.0
Common Equity: Common Stock ($1 par)	25.0	50.0
Retained Earnings	72.3	437.0
Total Liabilities and Net Worth	$117.0	$1,242.0
Current Ratio	5.5 to 1	1.71 to 1
Debt Ratio	16.8%	60%

dividend check revealed that stockholders show an overwhelming preference for a policy of high dividends as opposed to a policy of a low payout. Leach stated that because of its acute need for current income, his university's trust fund would be forced to sell its Genetic Industries stock if the dividend were cut significantly. He also noted that his trust, like many others, was permitted to spend only income, not principal, so that the trust would not have the option of selling some of the stock and spending the proceeds in lieu of dividends. For this trust, dividends and capital gains are not interchangeable, so it would have to reinvest in another company that paid high dividends. Leach was sure that a number of other institutional holders were in the same position, and, based on the answers to the questionnaires sent to individual stockholders, he believed that many of them would also sell their stock in the event of a sizable dividend cut. According to Leach, the liquidation of Genetic Industries stock from so many portfolios would have a disastrous effect on the stock price.

At this point, Rose stated that she had to agree with Leach's arguments. As corporate secretary, Rose handled correspondence with stockholders. In this capacity she had gained a very distinct impression that the majority of stock-holders did indeed want dividends and would sell their holdings if dividends were eliminated or reduced materially.

Fred Cantrell, production manager of the special seeds division, who, like Rosenblum, was brought into Genetic Industries when his firm was acquired, joined the discussion in favor of the payout reduction. Cantrell argued that the company's dividend policy was responsible for the type of stockholders the firm has. He suggested that if the firm had retained all of its earnings rather than paying out 60 percent in dividends, acquisitions could have been made for cash rather than by issuing new stock. With fewer shares of stock outstanding, earnings per share would be higher today and would have shown a higher growth rate over the past decade. This higher growth rate, according to Cantrell, would have induced growth-oriented institutions and individual investors to purchase Genetic stock. Cantrell concluded by saying that he believed the high dividend policy of past years was a mistake, but a mistake that could be rectified by changing the policy at the present time. He discounted the argument that the price of the stock would be depressed if the dividend were cut. Rather, Cantrell argued, aggressive investors would more than take up the slack caused by possible liquidations of income-seeking investors, with the result that the price of the stock would increase, not decrease, if dividends were cut.

The discussion continued for almost an hour past the scheduled adjournment time and terminated only because Rosenblum had to catch a plane to Mexico City where she was to make a presentation to an Organization of American States Conference on agriculture regarding newly developed types of feed grains that showed great potential for Latin American production. Before adjourning, however, the board directed Gerald Lafferty, vice-president of finance, to study the whole question of dividend policy and to make a report at the next directors' meeting, scheduled to be held in one month. Lafferty was given explicit directions to study the following alternative policies:

1. A continuation of the present policy of paying out 60 percent of earnings.
2. A policy of lowering the present payout to some percentage below 60 percent (for example, 20, 30, or 40 percent) and maintaining the payout ratio relatively constant at this new figure.
3. Establishing a dollar amount of dividends, say one dollar a year, and maintaining the dividend at this rate. As earnings fluctuated, the dividend payout ratio would fluctuate. Eventually, the dollar dividend would be increased, assuming that earnings continued to rise. If this policy is adopted, the question of the initial dividend in relation to current earnings, or the payout ratio, must also be settled.
4. Setting a relatively low dividend payout, say 50 cents per share, and supplementing this regular dividend with an extra dividend that would depend on the availability of funds and the need for capital. Again, the matter of total payout would arise.

The directors also asked Lafferty to consider whether or not the dividend policy, whichever was decided upon, should be announced. Rosenblum and Cantrell both expressed the opinion that dividend policy should not be announced, citing the company's present position as an example of how an announced policy could cause the firm to feel "locked in" and force it to take actions that otherwise would be undesirable.

As Lafferty was leaving the meeting, Cantrell asked him to include in his report an analysis of the firm's past growth rate in sales, total earnings, and earnings per share, as well as a statement of how the earnings per share figures might have differed if the firm had followed a different payout policy (see Table 2).

Cantrell promised to send Lafferty some figures on payout ratios and price-earnings ratios that he had seen in a brokerage house report a few days before. These figures are given in Table 3.

Table 2   Selected Information

Year	Sales (Millions)	Earnings After Taxes (Millions)	Earnings Per Share	Dividends Per Share	Average Stock Price During Year
1980	$1,890	$104.3	$2.09	$1.25	$14.63
1977	1,060	61.5	1.71	1.03	13.68
1972	543	31.2	1.25	0.75	6.75
1967	189	7.6	0.76	0.46	4.95

Table 3   Selected Stock Market Data

	Payout	P/E
Playboy	17%	25X
Uniroyal	0%	19X
Hewlett Packard	11%	17X
Datapoint	0%	16X
Texas Instruments	30%	13X
Xerox	40%	10X
ATT	67%	8X
Allied Stores	45%	6X

Questions

1. Evaluate the advantages and disadvantages of each of the four dividend policies, considering each as it applies in this specific case to Genetic Industries. Use a hypothetical graph showing investment opportunity schedules and a cost of capital schedule to illustrate your analysis.
2. Evaluate the advantages and disadvantages of having an announced dividend policy.
3. What effect does the payout policy have on the growth rate of earnings per share? Explain in terms of the formula

   $$g = br,$$

   where b equals the percentage of earnings retained and r equals the average rate of return on retained earnings.
4. Could the figures in Table 3 be considered proof that firms with low payout ratios have high price-earnings ratios? Justify your answer.
5. How does the firm's debt position affect the dividend policy?
6. Evaluate Cantrell's argument that a reduction in the dividend payout rate would increase the price of the stock versus Leach's opinion that such a reduction would drastically reduce the price of the stock.
7. Might stock dividends be of use here? Explain.
8. What specific dividend policy should Cantrell recommend to the board of directors at its next meeting? Fully justify your answer.
9. The tax law was changed in 1981 to reduce the top federal tax rate on dividends from 70 percent to 50 percent, and the top federal capital gains tax rate from 28 percent to 20 percent. How might these changes have affected Genetic Industries' optimal payout ratio?

Case **36:** *Timing of Financial Policy*

Michigan Engine Works, Inc.

Michigan Engine Works, Inc., a large manufacturer of engines used in lawn mowers, boats, power tools, and the like, was almost acquired in 1981 by Omega Industries, a major conglomerate. Michigan Engine's management resisted the merger, and with the aid of the Hooper Foundation, a nonprofit organization established by Charles Hooper, founder of Michigan Engine Works, the takeover bid was successfully warded off. However, the foundation's trustees indicated some dissatisfaction with Michigan Engine's performance during the past few years. They noted that, although sales have been expanding rapidly, earnings, dividends, and the price of the company's stock have not been keeping pace. Michigan Engine Works' management, in return for the foundation's aid in resisting the takeover, agreed to undergo a thorough review of present management practices and policies and to make whatever changes seemed necessary for improving the firm's performance.

To aid in making the review, Michigan Engine retained the management consulting firm of Andrew B. Lytle and Company. One aspect of ABL's survey is an appraisal of policy decisions in the major functional areas, including the financial area. For purposes of the study, ABL has divided the finance function into two parts: (1) internal operations, encompassing the effectiveness of financial controls over the various divisions, capital budgeting, and credit policy; and (2) external financing policies, comprising principally the methods used in obtaining funds and the timing of financial policy. Margaret Smallwood, the ABL partner who is directing the Michigan Engine Works study, is well aware of the sensitive nature of her report, in particular, the effect it will have on the career of John Ridge, financial vice-president. If Smallwood's report is favorable, Ridge will be given a substantial salary increase and additional corporate responsibilities. If the report is unfavorable, Ridge's progress will be arrested; in fact, given the pressures now on the company, there is even a possibility that Ridge will be fired.

Smallwood notes that Ridge has an accounting background. Ridge was brought into Michigan Engine Works as controller from the accounting firm of Pierce Bettenhauser in 1958. He was promoted to vice-president of finance in 1964. Smallwood is also aware that Ridge attended an executive development program at Midwestern University during the academic year 1969–1970. Ridge finished at the top of his class at Midwestern, and his performance in the area of corporate finance was especially meritorious.

Smallwood's analysis indicates that Michigan Engine's internal financial operations are excellent. The company has a well-organized system of financial controls, and its capital budgeting procedures are as modern as any that Smallwood has ever encountered. Smallwood has not completed her appraisal of Michigan Engine's external financing policies, but she has assembled the following information on the company's past financing arrangements.

1960 Financing

In early 1960, Michigan Engine Works required a substantial amount of new external funds. From 1956 through 1959, sales had grown at a rate of about 5 percent a year, but earnings had been relatively constant, held down because: (1) research and development expenditures were very high during this period; (2) new plant facilities had been required to produce the products generated by the research and development program; and (3) the start-up cost of these new facilities had not yet been offset by increased revenues.

The price of the stock in 1960 was approximately ten dollars per share, while earnings per share were one dollar. Other firms in the industry were selling at price-earnings ratios of about 18, but the rest of the industry had been showing significantly better growth trends in earnings per share. Michigan Engine's debt ratio in 1960 was 30 percent as compared to 38 percent for the industry.

The company needed to increase net assets from $80 million to $104 million, or by approximately 30 percent. Since four million dollars of these funds would be obtained from earnings retained during 1960, approximately $20 million in new external funds would be required. The first alternative open to the company was to issue commercial paper with a current interest rate of 4½ percent. A second alternative was 5 percent, long-term, nonconvertible bonds. A third option was to sell common stock to net the company nine dollars per share. On the recommendation of Ridge, Michigan Engine Works sold $10 million worth of common stock and obtained the other $10 million in the form of long-term bonds.

1962 Merger Financing

The additional production facilities that were opened in 1960 enabled Michigan Engine Works to take advantage of the new products developed earlier under the research and development program. Earnings increased from one dollar to four dollars per share, and the price of the stock rose from $10 to $88. In 1962 the investment community regarded Michigan Engine as a growth company because of its recent earnings pattern, but the firm's management believed that this label was probably inaccurate. Since increased competition from other companies was cutting into profit margins, and because no new products were in sight in the research and development department, management expected growth to stabilize at about 5 percent a year, which would be in line with the national growth rate.

Michigan Engine Works needed no additional outside funds to finance internal operations in 1962, but it did need to finance a merger acquisition. The owner of Turner Products Company, a manufacturer of motor housing units and one of Michigan Engine's major suppliers, wanted to sell his company and retire. Management decided that the acquisition should be made. In the past, the firm had experienced difficulty at certain times in receiving a steady supply of high-quality motor housings, and management felt that acquiring Turner Products would eliminate this problem.

The agreed-upon price for Turner Products was $25 million. Douglas Turner was willing to either sell out for cash or accept Michigan Engine Works' stock with a value of $25 million. Ridge recommended the cash purchase, and this method of acquisition was agreed to by Michigan Engine's board of directors. Since the firm had no excess cash at the time, the $25 million was borrowed from a life insurance company on a 15-year, 5 percent loan. At the time, short-term bank loans were available at a $4\frac{1}{4}$ percent rate of interest.

1965 Refunding

Early in 1965, Ridge planned to reduce Michigan Engine Works' debt ratio by retiring $25 million of 5 percent, long-term debt. He had planned to finance the refunding by issuing $25 million of $4\frac{1}{2}$ percent commercial paper. After listening to President Johnson's "guns and butter" speech, Ridge reconsidered the proposal and decided that the inflationary pressures that could be expected from such a presidential policy would lead to rising interest rates. He therefore deferred the refunding proposal until a time when circumstances would be more favorable.

1969 Financing

Michigan Engine Works' steady, though not spectacular, growth required additional financing in 1969. The stock had been split three for one in 1964, and in 1969 it was selling for $35 and earning $2.20 per share. The industry average price-earnings ratio at the time was 16. A policy of retaining most of its earnings had enabled Michigan Engine to reduce its debt ratio from 44 percent in 1966, to 35 percent, which was lower than the industry average of 37 percent.

Michigan Engine's total assets in 1969 were $148 million. The company needed $15 million over and above the amount that would be generated by retained earnings to finance its continued growth. The required funds could have been obtained by using short-term debt at an interest rate of 9 percent; long-term, nonconvertible debt at an 8⅓ percent interest rate; or common stock that would be sold to net the company $33 per share. On Ridge's recommendation, long-term debt was used to obtain the $15 million.

1972 Financing

Ridge expected a continuing rise in the level of interest rates in 1972, so he decided that refunding short-term debt with long-term debt would be a good idea. Therefore, upon his recommendation, Michigan Engine Works issued $25 million of nonconvertible bonds with an interest rate of 7¼ percent. The proceeds were used to refund $25 million of short-term debt with a current rate of 6 percent.

1974 Operations

In 1974, Michigan Engine Works faced the necessity of expanding its facilities to meet an increased demand for the firm's products. Ridge estimated that $20 million in externally-generated funds would be needed for expansion purposes. This amount could be obtained through a bond issue with an interest rate of 8 percent, or through a floating rate term bank loan with a current rate of 9 percent.

To stimulate the economy, the Federal Reserve Board had been increasing the money supply each year from 1970 to 1973, during which time the federal government was running sizable deficits. However, in 1974 the Fed tightened credit drastically. Believing that these actions, combined with energy shortages, would lead to a period of recession, Ridge argued strenuously that this was a time to cut back on capital expenditures. He recommended no expansion and no new financing.

1975 Financing

Anticipating a business upturn in 1975 or 1976, Ridge proposed in early 1975 that Michigan Engine Works undertake a major capital investment program. With the slack in the economy and the decrease in the rate of inflation, the company could obtain favorable contracts for capital equipment. External funds of $20 million were needed to finance the expansion. On Ridge's recommendation, Michigan Engine sold 25-year bonds having a floating rate set three-quarters of 1 percent above the prime rate. The prime rate at time of issue was 8 percent, so Michigan Engine Works' initial rate was 8¾ percent. Long-term debt with a fixed rate could have been sold at an interest rate of 10 percent.

1977 Financing

Although worried that the economy was showing signs of overheating in mid-1977, and possibly heading toward a slowdown of business activity, Ridge recommended that a plant modernization and retooling project be undertaken as soon as possible instead of waiting until late 1978. The project was mandatory to comply with federal safety and pollution regulations for small gasoline engines, but the company enjoyed some flexibility in timing the construction since the rules would not apply until July 1, 1979. Ridge reasoned that inflationary expectations were increasing and would only serve to drive up interest rates and depress real earnings and stock prices. The terms under which the $20 million external capital required to finance the project could be acquired now are likely to show a significant deterioration if prompt action is not taken.

The company's debt ratio is approximately equal to the industry average (40 percent debt) and the market value/book value ratio for the stock is 1.00. Short-term interest rates are around 6 percent while long-term capital is available at 9 percent. On Ridge's recommendation, Michigan Engine Works issued $20 million of 9 percent debentures to finance the modernization program.

1981 Operations

In the euphoria surrounding Ronald Reagan's election victory and his success in getting his economic program through the Congress, the company was placed under great pressure to expand its operations. Ridge urged the board of directors to proceed cautiously because he was worried that the money supply growth targets of the Federal Reserve Board were unduly restrictive and would lead to a negative growth period for the economy. He also believed that the tax revenue projections were optimistically biased and that excessive Federal deficits were likely to continue in spite of the massive budget cuts. For these reasons, Ridge recommended that no new external financing be undertaken, that the dividend be maintained at its present level to build up liquidity and retained earnings, and that production targets for the company be revised downward with the emphasis on consolidation and retrenchment. The board of directors agreed to his recommendation that no new external financing be obtained, but it elected to follow its customary policy and increase the dividend by 5 percent, and to continue operating on the basis of currently targeted sales levels.

Questions

1. Using Figure 1 as a reference, evaluate the decisions Ridge made from 1960 to 1981.

Figure 1   Long- and Short-Term Interest Rates, 1953-1981

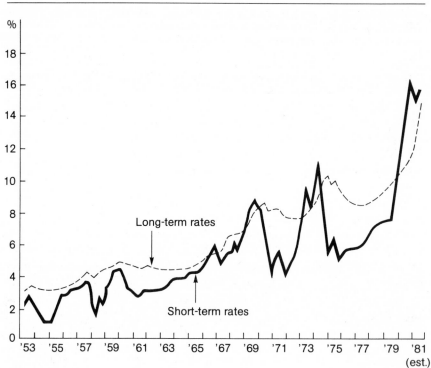

Note: Short-term rates are measured by four- to six-month A-rated commercial paper and
        long-term rates by A-rated corporate bonds.

Sources: *Federal Reserve Bulletin*, U. S. Department of Commerce, *Moody's Investors Service*.

2. Do his decisions seem to be improving over time?
3. How should Margaret Smallwood evaluate John Ridge's overall perform-
    ance, and what recommendation should she make in terms of Ridge's
    future? Give adequate consideration to both internal financial operations
    and external financing operations.

Part **5**: Other Topics in
Financial
Management

Case 37: *Mergers*

Armada Corporation

Armada Corporation, whose balance sheet is shown in Table 1, is a company with an honored past. A pioneer in microwave ovens in the sixties, Armada now produces and distributes a full line of stoves, refrigerators, and freezers, all of which use state-of-the-art electronic components. Since this type of equipment is a durable good whose purchase can be postponed, sales in the industry as a whole tend to fluctuate with changes in the economy. However, during the past decade, only the 1978 slump interrupted the company's relatively steady growth (see Table 2). Long recognized as a leader in developing managerial talent, Armada has a strong, balanced team of management personnel; in fact, the company has more people qualified for responsible positions than it has openings. For this reason, Armada's management is considering expanding its operations so that it can utilize its managerial talents to the fullest capacity.

Armada's board of directors asked William DeLoach, assistant to the president, and Robert Bryan, a partner in the consulting firm of Thornton, Ingman, and Associates, to prepare a report on the feasibility of embarking on an expansion program. DeLoach has an excellent knowledge of Armada's strengths and weaknesses, while Bryan has considerable experience in helping firms locate suitable merger partners and then consummate "happy marriages." The two men are a well-balanced team for purposes of formulating company policy, whether it be for external or internal expansion.

DeLoach and Bryan initially concluded that it is in Armada's best interest to expand. Having reached this decision, they next considered implementing it either through mergers or through internal growth. After a careful review of the advantages and disadvantages of these two methods of expansion, they decided that Armada is already expanding its normal product lines about as rapidly as possible. Therefore, if it opts to seek a faster internal growth rate, the company will have to start new divisions in new product areas. However, even though it has the depth to supply management teams to newly formed

Table 1 Balance Sheet

Year Ended December 31, 1982 (in millions)		
Current Assets	$382.00	
Fixed Assets	410.00	
		$792.00
Current Liabilities[a]	$ 87.00	
Long-Term Debt	155.00	
Common Equity (10 million shares out)	550.00	
		$792.00

a. Includes $70 million in 10 percent bank notes payable, which are a "fixed" component of the firm's structure.

divisions, starting up these divisions would be a relatively long, drawn-out process. Further, since the company would have little or no experience in the new areas, there is the strong possibility that costly mistakes would be made; thus, the risk of internal expansion into new product lines is relatively high.

A merger program, on the other hand, would enable Armada to meet its growth objectives much faster, because new facilities, products, processes, plants, and productive organizations can be acquired in operating condition. Further, assuming that the prospects of the acquired company are carefully checked before consummating the merger, risk can be reduced. Finally,

Table 2 Statistical Data

Year	Sales (in millions)	Net Income after Taxes (in millions)[a]	Earnings Per Share	Dividends Per Share	Average Price of Stock
1982	$672.30	$50.0	$5.00	$2.60	$55
1981	595.62	44.3	4.43	2.40	50
1980	551.22	41.6	4.16	1.80	44
1979	500.13	37.2	3.72	1.80	41
1978	255.89	(4.1)	(0.41)	1.80	29
1977	420.63	31.2	3.12	1.80	38
1976	385.86	28.7	2.87	1.60	34
1975	326.70	24.3	2.43	1.60	29
1974	317.50	23.4	2.34	1.60	27
1973	295.77	22.0	2.20	1.27	25
1972	285.67	21.1	2.11	1.27	24

a. Assumes a 48 percent marginal tax rate.

DeLoach and Bryan believe that there are potential merger candidates whose current earnings are being held down by relatively poor management, and, if Armada takes over such a company and replaces its management with Armada personnel, earnings can be increased. In other words, DeLoach and Bryan think that, in some cases, they would be able to purchase more production capacity per dollar via merger than through internal expansion. They recognize that it is also possible to pay too much when acquiring a firm, but they are confident that Armada will be able to separate good from bad mergers, and to negotiate a favorable settlement.

Armada can use either of two methods in its acquisition program: (1) it can negotiate and reach an agreement with the management of the target firm, or (2) it can make a direct tender offer to the target firm's stockholders. If the negotiated method is used, the actual acquisition may take place by purchase of assets, by a subsequent "friendly" tender offer for the stock, or by a vote of stockholders and agreement to swap shares of the target firm for those of Armada. Of course, the acquisition may fail regardless of the procedure followed; the target firm's stockholders may not tender their shares, or they may vote against a merger whether both managements agree to it or not.

Aside from the synergistic aspects of proposed mergers—and DeLoach and Bryan recognize that synergy is of the utmost importance—the terms of any merger with a firm in a high growth industry would boost Armada's total growth rate. Such a firm is likely to be selling at a higher price-earnings ratio than Armada is, which would cause an initial dilution of earnings per share. On the other hand, Armada might purchase a company that has relatively poor growth prospects and is selling at a low price-earnings multiple. This would provide Armada with an immediate earnings increase. Figure 1 shows both possible situations: merger with a high growth firm and merger with a low growth firm.

Rather than generalize about these factors in their report, DeLoach and Bryan decided to discuss the terms that might be applied to four potential merger candidates that have come to their attention. Statistics on the four firms in question are presented in Table 3, along with statistics on Armada for comparison. A brief description of each company follows:

World-Wind Company produces, sells, and leases washers and dryers. The firm is generally recognized as a laggard in its industry. Its chief weaknesses, aside from top management, are thought to lie in product design, production processes (production costs are higher than they should be), and the lack of an adequate sales financing plan. Also, a lack of investment opportunities has led to an excessive cash buildup. The company has a strong dealer distribution system with a good maintenance and repair service reputation. Bryan is aware that at least two other firms considered acquiring World-Wind but decided against the purchase because World-Wind's deep-seated problems would put a

Figure 1   Effect of Merger on Armada's Future Earnings: High and Low Growth Companies

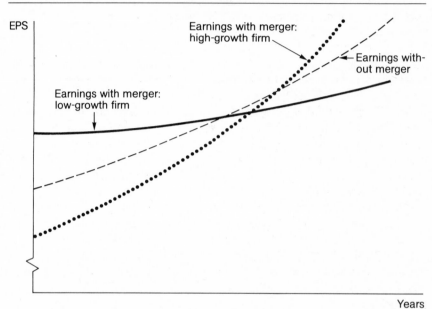

drain on the time and energy of their own management. World-Wind's management is approaching retirement age and would not resist a merger.

Corcoran Systems, Inc. manufactures, installs, and services a high-speed centralized vacuum cleaning system now used in a number of governmental agencies and private businesses. Madelyn Corcoran, chairman of the board and the designer of the system, would probably resist a merger offer, but Corcoran has direct control of only 15 percent of the stock, with the other stock being widely distributed. To take over Corcoran Systems, Armada would probably have to overcome the resistance of management and resort to a tender offer.

Scotch's, Inc. runs a chain of retail outlets which sells kitchen and bathroom equipment, hardware items, and other materials used in the do-it-yourself market. Although the company's locations are good and the company is relatively well run, the do-it-yourself supply business is one that prospers when the economy as a whole is down because laid-off workers have more time to repair their own homes and people generally avoid the purchase of new homes. Rumors have recently been circulating that Wacht's, a major building

Table 3 Comparative Statistics

Year Ended December 31, 1982

| | Per Share | | | | | Shares Out-standing (millions) | Debt Ratio | Beta Coefficient | P/E |
	Earnings	Last Dividend	Growth Rate	Book Value	Market Price				
World-Wind Company	$4.20	$2.50	4%	$43	$23	9.5	12%	0.8	5.5
Corcoran Systems, Inc.	2.00	1.20	10%	18	30	4.5	35%	1.6	15.0
Scotch's, Inc.	2.08	1.00	3%	13	10	2.0	24%	0.5	4.8
Christy Mathison Corporation	3.20	—	18%	14	65	10.0	50%	1.9	35.0
Armada Corporation	5.00	2.60	9%	38	55	10.0	30%	1.3	11.0

Note: The beta coefficients are based on historic returns data which compare a firm to "the market." Investors are assumed to expect these relationships to continue.

Except for Christy Mathison, the reported growth rates are expected to remain constant in the future. Further, these growth rates are based on Bryan's and DeLoach's appraisals of each company's prospects assuming that it continues to operate as an independent entity.

supply company, is planning to make a tender offer for Scotch's stock and that Scotch's is opposed to this merger. DeLoach and Bryan think that Scotch's management may welcome a merger offer from Armada to avoid being taken over by Wacht's. A merger with Scotch's would tend to have a stabilizing effect upon Armada's post-merger earnings.

Christy Mathison Corporation is a new firm engaged primarily in the production of high quality television sets. The company also has research and development contracts with a number of major corporations which use television for both process control and plant security systems, as well as long-term contracts with the government for research on television for use in space exploration and spy satellites. In addition to the company's own growth and earning potential, DeLoach and Bryan believe that some of the electronic processes being developed by Christy Mathison would also benefit Armada's own product line. Forty percent of Christy Mathison's common stock is owned by its board chairman, Christian Mathison, with its president owning an additional 20 percent. While these men have indicated that they are willing to discuss a merger, they have made it clear that they will agree only if the price is relatively high.

Questions

1. Using a DCF dividend model, determine the appropriate independent, or "stand alone," value for each merger candidate. Assume that Christy Mathison's recent growth will last for six more years, with no dividend paid during this period, after which growth will fall to 7 percent with 50 percent of earnings being paid out as dividends. In other words,

    $D_t = \$0$ for years 1 to 6, but $D_7 = 0.5 \ (EPS_7)$
    $= 0.5 \ (EPS_6)(1.07)$.

   Further, assume that the expected return on an average stock (K_m) is 12 percent and that the appropriate risk-free rate is 9 percent.

2. The production, operating, and marketing managers have estimated total 1982 postmerger earnings for each candidate:

Armada Plus	Pro Forma Total Post-Merger Earnings, 1982 (Millions)
World-Wind Company	$94.5
Corcoran Systems, Inc.	61.0
Scotch's, Inc.	59.6
Christy Mathison Corporation	99.3

Using this information and Table 3, complete Table 4.

Table 4   Exchange Ratios and Projected Earnings

	Exchange Ratio Based on 1982 Total Earnings[a]			
	Current Market Value	Current EPS	Maximum	Minimum
World-Wind Company	0.42	0.84	0.94	0.77
Corcoran Systems, Inc.		0.40	0.49	
Scotch's, Inc.	0.18			0.38
Christy Mathison Corp.	1.18	0.64	0.99	0.48

a. These exchange ratios are derived by using the formulas developed in Eugene F. Brigham, *Financial Management* (Hinsdale, Ill.: The Dryden Press, 1982), Chap. 20.

Hint: The maximum exchange ratio equates Armada's current EPS to the expected postmerger EPS and therefore defines the upper limit Armada can offer a merger candidate without diluting the current Armada shareholders' earnings:

$$ER_{max} = \frac{TE - EPS_A(N_A)}{EPS_A(N_T)}$$

where: TE = the consolidated total earnings,
EPS_A = Armada's pre-merger earnings per share,
N_A = the number of Armada shares outstanding, and
N_T = the number of the merger candidate's shares outstanding.

Conversely, the minimum ER equates the merger candidate's pre-merger EPS to the expected postmerger EPS. No merger would be likely to take place if shareholders expected their earnings to fall:

$$ER_{min} = \frac{EPS_T(N_A)}{TE - (N_T)EPS_T}.$$

Discuss the significance of these exchange ratios in terms of their implications for negotiations. Suggest an appropriate ER for each firm.
3. Specifically address such issues as relative size of the firms, changes in overall risk characteristics, possible effects on the cost of capital, synergis-

tic effects, changes in growth potential, financing economies, and so on, as they apply to the merger candidates.

4. After DeLoach and Bryan had received the earnings estimates and exchange ratio ranges, they arranged meetings with the management of each firm. From those discussions evolved the following tentative exchange ratios:

	ER	Explanation
World-Wind Company	0.620	
Corcoran Systems, Inc.	0.627	Armada must offer a 15 percent premium over market to obtain the stock.
Scotch's, Inc.	0.260	
Christy Mathison Corporation	1.420	Mathison's management is not willing to merge unless Armada pays a 20 percent premium over market value.

Compute the cash cost of each merger based on these exchange ratios and then suggest appropriate ways of financing each (i.e., debt or equity).

5. Calculate the pro forma expected earnings per share for 1982 for each proposed merger. Assume that the following schedule is an accurate representation of market response to each merger and then calculate the pro forma postmerger stock price.

Merger Candidate	Expected P/E
World-Wind Company	10.50
Corcoran Systems, Inc.	12.50
Scotch's Inc.	11.00
Christy Mathison Corporation	13.50

6. Finally, recommend and justify your choice of merger candidate(s).

Case 38: *Reorganization*

Miller Hardware and Supply

In 1940, Stanley Miller opened a small hardware store in downtown Hartford, Connecticut. Business conditions were difficult because inventory and materials were hard to get during World War II, but Miller Hardware grew and prospered even during those years because of Stanley Miller's devotion to the business. In 1962, Miller turned the store over to his son, Gerald, who had withdrawn from college at the end of his sophomore year to get married. Gerald had spent much of his youth in the hardware store, knew his father's customers well, and agreed completely with his father's business philosophy. Like his father, Gerald loved the personal contact inherent in a small store atmosphere, and he continued Miller's reputation for friendly, personal service.

Gerald's former college roommate, Mark Thornton, had completed his undergraduate studies and then gone on to graduate school. He received his M.B.A. in 1963, and returned to the Hartford area to look for a job in the building supply business, which was then entering a cyclical boom period. Thornton was an aggressive entrepreneur whom Gerald remembered as being quite a "wheeler-dealer" in college.

Realizing his own conservative bent, Gerald felt that Thornton would be a good addition to Miller Hardware. This feeling was reinforced when Thornton convinced him of the potential in the building supply business. Accordingly, in 1964, Thornton was appointed vice-president of Miller Hardware and given the responsibility for developing a building supply division.

Miller Hardware expanded rapidly during the late 1960s and early 1970s. The downtown store maintained a steady but unspectacular record of growing sales. Two new branch hardware stores, which were opened in suburban shopping centers, enjoyed good growth in both sales and profits. Meanwhile,

Source: This case was authored by Arthur L. Herrmann, Professor of Finance at the University of Hartford.

the building supply division simply mushroomed. Thornton opened four building supply yards, one each on the north, south, east, and west sides of Hartford, and by 1972 the building supply division accounted for almost 70 percent of the firm's total sales.

The expansion was financed largely through retained earnings and debt. However, because several members of the Miller family wanted an assured income, in 1972 the company was recapitalized with $3.5 million of retained earnings being converted into preferred stock and 7 percent subordinated debentures.

The mid-1970s witnessed drastic changes in both the hardware and the building supply industries. Sales fell off rapidly, not only in the downtown hardware store but also in the suburban branches. In addition, the building supply division was subjected to keen competition from discount supply outlets, which were springing up all over the Hartford area. Miller was forced to cut prices in order to compete, so profits fell drastically. These problems were compounded in 1974–1975 when the country experienced a major recession that was especially severe in the building industry.

The company was able to survive the 1974–1975 recession by obtaining a long-term loan from Central Connecticut Bank and Trust Company. The loan was secured by a first mortgage on the company's fixed assets. Unsecured short-term loans were also obtained from the bank on occasion. The added burden of this debt left Miller in a weakened financial condition when the 1980 recession struck the building business. Miller's 7 percent debentures, as shown in Table 1, are subordinated to the bank loans. The mortgage had a balance of $1,987,500 in June 1981, while the unsecured bank debt amounted to $800,000.

As a result of declining sales in 1980, and because the company had failed to cancel orders as sales declined, Miller Hardware's inventory increased from $755,000 to an alarming $1,642,500. At the same time, accounts receivable more than doubled from the average 1980 level of $602,000, to $1,550,000; whereas receivables had previously represented about 30 days' sales, in the spring of 1981 they stood at 72 days' sales outstanding. Further, accounts that were probably uncollectible rose from 3 percent to 11 percent of total receivables, as many small contractors were being forced into bankruptcy.

These frightening statistics resulted almost totally from the building supply division. Although the hardware operation was having problems, it was basically sound. However, the building supply operation was in serious trouble, and it was pulling the entire firm down with it.

The decrease in cash flow caused Miller to delay payments on its own accounts payable. News of the company's troubles spread fast, causing potential sources of new capital to dry up. The family—Gerald, his two sisters, and several other relatives, all of whom relied on income from the business—was

Table 1   Balance Sheet

June 1, 1981

Assets

Cash	$ 23,000
Accounts receivable	1,550,000
Inventory	1,642,500
Miscellaneous	87,000
Total current assets	$ 3,302,500
Net fixed assets	$ 8,673,500
Total assets	$11,976,000

Liabilities and Equity

Accounts payable	$ 1,017,500
Note payable (Kinzer Lumber)	289,000
Taxes (state and federal)	327,000
Bank notes payable	800,000
Other current liabilities	244,000
Wage claims	55,000
Preferred dividend arrearages	119,000
Total current liabilities	$ 2,851,500
Mortgage payable	1,987,500
Subordinated debentures (7%)[a]	992,000
Total liabilities	$ 5,831,000

Equity Accounts

Preferred stock ($25 par, 100,000 shares)	$ 2,500,000
Common stock ($100 par, 45,000 shares)	$ 4,500,000
Retained earnings	(855,000)
Total net worth	$ 6,145,000
	$11,976,000

a. Subordinated to the unsecured bank notes payable.

alarmed by these developments. Because preferred dividends had not been paid, issuing any more common stock was virtually precluded, even if equity investors could be found.

The senior loan officer of Central Connecticut Bank and Trust became worried and called Gerald Miller when the $300,000 portion of the unsecured $800,000 short-term note was not paid on its March 1, 1981, due date. Miller reported this to Mark Thornton, who said that he would take care of it.

Thornton subsequently obtained a 90-day extension of the $300,000 portion of the note, that is, until June 1st. The remaining $500,000 portion of the bank loan was not due until late in 1981.

In January 1981, Kinzer Lumber, Miller's largest supplier, had insisted on receiving a note, secured by a blanket lien on the company's inventory, to cover the $289,000 overdue portion of the account that the building supply division owed it. The note at this time (July 1981) was almost 60 days overdue.

Despite the firm's present troubles, Thornton convinced Gerald Miller that there were legitimate reasons for optimism. All of the leading economic indicators suggested an upturn in home-building starts for late 1981 and 1982. In addition, Thornton was about to finalize the largest contract the firm had ever received, a $1,250,000 deal with the B. F. Sheppard Company, a waste processing firm that was building a major regional plant in nearby Windham County. Once this contract was finalized, supposedly by November 1st, Thornton felt that the current dilemma would be solved. Shipments to B. F. Sheppard would reduce inventories and build up the cash account, which would permit a reduction in the most pressing debts.

In June, Kinzer Lumber's credit manager met with his financial vice-president to discuss Miller's current financial status. Since their note was overdue, they were aware that they had a basis for forcing Miller into involuntary bankruptcy under Chapter 11 of the Federal Bankruptcy Act. At the conclusion of their meeting, the two men decided to notify Gerald Miller that they were giving serious consideration to filing a petition for bankruptcy in Federal Bankruptcy Court. Since Miller Hardware had been a long time, valued customer, they felt they owed him this courtesy.

To forestall being thrown into involuntary bankruptcy, Gerald Miller began considering a voluntary reorganization. If he could effect a reorganization, he might be able to accomplish three important objectives: (1) pay the bank note; (3) become current on the accounts payable, which would permit a reestablishment of credit lines before the predicted business upturn; and (3) repay the note to Kinzer Lumber, thus eliminating the threat of involuntary bankruptcy.

A reorganization would require additional capital, and, with this in mind, Gerald's banker put him in touch with a strong midwestern company, Dayton Industries, that wanted to acquire a building supply distributor on the eastern seaboard. It was agreed that at least $2,000,000 in additional capital would be required for Miller to become current on current liabilities (this included the $289,000 owed Kinzer Lumber) and to regain a solid position from which to take advantage of the expected upturn in the economy. Dayton offered to invest the required funds by purchasing 23,000 shares of common stock for a total cost of $2.355 million. However, the Miller family would have to agree to the retirement, without compensation, of the $2.5 million of preferred stock, cancellation of the $119,000 of preferred dividend arrearages, and the giving of

23,000 of their 45,000 shares of common stock back to the company for reissuance to Dayton. Thus, Dayton would own 51.1 percent of the common stock after the reorganization. Once in control, Dayton's management intended to replace Thornton and to put their own person in charge of the building supply operation, but they planned to let Gerald Miller continue to manage the hardware business.

Before offering the financial package to Miller, Dayton had called in a national consulting firm to do a valuation appraisal of the business. Using a profit margin of 8 percent and an estimated sales figure of $10,153,125 (which assumed a business upswing), the consultants predicted that earnings after taxes and after interest is paid, for a "normal" year, would be $812,250. Applying a capitalization multiplier of 12 times, which was typical for the industry, they valued Miller Hardware as a going concern at $9,747,000. This figure is the estimated total value of the firm, not simply the value of the common equity.

Dayton planned to borrow the $2,355,000 needed for the investment. If the deal were completed, Dayton's total liabilities and net worth would amount to $77,000,000, consisting of $27 million in debt and $50 million in equity.

While Miller and Dayton were holding their discussions, Kinzer Lumber was still considering forcing Miller into involuntary bankruptcy. Its management had come to the conclusion that Miller Hardware had a gross liquidation value of $7,185,600, or 60 percent of book value. (Of the total proceeds, $5 million was expected from the sale of fixed assets.) The fees and administrative expenses associated with the bankruptcy proceedings would be about 20 percent of the gross liquidation proceeds. Thus, it appeared that Kinzer Lumber could surely recover its $289,000 loan by forcing Miller into bankruptcy. On the other hand, if they held off, and if the Dayton deal fell through, the situation might deteriorate still further, with Kinzer Lumber ending up having to take a loss.

Kinzer's credit manager noted that, under the new Bankruptcy Act, Kinzer Lumber needed only to show that Miller was "generally not paying debts as they matured" in order to force an involuntary proceeding. He was, however, concerned about how things would be handled in the courts because the revised code incorporated a shift in philosophy from the absolute priority doctrine toward the relative priority doctrine. These doctrines and their ramifications are important to Kinzer since they have a direct impact on who shall bear the losses associated with bankruptcy. The absolute priority doctrine that had been stressed under the old Bankruptcy Act states that claims must be paid in strict accordance with the priority of each claim, regardless of the consequences to other claimants. The relative priority doctrine is more flexible since it gives a more balanced consideration to all claimants. Under the old absolute priority doctrine, liquidations were more likely to be ordered by the courts because they generally permitted senior creditors (like Kinzer) to be paid off sooner, but often at the expense of junior creditors and stockholders. Under the relative priority doctrine, senior creditors are more likely to be required to wait for payment in order to increase the chances of providing some value to junior creditors and stockholders.

Also of importance to Kinzer Lumber, under the new Bankruptcy Code there is more flexibility, and thus broader scope for informal negotiations between a company and its creditors and stockholders. Under the new law, it is much more likely that the current management team would be permitted to remain in control of the company. Kinzer's credit manager believed that these changes were against the best interest of his firm, but there was not much that could be done about them.

The financial vice-president of Kinzer Lumber was not entirely convinced that the change in the Bankruptcy Act had any material bearing on Kinzer Lumber's position, or on the action it should take regarding Miller Hardware. He recognized that additional classes of priority payments for liquidation cases were added under the new code, but none of these was among the claims against Miller. So, while the procedures and some of the provisions of the law would be changed, he believed that the strategies of both Kinzer Lumber and Miller Hardware would still be valid, and the choices for all parties would remain substantially the same.

Assume that you are a loan officer for Central Connecticut Bank and Trust charged with the task of writing up a report for the Senior Loan Committee's quarterly review. As a part of your report, answer the following questions.

Questions

1. What was the basic cause of Miller's failure?
2. If Miller is forced into involuntary bankruptcy and liquidation, what will be the priority of claims, the amount owed to each group of claimants, and the amounts received by each group? Assume that assets can be sold for $7,185,600 and that administrative costs are 20 percent of gross proceeds. (Note: Preferred dividend arrearages are included with general creditors in bankruptcy.)
3. Assuming that reorganization takes place, prepare a pro forma balance sheet showing Miller Hardware's position after Dayton's takeover. Assume that all current liabilities except the non-past due bank loans are paid. Use the June 1, 1981 values for all assets except cash and fixed assets, and use the estimated going concern market value of the firm as the total asset value. Reduce fixed assets to force a balance on the assets side, and determine the cash balance as the current cash on hand, plus cash received from Dayton, minus cash paid out. Eliminate the retained earnings account, and balance the refinancing with a "paid-in capital" account. Paid-in capital is found as a forced figure: the value that will force the liabilities/capital side of the balance sheet to equal the asset side.

4. Discuss the pros and cons of forcing Miller Hardware into bankruptcy. Would you recommend that Kinzer Lumber proceed with the forced bankruptcy?

5. Analyze the reorganization plan from the viewpoint of a Dayton Industries director, strictly as an investment proposal, disregarding any strategic benefits to Dayton.

6. Would you recommend that Miller Hardware accept Dayton's offer of reorganization? Specifically address the relative position of the Miller family in reorganization as opposed to their position in a liquidation.

7. The SEC is required to examine certain reorganizations to ensure the fairness and feasibility of the reorganization. Is this test required in the present reorganization proposal? Explain.

8. The going rate of interest on debentures such as those of Miller Hardware in 1981 was approximately 16 percent versus a coupon rate of only 7 percent. Assume that these bonds have a 20-year maturity. From an economic standpoint, under the fairness standard, should they be paid off at par in the event of liquidation?

Case 39: *Multinational Finance: Capital Budgeting under Uncertainty*

Geodyne Exploration

Charles Morgan, vice-president of finance, is preparing a report for the monthly directors' meeting of Geodyne Industries, Inc. A number of important issues are on the agenda, and Morgan himself has not finalized his own opinions, particularly on those topics related to what some of the directors call the "foreign aid project." The government of Rudibia, one of the new West African nations, has agreed to give Geodyne Exploration, the oil field drilling subsidiary of Geodyne Industries, some important offshore oil concessions, provided Geodyne agrees to take on one of the four investment projects listed in Table 1. Project A involves the development of a rubber plantation which, although it will not produce any income for ten years, is expected to be worth approximately $349 million at the end of the tenth year. Project B, the construction of a deepwater seaport facility, has prospects of revenues amounting to $11.985 million a year. Project C calls for the construction and operation of an airport facility from which revenues should increase as Rudibia's economic development progresses. Project D involves the development of a strip mining operation in the central highlands. Its revenues will be highest in the first year; however, the mine will be completely exploited after four years.

The projects have all been examined by the World Bank, an organization supported by the United States and other industrialized nations to finance economic development. The bank's estimates of the cash flows for each of the projects are given in Table 1. Its economists, who took the potential oil resources into consideration when they made the study, judged all four projects to be economically feasible. Although the projects admittedly carry a high risk, the bank is willing to finance any of them. However, its funds are sufficient to lend the Rudibian government the amounts necessary to complete only three of the four projects. Rudibia has therefore tied the granting of the oil concession to investment in one or more of the listed projects.

It should be noted that the cash flows in each year for each project are equally risky, although the cash flows for different years are not equally risky, i.e., the

Table 1   Cash Flows from Alternative Investment Projects
            as Estimated by the World Bank

Cost of Project Returns in Years	Rubber Plantation A ($44,000,000)	Deepwater Seaport B ($50,240,000)	Airport Facility C ($50,000,000)	Strip Mine D ($46,800,000)
1	0	$11,985,000	$ 8,284,000	$30,000,000
2	0	11,985,000	9,234,000	20,110,000
3	0	11,985,000	10,284,000	10,410,000
4	0	11,985,000	11,484,000	6,570,000
5	0	11,985,000	12,984,000	0
6	0	11,985,000	14,684,000	0
7	0	11,985,000	16,634,000	0
8	0	11,985,000	18,884,000	0
9	0	11,985,000	21,484,000	0
10	$348,741,000	11,985,000	24,534,000	0

expectation of one dollar is equally uncertain for each project, but one dollar expected in year 1 is not necessarily as uncertain as one dollar expected in year 10.

Some of the directors of Geodyne consider the four projects to be "foreign aid." They think that the costs are likely to be underestimated and the returns overestimated, with the result that Geodyne will lose heavily on any project it undertakes. Other directors are impressed with the research done by the bank's economists, whose report hints that the projects' costs are very conservatively estimated while their revenues may well run double those shown in the table.

Morgan tentatively concludes, first, that the projects all carry considerable risk and, second, that no one of them is obviously better than any other. His personal preference is not to undertake any of the projects and, therefore, not to be granted the oil concession. However, a majority of the board members have indicated that they favor taking on one of the projects in order to obtain the concession. Several board members have even suggested that all of the projects look interesting, and, given Geodyne's large cash flows and unused borrowing capacity, these directors will probably suggest that Geodyne take on more than one of the projects. A spokesman for this group recently sent Morgan a memorandum indicating that, according to his rough estimates, each of the listed projects has a rate of return in excess of the 16 percent cutoff point Geodyne uses in capital budgeting. He also points out that if Geodyne does not undertake the Rudibian venture, it will probably have to increase cash dividends to get rid of its cash flows from operations.

Another topic that is likely to be brought up at the forthcoming directors' meeting is the cutoff rate of return itself. Geodyne has been using 16 percent as the cutoff point, or "hurdle rate," for all projects. This procedure has been criticized by some directors in the past on the grounds that less risky projects should be subject to a lower cutoff point, while higher risk projects should have to pass a higher hurdle rate. Walter Hart, president of a major bank and a long-term board member of Geodyne Industries, advocates the use of differential rates for different risk projects, and he recently sent Morgan the figures shown in Table 2. These figures, according to Hart, support his contention that projects with differing degrees of risk should be capitalized at different rates. Morgan believes that, although the four projects are not equally risky, in general they are all about as risky as the riskiest companies on Hart's list.

Another recommendation that Morgan is considering in terms of his report came in a telephone call he just received from Raymond Watson, president of Geodyne. Watson suggested that, assuming Geodyne goes ahead and takes on one of the projects in order to obtain the oil concession, the project should be either B, the deepwater seaport, or C, the airport installation. His argument is that these two projects tie in quite well with the oil concession, because if the oil drilling turns out to be successful, the economy of Rudibia will boom. In

Table 2 Cost of Capital Estimates for U.S. Firms
with Different Degrees of Risk

Justice Department Studies[a]	Required Rate of Return	Risk Index (1 = lowest)
Large public utilities	11%	1.8
Grocery chains	12	2.4
Major chemical producers	14	2.8
U.S. computer corporations	15	2.8
International oil companies	16	3.2
Smaller computer companies	21	4.8
Small oil drilling and exploration companies	26	6.8
Public Utility Rate Case[b]		
Short-term government bonds	11.5	1.0
Long-term government bonds	13.0	1.2
Long-term electric utility bonds	14.5	1.6
Electric utility stocks	17.0	3.2
(electric utilities: average of bonds and stocks)	11.5	2.0
Industrial stocks: major firms	18.0	3.6
(industrials: average of bonds and stocks)	15.5	2.8
Small industrial company stocks	23.0	5.6

a. Figures developed as a table in a recent antitrust case.

b. Figures presented in a recent case before a utility commission seeking to determine a proper rate of return for a large electric utility company. It should *not* be assumed that a U.S. utility company and a Rudibian utility carry the same degree of risk.

this event, both the seaport and the airport should be highly profitable. Thus, Geodyne's earnings would be improved substantially by a major strike in the oil drilling operations. Earnings would flow in from the oil itself, and the resultant economic boom would cause the seaport or airport investment to turn out better than anticipated. These higher earnings would naturally be reflected in the price of Geodyne's common stock.

Geodyne has already spent $75 million on geologic surveys for the offshore oil concession. These expenditures include seismographic work and the drilling of one exploratory well. Seismographic data indicate a high probability of a sizable oil strike, and the one well that was drilled did produce a substantial flow of oil. Assuming that Geodyne goes ahead with the project, it must spend an additional $10 million on exploratory wells to determine the size of the oil field. This drilling will take about one year to complete. Depending on the size of the field, the project may or may not be commercially feasible. It is estimated that the chances are 65 percent that the exploratory drilling will lead to the conclusion that the field is commercially profitable. There is a 35 percent probability that the additional drilling will indicate that the field cannot be developed commercially and that Geodyne should not go on with the project. Assuming that the field can be developed, an additional $29 million must be spent to provide storage facilities, transportation facilities, and development wells. If the firm goes on with the offshore oil project, expected returns are as follows:

Probability	Annual Returns (in millions)
.10	$ 1.5
.20	6.0
.40	12.0
.20	19.0
.10	29.0

Geodyne is not sure how long the annual returns will continue, but probability estimates are as follows:

Cumulative Probability	Life of the Offshore Oil Project (in years)
1.00	5
.85	10
.65	20
.35	30
.15	35

Because of the obvious uncertainties in the offshore venture, Geodyne officials feel that this project is more risky than the average project taken on by the company.

Geodyne must commit itself to a "foreign aid" project before it goes ahead with the additional exploratory well. It cannot wait until the results of the exploratory drilling are available before deciding on the special government project. If the company is to continue with the offshore oil concession project, it must commit itself to at least one of the four projects at this time.

Questions

1. How would the information in Table 2 affect the decision regarding which project to select?
2. What is the expected rate of return on the remainder of the expenditures for the offshore oil project? How should the sunk costs of $75 million be taken into account? (Hint: generate the expected annual returns and then the expected cash flows over time to calculate the IRR. Assume: (a) that all outlays are made immediately and inflows begin in one year; and (b) that the appropriate cost of capital for the project is 16 percent.)
3. Assume that Geodyne Industries, Inc. goes ahead with one of the four projects. Calculate the internal rate of return for projects A and C. (Hint: try 21 percent for project C.) The internal rates of return are 20 and 22 percent for projects B and D, respectively. Based on these criteria, which project should Geodyne undertake?
4. Consider now the timing of the cash flows of the projects. What bearing does this have upon the investment decision?
5. Calculate the rate of return that Geodyne would realize if it accepts (a) project A or (b) project D, in combination with the oil drilling project. Undertaking project B and the oil project makes the IRR 22.56 percent and for project C with the oil venture this value is 23.19 percent. Which combination of projects appears to be the better investment alternative?
6. Morgan believes that the values given in Table 2 are valid for those types of companies in the United States, but he does not feel that they are a suitable basis for an accept/reject decision for a Rudibian project. Rather, he feels that he should employ the Capital Asset Pricing Model (CAPM) to account for the amount of risk that is inherent in each project.[1] After careful consideration, he has derived the following values for use in the CAPM:

---

1. The CAPM is a procedure for estimating the riskiness of a specific security held in a portfolio of securities. It has been used, as Morgan is doing, to measure the riskiness of a major capital budgeting project.

$$k_i = R_F + b_i(k_M - R_F)$$
$$= 13\% + b_i(18 - 13) = 13.0\% + b_i(5.0\%)$$

where k_i = risk-adjusted discount rate appropriate for the ith project,
R_F = riskless rate of interest,
k_m = expected return on "the market,"
b_i = the beta coefficient of the ith project.[2]

The beta coefficients that Morgan has determined for the projects are:[3]

Project	Beta Coefficient
A	2.4
B	2.1
C	2.2
D	2.0

Given this information, calculate the risk-adjusted discount rates for projects A and D. For projects B and C, the values are approximately 23.5 and 24 percent, respectively.

7. George Barnard, president of Lasertech, Inc., and a director of Geodyne, has called Morgan's attention to the hurdle rate of 16 percent (Geodyne's cost of capital currently used for all projects). Since the IRRs of all five projects exceed 16 percent, he asks why, especially in view of Geodyne's ample cash flows and funds for investment, all of the projects should not be accepted? Morgan, like Hart, disagrees with this thinking, contending that none of the "foreign aid" projects gives Geodyne an adequate return for the amount of risk the company would be taking.

Morgan plans to illustrate his point by referring to Figure 1, which shows that, while all four projects' returns lie above the line representing Geodyne's weighted average cost of capital (k_a), they are below the security market line (SML), which represents the minimum amount of return that a firm should require for a specified amount of risk. For example, project B's beta coefficient is 2.1, so the minimum expected return that would make the project acceptable is 23.5 percent. Since the project's expected return is only 20 percent, the firm is not receiving adequate compensation for the amount of risk inherent in the investment, and, if accepted, the project would raise the firm's cost of capital.

2. A beta coefficient is an index of the relative riskiness of an asset as compared to other assets. For an "average" asset, $b = 1.0$. High risk assets have $b > 1.0$; low risk assets have $b < 1.0$.

3. These betas were subjectively estimated, although Morgan did examine the limited available market data on stock in developing nations when he was making his beta estimates.

Figure 1

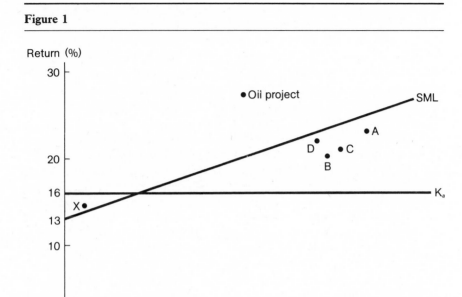

On the other hand, the oil project has a beta of 1.4, a required return of 20 percent, and an expected return of 27 percent; since the expected return exceeds the risk-adjusted required rate of return (the project's own cost of capital), it should be accepted. Of course, the oil project cannot be accepted unless one of the "foreign aid" projects is accepted in conjunction with it.

Therefore, calculate for Morgan the weighted average beta coefficients for projects A and D in conjunction with the oil drilling project. For projects B and C, each combined with the oil project, the weighted beta coefficients are 1.85 and 1.91, respectively. Which project combination is the most advantageous? (Hint: plot these values, and those found in Question 5, on Figure 1 to better illustrate the relative positions of the investment proposals.)

8. Often, due to its ample cash flows, Geodyne projects an excessive amount of cash on hand over and above the amount required for daily operations. Morgan invests the excess in earning assets rather than holding it in cash. Project X in Figure 1 represents a potential investment (not previously discussed in this case) that Morgan has investigated thoroughly. Bauer-Karbach Gmbh, a foreign company with a tight cash position due to its

recent expansion program, requires a loan of $50 million. Bauer-Karbach contacted Morgan in hopes of borrowing the funds from Geodyne.

After determining that his company had sufficient funds to meet the loan request, Morgan calculated that the investment would have a beta coefficient of 0.2, while the interest rate would be 15 percent. He felt that the beta of 0.2 was appropriate for several reasons: (a) Morgan has had a long history of successful dealings with Bauer-Karbach; (b) Bauer-Karbach is a very stable, profitable firm; and (3) the loan can be called for repayment any time ratios indicate a deteriorating situation. In combination, these factors make the loan a very low risk investment proposal.

The problem that faces Morgan is that, although the Bauer-Karbach proposal has a very small amount of risk and a return in excess of that required by the SML, the percentage return lies below the average cost of capital (or hurdle rate) of 16 percent that Geodyne presently employs. He sees this as an excellent opportunity to illustrate the desirability of using risk-adjusted discount rates rather than a constant rate for project selection.

Morgan plans to point out that none of the individual "foreign aid" projects should be accepted, as their returns are not sufficient for the high degree of risk involved. Only when these individual projects are combined with the oil drilling project do they offer sufficient return to compensate for their risk. With the same argument, Morgan contends that Project X should be accepted, as its return is in excess of the required rate of 14 percent read from the SML.

Do you think Geodyne should extend the loan to Bauer-Karbach Gmbh? Discuss from the viewpoint of the directors and of Morgan.

9. What are the NPVs of Projects A and D, using the risk-adjusted discount rates determined in Question 6? (Use $k_A = 25$ percent and $k_D = 23$ percent if you did not answer Question 6.) Based on this criterion, which project should Geodyne undertake? The NPVs for projects B and C are negative, ($5,418,750) and ($5,569,392), respectively.

10. Defend or criticize Raymond Watson's suggestion to accept Project B or C as Geodyne's "foreign aid" project.

11. What additional information would be useful to the directors in making the investment decision? Discuss the feasibility of obtaining such information, and specific applications if it could be obtained.

12. Based on your answers to the previous questions, which project(s), if any, should Geodyne accept? Remember that at least one "foreign aid" project must be accepted in order to receive the oil concession from Rudibia.

Case 40: *Multinational Business Finance: Capital Budgeting*

Russo Winery, Inc.

"This will have a phenomenal impact on the credibility of California wines," exclaimed Ettore Russo. Russo had just received news of the results of the centennial tasting held in London. In the summer of 1976, Reginald Lumley, a prominent wine merchant, brought the leading wine experts of the world together to participate in a blind tasting of some of the most outstanding wines of the past century. To pacify Americans during their bicentennial celebration (and, some claimed, to put the Americans in their place once and for all) Lumley included some California wines in the group. As the identity of the bottles was revealed and their respective votes tabulated, gasps of *mon dieu* echoed throughout the tasting room. The clear-cut winner, selected blindly by the connoisseurs, was a moderately-priced California wine, Stags Leap Cabernet Sauvignon, 1974.

Besides his personal love of California wines, Russo had other reasons to be extremely pleased with the outcome of this tasting; he was president of Russo Winery, Inc., one of the largest and most profitable vineyards in California. Russo Winery's success was due in a large part to Ettore Russo's expertise in mass production of quality wine. A graduate in oenology of the University of California at Davis, Russo had revolutionized the industry by using stainless steel vats instead of the traditional oak lined casks for fermentation. This switch allowed much greater efficiency in production.

Russo's expectations of the impact of the centennial tasting proved true, as demand for California wine in foreign markets increased rapidly. Up to this time Russo had been serving as a private consultant to a number of foreign vineyards regarding implementation of the fermentation and production processes which had made Russo so successful. In 1977 Russo Winery decided to expand these foreign operations beyond the scope of consulting by establishing overseas subsidiaries. Because of the success of this initial venture, Russo Winery established a special foreign investment team, headed by a vice-president and close personal friend, Carl Marks.

In the winter of 1981, Marks began to evaluate a proposal for establishing a subsidiary in the South American country of Pacifica. The climate, soil, and grape quality were similar to those in California, but the country lacked the technical skill necessary for commercial production of wine. The wines currently produced were distributed only to local villages because yield was small and quality inconsistent. After personal inspection of the vines, Marks concluded they were 5–7 years old, the prime age for quality grape yield. A typical vine maintains this prime state for approximately 20 years at which time it must be replanted.

At this time Pacifica appears to be on the verge of a marked long-term economic expansion. The Minister of Industry and Trade assured Marks of his country's commitment to establishing Pacifica as a wine producer and exporter. As an inducement to locate in Pacifica, he offered Russo Winery, Inc. a 10 percent reduction in their tax rate (from the normal 50 percent to 40 percent).

Estimates of the required capital investment in the proposed Russo-Pacifica facilities to be constructed in 1982 are shown in Table 1. The uncertainty about the required investment outlay is primarily the result of unpredictable construction costs, inflation, and the shortage of skilled labor.

The estimated before-tax profits from operations (in Pacifican pesos) for a 20-year period are shown in Table 2. It is recognized that these estimates, especially those for the later years, are not firm. Russo Winery's own cash inflows from these earnings are subject to additional uncertainty. Apart from the repatriated earnings from the Russo-Pacifica operation, the parent firm will receive $200,000 per year in technical and supervisory fees. These management fees are expenses of Russo-Pacifica that have already been subtracted from the expected gross revenues to get the estimated cash flows in Table 2. Thus, there is no Pacifican tax on this income to the parent. However, it will be fully taxed to Russo Winery when it is received.

The expected economic life of the initial production facilities, without any additional major investments, should be approximately 9 years, although a

Table 1 Probability Distribution of Russo-Pacifica Investment Requirements (in thousands of U.S. dollars)

Cash Investment Required	Probability
$1,000	0.05
2,500	0.20
3,000	0.50
3,500	0.20
5,000	0.05

Table 2   Estimated Annual Earnings of Russo-Pacifica
(in thousands of Pacifican Pesos)

Year	Profit Before Tax	Pacifican Tax (40 percent)
1982	P(30)	P 0
1983	60	24
1984	250	100
1985	450	180
1986–1991	490	196
1992–1997	550	220
1998–2001	500	200

longer life of up to 20 years is possible under favorable operating conditions. The productive capacity of the vineyards will be maintained to some extent by partial reinvestment of earnings as required by Pacifican law. There also exists the possibility, however remote, that the government of Pacifica might nationalize the operation. Nationalization of foreign firms has not occurred there in the past despite the fact that the government is strongly nationalistic and independent. The president of Pacifica has given assurances that the hands-off policy will not be changed, and, in the unlikely event of nationalization, the firm will be given fair compensation for the vineyard. Despite the obvious uncertainties involved, Marks concluded that the present political situation in Pacifica is stable and conducive to foreign investment.

In conjunction with the vice-president of production, Giovanni Russo, Ettore's younger brother, Marks developed estimates of the project life and conditional expected values of the vineyard at the end of each possible project life. These estimates are shown in Table 3. Although the estimates for the project's life reflect, to the extent possible, the risk of expropriation of the vineyard by the Pacifican government, no attempt has been made to estimate

Table 3   Probability Distribution of Project Life and Salvage Value of Vineyard
(in thousands of Pacifican Pesos)

Cumulative Probability Project Life	Project Life	Expected Value at End of Project Life
1.0	2 years	550
0.8	4 years	550
0.4	10 years	300
0.3	15 years	150
0.2	20 years	75

the amount of compensation to be received if the vineyard is nationalized. Thus the estimates for the terminal value of the vineyard reflect only its expected value under the assumption of no expropriation.

At the time of Marks's study, the official exchange rate was $5 to one Pacifican peso. The Central Bank of Pacifica is attempting to stabilize the rate at this level. However, because of inflationary pressures on the peso and the deficiency of adequate foreign currency reserves, there is a good chance that the exchange rate will fall substantially. The magnitude of change is uncertain and will depend largely on the Pacifican government's ability to control inflation. Under current estimates, the exchange rate will remain at $5 for P1 in 1982, fall to $4.50 in 1983, and then stabilize at $4.00 for P1 in 1984. This downward shift in the exchange rate will result in a reduction in the dollar value of repatriated earnings. In addition, the translated book value of Russo-Pacifica will be reduced by approximately $175,000 in both 1983 and 1984.

Marks's next task is to estimate the cash inflows to the parent firm. These inflows will include repatriated earnings plus the $200,000 supervisory fee. Moreover, the projected gross inflows must show a negative entry of $300,000 per year to account for the lost Russo export sales. Since income from other Russo subsidiaries is consolidated with that from domestic operations, Marks is assuming that the same practice will apply to Russo-Pacifica.

The initial plans call for the establishment of Russo-Pacifica as a wholly-owned subsidiary of Russo Winery, but a joint venture with Pacifican investors is also being investigated. Although a foreign partner can provide knowledge of the local economy, politics, customs, and quick entry into Pacifican markets, Russo and Marks fear the restrictions a foreign partner might wish to impose regarding dividend policy, export sales, intercompany transfer pricing strategy, and financing policies.

The present proposal is to begin the Pacifica vineyard with 50 percent equity and 50 percent debt. The 50 percent equity financing will come directly from the parent; about one-half of that amount is in the form of stainless steel vats and other equipment. The 50 percent debt financing could be obtained from several sources. The Central Bank of Pacifica has indicated a willingness to lend the equivalent of $1.5 million at an interest rate of 14 percent. No parent company guarantee would be involved in this loan. Russo-Pacifica could also obtain up to $1.5 million from U. S. banks at an interest rate of approximately 11 percent. However, a parent company guarantee would be required. In addition, funds could be raised in the Eurodollar or Eurobond markets at 10 and 10½ percent, respectively, again with the obligation guaranteed by the parent firm.

Because there are several alternative sources of capital, each with a different cost, there has been considerable debate over the appropriate cost of capital for this project. Russo Winery's average cost of capital for U. S. investments of this type is 12 percent, but specific projects range from a low of 10 percent to a high of 15 percent. One of Marks's assistants has suggested that cash flows be discounted at 15 percent, Russo Winery's required rate of return for high risk projects in the United States. Another staff member has argued that an even higher cost of capital should be used because the project is overseas and thus is subjected to political risks. A third analyst suggested that the cost of capital cannot be determined until the method of financing has been decided. Marks is also uncertain about the appropriate cost of capital and wonders about the possibility of using a lower than average cost of capital for this project because of possible portfolio effects (the world economy and the U. S. economy may, over the next 10 to 12 years, move in somewhat divergent directions).

Questions

1. Compute the net present value of the project to Russo Winery, Inc., at the beginning of 1982. Assume: (a) the vineyard is established as a wholly-owned subsidiary; (b) Russo-Pacifica income is consolidated with parent firm income; and (c) the discount rate is 15 percent. Note the following conditions on taxes and repatriated earnings: (a) repatriated earnings are 75 percent of the net profit (after local taxes) of Russo-Pacifica before U. S. taxes; (b) the 48 percent U. S. tax rate is applied to the total earnings of the subsidiary before local taxes; and (c) Russo Winery is given a U. S. tax credit equal to the amount of Pacifican taxes paid on the portion repatriated. Ignore the devaluation in the book value of the assets of the subsidiary in your tax and cash flow calculations. (Hint: calculate the present value of the cash flows to Russo Winery and then generate the expected value of the flows over time. Also generate the expected terminal value of the vineyard at the end of the project life.)

2. How would the NPV of the project be affected if Russo Winery chose to receive its returns from the Pacifica vineyard in the form of dividends rather than to consolidate the Pacifica income with domestic income? Give only the probable direction of the change. Under what condition would Russo Winery prefer to consolidate income rather than to receive dividends? Does this situation appear to exist in the present case?

3. Evaluate the options of a wholly-owned subsidiary versus a joint venture with Pacifican investors. Is there any advantage to employing the higher cost local debt rather than the other sources?

4. Design and justify an appropriate financing mix for the project. (The 50-50 debt-equity mix and the exclusion of joint venture partners need not be used.) Be sure to indicate the effects of the following factors, among others, on the financing program: (a) relative rate of inflation in the U. S. and Pacifica; (b) quotas on U. S. direct investments; and (c) the chance of expropriation.

5. What cost of capital do you feel is appropriate for this project? Why? Would a better way to adjust for foreign uncertainty and risk be to adjust the cash flows directly and then discount at the rate appropriate for U. S. investment?

6. Which are the most relevant cash flows to consider, cash flows to Russo Winery or the operating cash flows of Russo-Pacifica? Explain.

7. What effect would the devaluation of the assets of Russo-Pacifica have on: (a) the parent firm's consolidated earnings; and (b) cash flows?

8. Should Russo Winery, Inc. go ahead with the project?

Case **41:** *Suggested Financing Alternatives*

Sampson Brothers

While investment banking firms have recently hired very few new employees, the positions they do fill are highly sought after and considered by many to be extremely lucrative. Prime candidates not only need to have knowledge of the financial markets, but also must have the ability to sell their firm's services to some of the most successful members of the financial community. Quite often, knowledge of oenology, ancestry, and a scratch golf game have just as much persuasive power in obtaining a client's business as do the actual services of Sampson Brothers.

Through an old family contact pulling the right strings, J. Pinkston Whitney, III was fortunate enough to obtain the job of assistant to Eleanor Freeman, a senior partner and managing officer at Sampson Brothers. Whitney received his bachelor's degree in history from a very expensive and prestigious Eastern school only two weeks ago, and this is his first day on the job. After a rather pleasant morning spent meeting various people around the office, including a number of rather attractive secretaries, Whitney was given his first task.

Freeman had been forced to miss her regular Thursday afternoon tennis match and to stay up until 3 a.m. Friday morning to finish some recommendations on the types of financing that a group of clients should use. Having completed the analyses and made her recommendations, that Friday morning Freeman turned over to Whitney the folder on each client and the recommendations on the type of financing that each should use. She then told Whitney to have the analyses and financing recommendations typed up and sent immediately to the respective client companies. Freeman and Rolf Swensen, her private secretary, were leaving for a weekend of uninterrupted dictation in Aspen, so she particularly emphasized that she should be contacted during the weekend only in the event of an emergency.

The first thing Whitney did was to detach the analyses and recommendations from the folders and give them to one of the secretaries to type. When the secretary returned the typed reports, Whitney discovered that he did not know which recommendation belonged to which company! He had folders on nine different companies and financing recommendations for nine companies, but he could not match them up. Whitney's major was history, so he could not be expected to match the financing recommendations with the appropriate companies. However, as a finance student, you should be able to help Whitney by telling him which companies in section B should use the financing methods in section A.

Questions

Section A

1. Leasing Arrangement
2. Long-Term Bonds
3. Debt with Warrants
4. Friends or Relatives
5. Common Stock: Nonrights
6. Preferred Stock (Nonconvertible)
7. Common Stock: Rights Offering
8. Convertible Debentures
9. Factoring

Section B

A. Lewis Brothers, Inc.
   This company, a women's retail clothing store chain in Atlanta, Georgia is incorporated, with each of the three Lewis brothers owning one-third of the outstanding stock. The company is profitable, but rapid growth has put it under severe financial strain. The real estate is all under mortgage to an insurance company, the inventory is being used under a blanket chattel mortgage to secure a bank line of credit, and the accounts receivable are being factored. With total assets of $7 million, the company now needs an additional $150,000 to finance a building and fixtures for a new outlet.
B. Carolina Edison Electric, Inc.
   Since Carolina Edison Electric, Inc., a major electric utility, is organized as a holding company, the Securities and Exchange Commission must approve all its security issues. Such approval is automatic if the company stays within conventional norms for the public utility industry. Reasonable norms call for long-term debt in the range of 55–65 percent, preferred stock in the range of 0–15 percent, and common equity in the range of 25–35 percent. Carolina Edison Electric currently has total assets of $1.5 billion financed as follows: $900 million debt, $75 million preferred stock, and $525 million common equity. The company plans to raise an additional $37 million at this time.

C. Georgia Girl Canning Company

Georgia Girl Canning Company is a large operation located in Dalton, Georgia that purchases peaches and other fruits from farmers in Georgia, Illinois, Tennessee, and Kentucky. These fruits are then canned and sold on 60-day credit terms, largely to food brokers and small retail grocers in the same four-state area. The company's plant and equipment have been financed in part by a mortgage loan, and this is the only long-term debt. Raw materials (fruits) are purchased on terms calling for payment within 30 days of receipt of goods, but no discounts are offered. Because of an increase in the popularity of vegetables and fruits, canned fruit sales have increased dramatically. To finance a higher level of output to take advantage of this increased demand, Georgia Girl Canning will need approximately $550,000.

D. Pritz Pickle Company

Pritz Pickle Company is a major packer of pickles and pickled products (horseradish, pickled watermelon rinds, relishes). The company's stock is widely held, actively traded, and listed on the New York Stock Exchange. Recently, it has been trading in the range of $18-$22 a share. The latest 12 months' earnings were $1.70 per share. The current dividend rate is 64 cents a share, and earnings, dividends, and the price of the company's stock have been growing at a rate of about 7 percent over the last few years. Pritz Pickle's debt ratio is currently 42 percent versus 25 percent for other large pickle packers. Other firms in the industry, on the average, have been growing at a rate of about 5 percent a year, and their stocks have been selling at a price-earnings ratio of about 10. Pritz Pickle has an opportunity to begin growing its own cucumbers, which would result in a substantial price savings and reduce the risk involved in having to compete for cucumbers in the open market. This vertical integration would require $20 million in cash for the necessary farms and equipment.

E. Rockledge Mining Company

Rockledge Mining needs $12 million to finance the acquisition of mineral rights to some land in southcentral New Mexico and to pay for some extensive surveys, core-borings, magnetic aerial surveys, and other types of analyses designed to determine whether the mineral deposits on this land warrant development. If the tests are favorable, the company will need an additional $12 million. Rockledge Mining's common stock is currently selling at $11, while the company is earning approximately $1 per share. Other firms in the industry sell at from 8 to 13 times earnings. Rockledge Mining's debt ratio is 30 percent, compared to an industry average of 35 percent. Total assets at the last balance sheet date were $120 million.

F. Lone Star Saloon and Dance Hall

Larry Perkins, a professor at the University of Florida, is an avid country and western music fan and square dancer. He has just learned that a recently developed downtown entertainment center still has a lease available for the original, renovated building of the First National Bank of Gainesville. The bank outgrew the building in the late fifties and the large open spaces and high ceilings would be ideal for a country and western nightclub. Perkins knows the market well and has often noted the lack of a real "kicker bar" in Gainesville, the closest being in Jacksonville. Perkins believes that if he can obtain approximately $50,000 for a sound system and interior decorations, he can open a small but successful operation in the old bank building. His liquid savings total $15,000, so Perkins needs an additional $35,000 to open the proposed nightclub.

G. Musselman Aircraft Corporation

Musselman Aircraft is a medium-sized aircraft company whose sales distribution is approximately 30 percent for defense contracts and 70 percent for nonmilitary uses. The company has been growing rapidly in recent years, and projections based on current research and development prospects call for continued growth at a rate of 10-12 percent a year. Although recent reports of several brokerage firms suggest that the firm's rate of growth might be slowing down because of the high price of fuel and the impact of the air traffic controllers' strike, Musselman's management believes, based on internal information, that no decline is in sight. The company's stock, which is traded on the Pacific Stock Exchange, is selling at 15 times earnings. This is slightly below the 17 times ratio of Standard & Poor's aircraft industry average. The company has assets of $35 million, a debt ratio of 25 percent (industry average 23 percent), and needs an additional $5 million over and above the retained earnings to support the projected level of growth during the next 12 months.

H. Beaty Yachts

Beaty Yachts is a closely held company that was founded in 1960 by Cecil Beaty to build a top quality line of sailboats. The company's debt ratio is 48 percent as compared to an average ratio of 36 percent for sailboat companies in general. The stock is owned in equal parts by ten individuals, none of whom is in a position to put additional funds into the business. Sales for the most recent year were $12 million, and earnings after taxes amounted to $720,000. Total assets, as of the latest balance sheet, were $9.6 million. Beaty Yachts needs an additional $4 million to finance expansion during the current fiscal year. Given the world-wide growth in leisure time activities and interest in sailing in particular, the firm can anticipate additional outside capital needs in the years ahead.

I. Puck Pen Corporation

Puck Pen is engaged in the manufacture of mechanical pens and pencils, porous pens, and a recently developed line of disposable lighters. Since the firm sells to a great many distributors and its products are all considered nondurable consumer goods, sales are relatively stable. The current price of the company's stock, which is listed on the New York Stock Exchange, is $25. The most recent earnings and dividends per share are $3.10 and $1.50, respectively. The rate of growth in sales, earnings, and dividends in the last few years has averaged 5 percent. Puck Pens has total assets of $400 million. Current liabilities, which consist primarily of accounts payable and accruals, are $28 million, long-term debt is $83 million, and common equity totals $289 million. An additional $33 million of external funds is required to build and equip a new disposable lighter manufacturing complex in central Pennsylvania and to supply the new facility with working capital.

Appendix A

Table A-1 Present Value of $1: PVIF $= 1/(1 + k)^m$

Period	1%	2%	3%	4%	5%	6%	7%	8%	9%	10%
1	.9901	.9804	.9709	.9615	.9524	.9434	.9346	.9259	.9174	.9091
2	.9803	.9612	.9426	.9246	.9070	.8900	.8734	.8573	.8417	.8264
3	.9706	.9423	.9151	.8890	.8638	.8396	.8163	.7938	.7722	.7513
4	.9610	.9238	.8885	.8548	.8227	.7921	.7629	.7350	.7084	.6830
5	.9515	.9057	.8626	.8219	.7835	.7473	.7130	.6806	.6499	.6209
6	.9420	.8880	.8375	.7903	.7462	.7050	.6663	.6302	.5963	.5645
7	.9327	.8706	.8131	.7599	.7107	.6651	.6227	.5835	.5470	.5132
8	.9235	.8535	.7894	.7307	.6768	.6274	.5820	.5403	.5019	.4665
9	.9143	.8368	.7664	.7026	.6446	.5919	.5439	.5002	.4604	.4241
10	.9053	.8203	.7441	.6756	.6139	.5584	.5083	.4632	.4224	.3855
11	.8963	.8043	.7224	.6496	.5847	.5268	.4751	.4289	.3875	.3505
12	.8874	.7885	.7014	.6246	.5568	.4970	.4440	.3971	.3555	.3186
13	.8787	.7730	.6810	.6006	.5303	.4688	.4150	.3677	.3262	.2897
14	.8700	.7579	.6611	.5775	.5051	.4423	.3878	.3405	.2992	.2633
15	.8613	.7430	.6419	.5553	.4810	.4173	.3624	.3152	.2745	.2394

16	.8528	.7284	.6232	.5339	.4581	.3936	.3387	.2919	.2519	.2176
17	.8444	.7142	.6050	.5134	.4363	.3714	.3166	.2703	.2311	.1978
18	.8360	.7002	.5874	.4936	.4155	.3503	.2959	.2502	.2120	.1799
19	.8277	.6864	.5703	.4746	.3957	.3305	.2765	.2317	.1945	.1635
20	.8195	.6730	.5537	.4564	.3769	.3118	.2584	.2145	.1784	.1486
21	.8114	.6598	.5375	.4388	.3589	.2942	.2415	.1987	.1637	.1351
22	.8034	.6468	.5219	.4220	.3418	.2775	.2257	.1839	.1502	.1228
23	.7954	.6342	.5067	.4057	.3256	.2618	.2109	.1703	.1378	.1117
24	.7876	.6217	.4919	.3901	.3101	.2470	.1971	.1577	.1264	.1015
25	.7798	.6095	.4776	.3751	.2953	.2330	.1842	.1460	.1160	.0923
26	.7720	.5976	.4637	.3607	.2812	.2198	.1722	.1352	.1064	.0839
27	.7644	.5859	.4502	.3468	.2678	.2074	.1609	.1252	.0976	.0763
28	.7568	.5744	.4371	.3335	.2551	.1956	.1504	.1159	.0895	.0693
29	.7493	.5631	.4243	.3207	.2429	.1846	.1406	.1073	.0822	.0630
30	.7419	.5521	.4120	.3083	.2314	.1741	.1314	.0994	.0754	.0573
35	.7059	.5000	.3554	.2534	.1813	.1301	.0937	.0676	.0490	.0356
40	.6717	.4529	.3066	.2083	.1420	.0972	.0668	.0460	.0318	.0221
45	.6391	.4102	.2644	.1712	.1113	.0727	.0476	.0313	.0207	.0137
50	.6080	.3715	.2281	.1407	.0872	.0543	.0339	.0213	.0134	.0085
55	.5785	.3365	.1968	.1157	.0683	.0406	.0242	.0145	.0087	.0053

Table A–1 (continued)

Period	12%	14%	15%	16%	18%	20%	24%	28%	32%	36%
1	.8929	.8772	.8696	.8621	.8475	.8333	.8065	.7813	.7576	.7353
2	.7972	.7695	.7561	.7432	.7182	.6944	.6504	.6104	.5739	.5407
3	.7118	.6750	.6575	.6407	.6086	.5787	.5245	.4768	.4348	.3975
4	.6355	.5921	.5718	.5523	.5158	.4823	.4230	.3725	.3294	.2923
5	.5674	.5194	.4972	.4761	.4371	.4019	.3411	.2910	.2495	.2149
6	.5066	.4556	.4323	.4104	.3704	.3349	.2751	.2274	.1890	.1580
7	.4523	.3996	.3759	.3538	.3139	.2791	.2218	.1776	.1432	.1162
8	.4039	.3506	.3269	.3050	.2660	.2326	.1789	.1388	.1085	.0854
9	.3606	.3075	.2843	.2630	.2255	.1938	.1443	.1084	.0822	.0628
10	.3220	.2697	.2472	.2267	.1911	.1615	.1164	.0847	.0623	.0462
11	.2875	.2366	.2149	.1954	.1619	.1346	.0938	.0662	.0472	.0340
12	.2567	.2076	.1869	.1685	.1372	.1122	.0757	.0517	.0357	.0250
13	.2292	.1821	.1625	.1452	.1163	.0935	.0610	.0404	.0271	.0184
14	.2046	.1597	.1413	.1252	.0985	.0779	.0492	.0316	.0205	.0135
15	.1827	.1401	.1229	.1079	.0835	.0649	.0397	.0247	.0155	.0099

16	.1631	.1229	.1069	.0930	.0708	.0541	.0320	.0193	.0118	.0073
17	.1456	.1078	.0929	.0802	.0600	.0451	.0258	.0150	.0089	.0054
18	.1300	.0946	.0808	.0691	.0508	.0376	.0208	.0118	.0068	.0039
19	.1161	.0829	.0703	.0596	.0431	.0313	.0168	.0092	.0051	.0029
20	.1037	.0728	.0611	.0514	.0365	.0261	.0135	.0072	.0039	.0021
21	.0926	.0638	.0531	.0443	.0309	.0217	.0109	.0056	.0029	.0016
22	.0826	.0560	.0462	.0382	.0262	.0181	.0088	.0044	.0022	.0012
23	.0738	.0491	.0402	.0329	.0222	.0151	.0071	.0034	.0017	.0008
24	.0659	.0431	.0349	.0284	.0188	.0126	.0057	.0027	.0013	.0006
25	.0588	.0378	.0304	.0245	.0160	.0105	.0046	.0021	.0010	.0005
26	.0525	.0331	.0264	.0211	.0135	.0087	.0037	.0016	.0007	.0003
27	.0469	.0291	.0230	.0182	.0115	.0073	.0030	.0013	.0006	.0002
28	.0419	.0255	.0200	.0157	.0097	.0061	.0024	.0010	.0004	.0002
29	.0374	.0224	.0174	.0135	.0082	.0051	.0020	.0008	.0003	.0001
30	.0334	.0196	.0151	.0116	.0070	.0042	.0016	.0006	.0002	.0001
35	.0189	.0102	.0075	.0055	.0030	.0017	.0005	.0002	.0001	*
40	.0107	.0053	.0037	.0026	.0013	.0007	.0002	.0001	*	*
45	.0061	.0027	.0019	.0013	.0006	.0003	.0001	*	*	*
50	.0035	.0014	.0009	.0006	.0003	.0001	*	*	*	*
55	.0020	.0007	.0005	.0003	.0001	*	*	*	*	*

*The factor is zero to four decimal places

Table A–2 Present Value of an Annuity of $1 per Period for n Periods:

$$PVIFA = \sum_{t=1}^{n} \frac{1}{(1+k)^t}$$

$$= \frac{1 - \frac{1}{(1+k)^n}}{k}$$

Number of Payments	1%	2%	3%	4%	5%	6%	7%	8%	9%
1	0.9901	0.9804	0.9709	0.9615	0.9524	0.9434	0.9346	0.9259	0.9174
2	1.9704	1.9416	1.9135	1.8861	1.8594	1.8334	1.8080	1.7833	1.7591
3	2.9410	2.8839	2.8286	2.7751	2.7232	2.6730	2.6243	2.5771	2.5313
4	3.9020	3.8077	3.7171	3.6299	3.5460	3.4651	3.3872	3.3121	3.2397
5	4.8534	4.7135	4.5797	4.4518	4.3295	4.2124	4.1002	3.9927	3.8897
6	5.7955	5.6014	5.4172	5.2421	5.0757	4.9173	4.7665	4.6229	4.4859
7	6.7282	6.4720	6.2303	6.0021	5.7864	5.5824	5.3893	5.2064	5.0330
8	7.6517	7.3255	7.0197	6.7327	6.4632	6.2098	5.9713	5.7466	5.5348
9	8.5660	8.1622	7.7861	7.4353	7.1078	6.8017	6.5152	6.2469	5.9952
10	9.4713	8.9826	8.5302	8.1109	7.7217	7.3601	7.0236	6.7101	6.4177
11	10.3676	9.7868	9.2526	8.7605	8.3064	7.8869	7.4987	7.1390	6.8052
12	11.2551	10.5753	9.9540	9.3851	8.8633	8.3838	7.9427	7.5361	7.1607
13	12.1337	11.3484	10.6350	9.9856	9.3936	8.8527	8.3577	7.9038	7.4869
14	13.0037	12.1062	11.2961	10.5631	9.8986	9.2950	8.7455	8.2442	7.7862
15	13.8651	12.8493	11.9379	11.1184	10.3797	9.7122	9.1079	8.5595	8.0607

16	14.7179	13.5777	12.5611	11.6523	10.8378	10.1059	9.4466	8.8514	8.3126
17	15.5623	14.2919	13.1661	12.1657	11.2741	10.4773	9.7632	9.1216	8.5436
18	16.3983	14.9920	13.7535	12.6593	11.6896	10.8276	10.0591	9.3719	8.7556
19	17.2260	15.6785	14.3238	13.1339	12.0853	11.1581	10.3356	9.6036	8.9501
20	18.0456	16.3514	14.8775	13.5903	12.4622	11.4699	10.5940	9.8181	9.1285
21	18.8570	17.0112	15.4150	14.0292	12.8212	11.7641	10.8355	10.0168	9.2922
22	19.6604	17.6580	15.9369	14.4511	13.1630	12.0416	11.0612	10.2007	9.4424
23	20.4558	18.2922	16.4436	14.8568	13.4886	12.3034	11.2722	10.3711	9.5802
24	21.2434	18.9139	16.9355	15.2470	13.7986	12.5504	11.4693	10.5288	9.7066
25	22.0232	19.5235	17.4131	15.6221	14.0939	12.7834	11.6536	10.6748	9.8226
26	22.7952	20.1210	17.8768	15.9828	14.3752	13.0032	11.8258	10.8100	9.9290
27	23.5596	20.7069	18.3270	16.3296	14.6430	13.2105	11.9867	10.9352	10.0266
28	24.3164	21.2813	18.7641	16.6631	14.8981	13.4062	12.1371	11.0511	10.1161
29	25.0658	21.8444	19.1885	16.9837	15.1411	13.5907	12.2777	11.1584	10.1983
30	25.8077	22.3965	19.6004	17.2920	15.3725	13.7648	12.4090	11.2578	10.2737
35	29.4086	24.9986	21.4872	18.6646	16.3742	14.4982	12.9477	11.6546	10.5668
40	32.8347	27.3555	23.1148	19.7928	17.1591	15.0463	13.3317	11.9246	10.7574
45	36.0945	29.4902	24.5187	20.7200	17.7741	15.4558	13.6055	12.1084	10.8812
50	39.1961	31.4236	25.7298	21.4822	18.2559	15.7619	13.8007	12.2335	10.9617
55	42.1472	33.1748	26.7744	22.1086	18.6335	15.9905	13.9399	12.3186	11.0140

Table A–2 (continued)

Number of Payments	10%	12%	14%	15%	16%	18%	20%	24%	28%	32%
1	0.9091	0.8929	0.8772	0.8696	0.8621	0.8475	0.8333	0.8065	0.7813	0.7576
2	1.7355	1.6901	1.6467	1.6257	1.6052	1.5656	1.5278	1.4568	1.3916	1.3315
3	2.4869	2.4018	2.3216	2.2832	2.2459	2.1743	2.1065	1.9813	1.8684	1.7663
4	3.1699	3.0373	2.9137	2.8550	2.7982	2.6901	2.5887	2.4043	2.2410	2.0957
5	3.7908	3.6048	3.4331	3.3522	3.2743	3.1272	2.9906	2.7454	2.5320	2.3452
6	4.3553	4.1114	3.8887	3.7845	3.6847	3.4976	3.3255	3.0205	2.7594	2.5342
7	4.8684	4.5638	4.2883	4.1604	4.0386	3.8115	3.6046	3.2423	2.9370	2.6775
8	5.3349	4.9676	4.6389	4.4873	4.3436	4.0776	3.8372	3.4212	3.0758	2.7860
9	5.7590	5.3282	4.9464	4.7716	4.6065	4.3030	4.0310	3.5655	3.1842	2.8681
10	6.1446	5.6502	5.2161	5.0188	4.8332	4.4941	4.1925	3.6819	3.2689	2.9304
11	6.4951	5.9377	5.4527	5.2337	5.0286	4.6560	4.3271	3.7757	3.3351	2.9776
12	6.8137	6.1944	5.6603	5.4206	5.1971	4.7932	4.4392	3.8514	3.3868	3.0133
13	7.1034	6.4235	5.8424	5.5831	5.3423	4.9095	4.5327	3.9124	3.4272	3.0404
14	7.3667	6.6282	6.0021	5.7245	5.4675	5.0081	4.6106	3.9616	3.4587	3.0609
15	7.6061	6.8109	6.1422	5.8474	5.5755	5.0916	4.6755	4.0013	3.4834	3.0764

16	3.0882	3.5026	4.0333	4.7296	5.1624	5.6685	5.9542	6.2651	6.9740	7.8237
17	3.0971	3.5177	4.0591	4.7746	5.2223	5.7487	6.0472	6.3729	7.1196	8.0216
18	3.1039	3.5294	4.0799	4.8122	5.2732	5.8178	6.1280	6.4674	7.2497	8.2014
19	3.1090	3.5386	4.0967	4.8435	5.3162	5.8775	6.1982	6.5504	7.3658	8.3649
20	3.1129	3.5458	4.1103	4.8696	5.3527	5.9288	6.2593	6.6231	7.4694	8.5136
21	3.1158	3.5514	4.1212	4.8913	5.3837	5.9731	6.3125	6.6870	7.5620	8.6487
22	3.1180	3.5558	4.1300	4.9094	5.4099	6.0113	6.3587	6.7429	7.6446	8.7715
23	3.1197	3.5592	4.1371	4.9245	5.4321	6.0442	6.3988	6.7921	7.7184	8.8832
24	3.1210	3.5619	4.1428	4.9371	5.4510	6.0726	6.4338	6.8351	7.7843	8.9847
25	3.1220	3.5640	4.1474	4.9476	5.4669	6.0971	6.4642	6.8729	7.8431	9.0770
26	3.1227	3.5656	4.1511	4.9563	5.4804	6.1182	6.4906	6.9061	7.8957	9.1609
27	3.1233	3.5669	4.1542	4.9636	5.4919	6.1364	6.5135	6.9352	7.9426	9.2372
28	3.1237	3.5679	4.1566	4.9697	5.5016	6.1520	6.5335	6.9607	7.9844	9.3066
29	3.1240	3.5687	4.1585	4.9747	5.5098	6.1656	6.5509	6.9830	8.0218	9.3696
30	3.1242	3.5693	4.1601	4.9789	5.5168	6.1772	6.5660	7.0027	8.0552	9.4269
35	3.1248	3.5708	4.1644	4.9915	5.5386	6.2153	6.6166	7.0700	8.1755	9.6442
40	3.1250	3.5712	4.1659	4.9966	5.5482	6.2335	6.6418	7.1050	8.2438	9.7791
45	3.1250	3.5714	4.1664	4.9986	5.5523	6.2421	6.6543	7.1232	8.2825	9.8628
50	3.1250	3.5714	4.1666	4.9995	5.5541	6.2463	6.6605	7.1327	8.3045	9.9148
55	3.1250	3.5714	4.1666	4.9998	5.5549	6.2482	6.6636	7.1376	8.3170	9.9471

Table A-3 Future Value of $1 at the End of n Periods: $FVIF = (1 + k)^n$

Period	1%	2%	3%	4%	5%	6%	7%	8%	9%	10%
1	1.0100	1.0200	1.0300	1.0400	1.0500	1.0600	1.0700	1.0800	1.0900	1.1000
2	1.0201	1.0404	1.0609	1.0816	1.1025	1.1236	1.1449	1.1664	1.1881	1.2100
3	1.0303	1.0612	1.0927	1.1249	1.1576	1.1910	1.2250	1.2597	1.2950	1.3310
4	1.0406	1.0824	1.1255	1.1699	1.2155	1.2625	1.3108	1.3605	1.4116	1.4641
5	1.0510	1.1041	1.1593	1.2167	1.2763	1.3382	1.4026	1.4693	1.5386	1.6105
6	1.0615	1.1262	1.1941	1.2653	1.3401	1.4185	1.5007	1.5869	1.6771	1.7716
7	1.0721	1.1487	1.2299	1.3159	1.4071	1.5036	1.6058	1.7138	1.8280	1.9487
8	1.0829	1.1717	1.2668	1.3686	1.4775	1.5938	1.7182	1.8509	1.9926	2.1436
9	1.0937	1.1951	1.3048	1.4233	1.5513	1.6895	1.8385	1.9990	2.1719	2.3579
10	1.1046	1.2190	1.3439	1.4802	1.6289	1.7908	1.9672	2.1589	2.3674	2.5937
11	1.1157	1.2434	1.3842	1.5395	1.7103	1.8983	2.1049	2.3316	2.5804	2.8531
12	1.1268	1.2682	1.4258	1.6010	1.7959	2.0122	2.2522	2.5182	2.8127	3.1384
13	1.1381	1.2936	1.4685	1.6651	1.8856	2.1329	2.4098	2.7196	3.0658	3.4523
14	1.1495	1.3195	1.5126	1.7317	1.9799	2.2609	2.5785	2.9372	3.3417	3.7975
15	1.1610	1.3459	1.5580	1.8009	2.0789	2.3966	2.7590	3.1722	3.6425	4.1772

16	1.1726	1.3728	1.6047	1.8730	2.1829	2.5404	2.9522	3.4259	3.9703	4.5950
17	1.1843	1.4002	1.6528	1.9479	2.2920	2.6928	3.1588	3.7000	4.3276	5.0545
18	1.1961	1.4282	1.7024	2.0258	2.4066	2.8543	3.3799	3.9960	4.7171	5.5599
19	1.2081	1.4568	1.7535	2.1068	2.5270	3.0256	3.6165	4.3157	5.1417	6.1159
20	1.2202	1.4859	1.8061	2.1911	2.6533	3.2071	3.8697	4.6610	5.6044	6.7275
21	1.2324	1.5157	1.8603	2.2788	2.7860	3.3996	4.1406	5.0338	6.1088	7.4002
22	1.2447	1.5460	1.9161	2.3699	2.9253	3.6035	4.4304	5.4365	6.6586	8.1403
23	1.2572	1.5769	1.9736	2.4647	3.0715	3.8197	4.7405	5.8715	7.2579	8.9543
24	1.2697	1.6084	2.0328	2.5633	3.2251	4.0489	5.0724	6.3412	7.9111	9.8497
25	1.2824	1.6406	2.0938	2.6658	3.3864	4.2919	5.4274	6.8485	8.6231	10.834
26	1.2953	1.6734	2.1566	2.7725	3.5557	4.5494	5.8074	7.3964	9.3992	11.918
27	1.3082	1.7069	2.2213	2.8834	3.7335	4.8223	6.2139	7.9881	10.245	13.110
28	1.3213	1.7410	2.2879	2.9987	3.9201	5.1117	6.6488	8.6271	11.167	14.421
29	1.3345	1.7758	2.3566	3.1187	4.1161	5.4184	7.1143	9.3173	12.172	15.863
30	1.3478	1.8114	2.4273	3.2434	4.3219	5.7435	7.6123	10.062	13.267	17.449
40	1.4889	2.2080	3.2620	4.8010	7.0400	10.285	14.974	21.724	31.409	45.259
50	1.6446	2.6916	4.3839	7.1067	11.467	18.420	29.457	46.901	74.357	117.39
60	1.8167	3.2810	5.8916	10.519	18.679	32.987	57.946	101.25	176.03	304.48

Table A–3 (continued)

Period	12%	14%	15%	16%	18%	20%	24%	28%	32%	36%
1	1.1200	1.1400	1.1500	1.1600	1.1800	1.2000	1.2400	1.2800	1.3200	1.3600
2	1.2544	1.2996	1.3225	1.3456	1.3924	1.4400	1.5376	1.6384	1.7424	1.8496
3	1.4049	1.4815	1.5209	1.5609	1.6430	1.7280	1.9066	2.0972	2.3000	2.5155
4	1.5735	1.6890	1.7490	1.8106	1.9388	2.0736	2.3642	2.6844	3.0360	3.4210
5	1.7623	1.9254	2.0114	2.1003	2.2878	2.4883	2.9316	3.4360	4.0075	4.6526
6	1.9738	2.1950	2.3131	2.4364	2.6996	2.9860	3.6352	4.3980	5.2899	6.3275
7	2.2107	2.5023	2.6600	2.8262	3.1855	3.5832	4.5077	5.6295	6.9826	8.6054
8	2.4760	2.8526	3.0590	3.2784	3.7589	4.2998	5.5895	7.2058	9.2170	11.703
9	2.7731	3.2519	3.5179	3.8030	4.4355	5.1598	6.9310	9.2234	12.166	15.916
10	3.1058	3.7072	4.0456	4.4114	5.2338	6.1917	8.5944	11.805	16.059	21.646
11	3.4785	4.2262	4.6524	5.1173	6.1759	7.4301	10.657	15.111	21.198	29.439
12	3.8960	4.8179	5.3502	5.9360	7.2876	8.9161	13.214	19.342	27.982	40.037
13	4.3635	5.4924	6.1528	6.8858	8.5994	10.699	16.386	24.758	36.937	54.451
14	4.8871	6.2613	7.0757	7.9875	10.147	12.839	20.319	31.691	48.756	74.053
15	5.4736	7.1379	8.1371	9.2655	11.973	15.407	25.195	40.564	64.358	100.71

16	6.1304	8.1372	9.3576	10.748	14.129	18.488	31.242	51.923	84.953	136.96
17	6.8660	9.2765	10.761	12.467	16.672	22.186	38.740	66.461	112.13	186.27
18	7.6900	10.575	12.375	14.462	19.673	26.623	48.038	85.070	148.02	253.33
19	8.6128	12.055	14.231	16.776	23.214	31.948	59.567	108.89	195.39	344.53
20	9.6463	13.743	16.366	19.460	27.393	38.337	73.864	139.37	257.91	468.57
21	10.803	15.667	18.821	22.574	32.323	46.005	91.591	178.40	340.44	637.26
22	12.100	17.861	21.644	26.186	38.142	55.206	113.57	228.35	449.39	866.67
23	13.552	20.361	24.891	30.376	45.007	66.247	140.83	292.30	593.19	1178.6
24	15.178	23.212	28.625	35.236	53.108	79.496	174.63	374.14	783.02	1602.9
25	17.000	26.461	32.918	40.874	62.668	95.396	216.54	478.90	1033.5	2180.0
26	19.040	30.166	37.856	47.414	73.948	114.47	268.51	612.99	1364.3	2964.9
27	21.324	34.389	43.535	55.000	87.259	137.37	332.95	784.63	1800.9	4032.2
28	23.883	39.204	50.065	63.800	102.96	164.84	412.86	1004.3	2377.2	5483.8
29	26.749	44.693	57.575	74.008	121.50	197.81	511.95	1285.5	3137.9	7458.0
30	29.959	50.950	66.211	85.849	143.37	237.37	634.81	1645.5	4142.0	10143.
40	93.050	188.88	267.86	378.72	750.37	1469.7	5455.9	19426.	66520.	*
50	289.00	700.23	1083.6	1670.7	3927.3	9100.4	46890.	*	*	*
60	897.59	2595.9	4383.9	7370.1	20555.	56347.	*	*	*	*

*FVIF > 99,999

Table A–4 Sum of an Annuity of \$1 per Period for n Periods:

$$FVIFA = \sum_{t=1}^{n} (1 + k)^{t-1}$$

$$FVIFA = \frac{(1 + k)^n - 1}{k}$$

Number of Periods	1%	2%	3%	4%	5%	6%	7%	8%	9%	10%
1	1.0000	1.0000	1.0000	1.0000	1.0000	1.0000	1.0000	1.0000	1.0000	1.0000
2	2.0100	2.0200	2.0300	2.0400	2.0500	2.0600	2.0700	2.0800	2.0900	2.1000
3	3.0301	3.0604	3.0909	3.1216	3.1525	3.1836	3.2149	3.2464	3.2781	3.3100
4	4.0604	4.1216	4.1836	4.2465	4.3101	4.3746	4.4399	4.5061	4.5731	4.6410
5	5.1010	5.2040	5.3091	5.4163	5.5256	5.6371	5.7507	5.8666	5.9847	6.1051
6	6.1520	6.3081	6.4684	6.6330	6.8019	6.9753	7.1533	7.3359	7.5233	7.7156
7	7.2135	7.4343	7.6625	7.8983	8.1420	8.3938	8.6540	8.9228	9.2004	9.4872
8	8.2857	8.5830	8.8923	9.2142	9.5491	9.8975	10.259	10.636	11.028	11.435
9	9.3685	9.7546	10.159	10.582	11.026	11.491	11.978	12.487	13.021	13.579
10	10.462	10.949	11.463	12.006	12.577	13.180	13.816	14.486	15.192	15.937
11	11.566	12.168	12.807	13.486	14.206	14.971	15.783	16.645	17.560	18.531
12	12.682	13.412	14.192	15.025	15.917	16.869	17.888	18.977	20.140	21.384
13	13.809	14.680	15.617	16.626	17.713	18.882	20.140	21.495	22.953	24.522
14	14.947	15.973	17.086	18.291	19.598	21.015	22.550	24.214	26.019	27.975
15	16.096	17.293	18.598	20.023	21.578	23.276	25.129	27.152	29.360	31.772

16	17.257	18.639	20.156	21.824	23.657	25.672	27.888	30.324	33.003	35.949
17	18.430	20.012	21.761	23.697	25.840	28.212	30.840	33.750	36.973	40.544
18	19.614	21.412	23.414	25.645	28.132	30.905	33.999	37.450	41.301	45.599
19	20.810	22.840	25.116	27.671	30.539	33.760	37.379	41.446	46.018	51.159
20	22.019	24.297	26.870	29.778	33.066	36.785	40.995	45.762	51.160	57.275
21	23.239	25.783	28.676	31.969	35.719	39.992	44.865	50.422	56.764	64.002
22	24.471	27.299	30.536	34.248	38.505	43.392	49.005	55.456	62.873	71.402
23	25.716	28.845	32.452	36.617	41.430	46.995	53.436	60.893	69.531	79.543
24	26.973	30.421	34.426	39.082	44.502	50.815	58.176	66.764	76.789	88.497
25	28.243	32.030	36.459	41.645	47.727	54.864	63.249	73.105	84.700	98.347
26	29.525	33.670	38.553	44.311	51.113	59.156	68.676	79.954	93.323	109.18
27	30.820	35.344	40.709	47.084	54.669	63.705	74.483	87.350	102.72	121.09
28	32.129	37.051	42.930	49.967	58.402	68.528	80.697	95.338	112.96	134.20
29	33.450	38.792	45.218	52.966	62.322	73.639	87.346	103.96	124.13	148.63
30	34.784	40.568	47.575	56.084	66.438	79.058	94.460	113.28	136.30	164.49
40	48.886	60.402	75.401	95.025	120.79	154.76	199.63	259.05	337.88	442.59
50	64.463	84.579	112.79	152.66	209.34	290.33	406.52	573.76	815.08	1163.9
60	81.669	114.05	163.05	237.99	353.58	533.12	813.52	1253.2	1944.7	3034.8

Table A-4 (continued)

Number of Periods	12%	14%	15%	16%	18%	20%	24%	28%	32%	36%
1	1.0000	1.0000	1.0000	1.0000	1.0000	1.0000	1.0000	1.0000	1.0000	1.0000
2	2.1200	2.1400	2.1500	2.1600	2.1800	2.2000	2.2400	2.2800	2.3200	2.3600
3	3.3744	3.4396	3.4725	3.5056	3.5724	3.6400	3.7776	3.9184	4.0624	4.2096
4	4.7793	4.9211	4.9934	5.0665	5.2154	5.3680	5.6842	6.0156	6.3624	6.7251
5	6.3528	6.6101	6.7424	6.8771	7.1542	7.4416	8.0484	8.6999	9.3983	10.146
6	8.1152	8.5355	8.7537	8.9775	9.4420	9.9299	10.980	12.135	13.405	14.798
7	10.089	10.730	11.066	11.413	12.141	12.915	14.615	16.533	18.695	21.126
8	12.299	13.232	13.726	14.240	15.327	16.499	19.122	22.163	25.678	29.731
9	14.775	16.085	16.785	17.518	19.085	20.798	24.712	29.369	34.895	41.435
10	17.548	19.337	20.303	21.321	23.521	25.958	31.643	38.592	47.061	57.351
11	20.654	23.044	24.349	25.732	28.755	32.150	40.237	50.398	63.121	78.998
12	24.133	27.270	29.001	30.850	34.931	39.580	50.894	65.510	84.320	108.43
13	28.029	32.088	34.351	36.786	42.218	48.496	64.109	84.852	112.30	148.47
14	32.392	37.581	40.504	43.672	50.818	59.195	80.496	109.61	149.23	202.92
15	37.279	43.842	47.580	51.659	60.965	72.035	100.81	141.30	197.99	276.97

16	42.753	50.980	55.717	60.925	72.939	87.442	126.01	181.86	262.35	377.69
17	48.883	59.117	65.075	71.673	87.068	105.93	157.25	233.79	347.30	514.66
18	55.749	68.394	75.836	84.140	103.74	128.11	195.99	300.25	459.44	700.93
19	63.439	78.969	88.211	98.603	123.41	154.74	244.03	385.32	607.47	954.27
20	72.052	91.024	102.44	115.37	146.62	186.68	303.60	494.21	802.86	1298.8
21	81.698	104.76	118.81	134.84	174.02	225.02	377.46	633.59	1060.7	1767.3
22	92.502	120.43	137.63	157.41	206.34	271.03	469.05	811.99	1401.2	2404.6
23	104.60	138.29	159.27	183.60	244.48	326.23	582.62	1040.3	1850.6	3271.3
24	118.15	158.65	184.16	213.97	289.49	392.48	723.46	1332.6	2443.8	4449.9
25	133.33	181.87	212.79	249.21	342.60	471.98	898.09	1706.8	3226.8	6052.9
26	150.33	208.33	245.71	290.08	405.27	567.37	1114.6	2185.7	4260.4	8233.0
27	169.37	238.49	283.56	337.50	479.22	681.85	1383.1	2798.7	5624.7	11197.9
28	190.69	272.88	327.10	392.50	566.48	819.22	1716.0	3583.3	7425.6	15230.2
29	214.58	312.09	377.16	456.30	669.44	964.06	2128.9	4587.6	9802.9	20714.1
30	241.33	356.78	434.74	530.31	790.94	1181.8	2640.9	5873.2	12940.	28172.2
40	767.09	1342.0	1779.0	2360.7	4163.2	7343.8	22728.	69377.	*	*
50	2400.0	4994.5	7217.7	10435.	21813.	45497.	*	*	*	*
60	7471.6	18535.	29219.	46057.	*	*	*	*	*	*

*FVIFA > 99,999

Appendix B

Part 1

Case 1

1.a. Key financial ratios for 1979: Current ratio 1.8; quick ratio 0.7; debt ratio 59.3 percent; times-interest-earned 1.5X; inventory turnover (cost) 3.6X; inventory turnover (sales) 4.2X; fixed assets turnover 12.1X; total assets turnover 2.0X; average collection period 54.0 days; profit margin 0.4 percent; gross profit margin 14.9 percent; return on total assets (ROA) 0.8 percent; return on equity 2.0 percent.

Case 2

3. Sales = $10.0 million.
6. No expansion: Profit$_{1984}$ = $1,195,378.
   Expansion: Profit$_{1984}$ = $2,336,000.

Case 3

1. 1979: $694,000; 1980: $844,000; 1981: $987,500.
3. $59,602 possible short-term debt.
7. $1,234,375 additional current liabilities.

Case 4

None.

Case 5

2. January: required financing $17,100.
   June: cash surplus $19,220.
3. January 5th: required financing $10,015.
   January 15th: required financing $19,715.
   January 30th: required financing $17,770.

Part 2

Case 6

2. Net gain from change in policy: $1,591.
3. Maximum that can be paid to reduce bad debts: $21,834.

Case 7

1.a. EOQ_A = 215 units per order.
2.b. Orders per year from B: 68.
3.a. Reorder point for manufacturer A = 525 units.
5. Average inventory using A: 2,208 units.

Case 8

1.b. Aggressive policy: Sales = $56,430,000; Industry average policy: Sales = $51,150,000; Conservative Policy: Sales = $48,000,000.

1.c. Aggressive policy: Current ratio 2.05:1; Debt/Assets 54 percent; Times-interest-earned 2.42X; Return on equity 14.68 percent.

Case 9

None.

Case 10

1. Present value of net after-tax cash inflows = $167,058.
3. Payback = 6.2 years.

Case 11

1. Initial investment = $36,081,550.
2. Net incremental after-tax cash flow: 1982 = $3,515,250; 1983 = $6,154,750; 1984 = $8,658,000; 1985 = $10,979,750; 1986-1990 = $12,399,750; 1991 = $17,019,750.
4. NPV = $13,550,760.

Case 12

1. CF bid = $505,361.41 per unit.

Case 13

1.a. $IRR_B \simeq$ 34 percent.
1.b. NPV at 26 percent cost of capital:
    A = ($217.28); B = $77,264.71; C = $89,996.72; D = ($59,867.31).
4. Optimal capital budget = $2,250,000.

Case 14

1.a. K_a = 11 percent.
4. Equipment depreciation in 1990 = $1,960.

Case 15

2. IRR_A = 14.91 percent; IRR_B = 22.52 percent; IRR_C = 27.17 percent.
3. NPV_A = ($5,027,374); NPV_B = $2,170,461; NPV_C = $6,305,817.

Part 3

Case 16

5.a. Accounts payable decline to $2.95 million.
5.b. Bank loan = $18.91 million.
5.c. Net savings = $1,015,350.

Case 17

1. Net Present Value = either $84,300,925 or $86,031,694.

Case 18

1. Flotation costs = 4.99 percent.
2. Flotation costs as a percentage of the funds raised = 10.6 percent or 9.6 percent.

Case 19

1. Number of new shares (millions): 0.495; 0.517; 0.573; 0.909; 4.500.
2. Rights required to buy new share: 7.74; 6.98; 4.40; 0.89.
4. Market value of stock ex rights: $48.00; $48.54; $47.87; $44.56; $25.72.
6. Market price/Share: $73.00; $72.60; $71.80; $66.80; $38.60.

Case 20

1. Sequoia Timber growth rate EPS = 7.75 percent;
Growth rate DPS = 8.45 percent;
Airhauser market/book ratio = 1.6798;
Carolina-Pacific payout ratio = 75.76 percent;
Airhauser P/E ratio = 11.64;
Carolina-Pacific cost of equity = 13.5 percent.

Case 21

1. 1982 EBIT = $60,613,200.
2. Debt ratio using: Bonds 28.48 percent; Preferred stock 17.72 percent; Common stock 17.72 percent.
3. Times-interest-earned using: Bonds 9.13X; Preferred stock 50.51X; Common stock 50.51X.
5. Earnings breakeven point = $253,513,120.

Case 22

4. Before-tax sinking fund = $192,749.
5. Breakeven point = $89,384,739.
6. Return on book equity using:
Debt = 14.48 percent;
Preferred stock = 18.40 percent;
Common stock = 12.66 percent.

Case 23

1. Leasing = $68,938; Buying = $65,325.

Case 24

1. Net proceeds from mortgage = $2,600,000;
   from sale and leaseback   = $2,866,500.
3. Nominal interest rate on lease = 12 percent; on mortgage = 14 percent.
5. IRR $\approx$ 16 percent.
6. Net profit after taxes: Lease = $386,130;
                           Mortgage = $292,500.

Case 25

9. Initial cash outlay = $75 million.

Case 26

2. N = 13 years.
4. Expected return = 13.05 percent.
5.a. k_a = 11.4 percent.
6. Conversion value = $1,140.

Case 27

1. Conversion value: Benson Petroleum   = $1,600;
                     Nazareth Steel   = $6,000;
                     Transnational Implement = $ 480.
2. Current Yield: Benson Petroleum   = 5.3 percent;
                     Nazareth Steel   = 1.4 percent;
                     Transnational Implement = 12.5 percent.

Part 4

Case 28

1. Breakeven point A =   70,000 units;
   Breakeven point B = 115,790 units.
2. 1983 EBIT = $25,006,000.
3. Times-interest-earned = 12.11X.
5. ROE = 43.35 percent.
6. k_s = 15.39 percent.

Case 29

1. Breakeven point A = 46,319 units;
   Breakeven point B = 53,243 units;
   Indifference sales level = 59,866 units.
3. Times interest earned = 3.92X;
   Debt ratio = 40.54 percent.

Case 30A

3. Expected ROE = 15.00 percent; σ_{ROE} = 6.71 percent; v = 0.45.
4. K_s = 15 percent.

Case 30B

4.   0% Debt; 150,000,000 total shares, AT&E Price = $20.00;
20% Debt; 128,734,000 total shares; AT&E Price = $17.29;
40% Debt; 102,105,000 total shares; AT&E Price = $15.26.

6.   Expected TIE = 4.46X;
σ_{TIE} = 1.99.

Case 31

1. $275,500 required.

Case 32

1.   Debt = 40 percent; preferred stock = 10 percent; common equity = 50
percent.

2.   Breaking points for common equity = $25 million; $30 million.

4. IRR_B = 14 percent;
IRR_D = 11 percent;
IRR_H = 10 percent.

Case 33A

3.c. Optimal capital budget = $750 million.

Case 33B

1.   New divisional indices: DS = 1.12;
MAN = 1.03;
TEL = 0.96.

Case 34

1.   P/E 1982 = 12.0X; Market value/Book value 1982 = 0.86; Growth rate
1977-1982 = 6 percent.

Case 35

None.

Case 36

None.

Part 5

Case 37

1.   World-Wind: P = $35.14.

5.   Corcoran Systems: P = $59.48.

Case 38

None.

Case 39

2.   IRR = 27.0 percent.

Case 40

1.   PV of cash inflows = $1,484.45.

Case 41

None.